Copyright © 2025 Maria Johnsen

All rights reserved.

ISBN 9798305569971

Library of Congress Control Number: 2025927730

Preface

The emergence of Agentic AI marks a pivotal moment in the evolution of artificial intelligence, transforming systems from passive tools into dynamic, autonomous agents capable of decision-making, learning, and meaningful interaction with the world. As the boundaries between human cognition and machine intelligence blur, the question of agency becomes not only a technical challenge but also a profound philosophical and ethical inquiry.

This book seeks to unpack the complex, multidisciplinary nature of Agentic AI, offering a comprehensive exploration of its theoretical foundations, practical applications, and societal implications. It is designed for a diverse audience engineers, researchers, ethicists, policymakers, and anyone intrigued by the rapid advancement of AI technologies.

Agentic AI differs fundamentally from traditional AI systems by introducing the ability to act independently, pursue goals,

Agentic AI

Maria Johnsen

and adapt to changing circumstances. These capabilities open up extraordinary opportunities in fields ranging from healthcare and education to space exploration and environmental sustainability. However, they also raise critical questions about trust, safety, regulation, and fairness. How do we ensure that autonomous systems act in alignment with human values? What are the risks of granting machines a level of decision-making power traditionally reserved for humans?

Each chapter in this book delves into a specific aspect of Agentic AI, from its conceptual underpinnings to its implementation challenges and real-world case studies. We examine the ethical dilemmas posed by autonomous agents, explore how they reshape industries and societal structures, and consider the psychological and philosophical dimensions of creating machines that exhibit agency.

As we navigate this transformative era, it is imperative to balance innovation with responsibility. Agentic AI has the potential to amplify human creativity, solve global challenges, and improve quality of life, but only if its development is guided by a clear understanding of its implications.

I invite you to embark on this journey into the heart of Agentic AI a field that is not just reshaping technology but redefining what it means to coexist with intelligent systems.

Together, let us explore the possibilities, confront the challenges, and envision a future where humans and autonomous agents collaborate for the betterment of society.

Table of Contents

Preface 4

Summary 18

Chapter 1 The Concept of Agency in AI 22

    Self-Directed Goals 24

    Applications of Agentic AI 26

Chapter 2 Historical Roots of Agentic Systems 31

    Early Automata: The Seeds of Agentic Thought 31

Chapter 3 Philosophy of Agency in Machines 41

Chapter 4 Components of Agentic AI 51

Chapter 5 Agentic AI vs Other AI Models 62

Chapter 6 Building Autonomy in AI Systems 72

The Foundation of Autonomy in AI Systems 73

6.1.1. Decision-Making...73

6.1.2. Learning and Adaptation..74

6.1.3. Goal Orientation..74

6.2. Enabling Decision-Making in Autonomous AI Systems 75

6.2.1. Classical Decision Theory 75

6.2.2. Reinforcement Learning (RL).....................................76

6.2.3. Decision Trees and Markov Decision Processes (MDPs) 77

6.2.4. Multi-Agent Systems 77

6.3. Goal-Oriented Behavior in Autonomous AI Systems 78

6.3.1. Define and Represent Goals......................................78

6.3.2. Decompose Goals into Subgoals 79

6.3.3. Monitor Progress and Adjust Strategies...............80

6.4. Ethical Considerations in Autonomous AI Systems ..81

6.4.1. Transparency and Accountability..........................81

6.4.2. Fairness and Bias..81

6.4.3. Safety and Security...82

Chapter 7 The Role of Reinforcement Learning in Agency..84

Chapter 8 Behavioral Modeling in Agentic AI 94

Chapter 9 Integrating Ethics into AI Agency........................103

Chapter 10 Balancing Control and Independence................111

    The Rise of Autonomous AI Systems...............................112

    The Need for Control...113

    The Case for Independence...115

    Striking a Balance...117

Chapter 11 Agentic AI in Healthcare......................................120

Chapter 12 The Rise of Agentic AI in Healthcare.................129

Chapter 13 Smart Cities and Infrastructure 138

    What Makes a City "Smart"?...138

    AI-Driven Urban Planning 140

    AI-Driven Infrastructure Management............................142

    Challenges of AI-Driven Urban Planning and Infrastructure Management..145

    The Future of AI-Driven Smart Cities..............................146

Chapter 14 Agentic AI in Defense and Security 148

Understanding Agentic AI 149

Autonomous Drones in Defense and Security.................149

AI-Enhanced Surveillance Systems 151

AI-Driven Threat Assessment..153

Challenges and Ethical Considerations 155

Chapter 15 Education and Learning Systems........................158

Adaptive Tutoring Systems: An Overview........................159

How Adaptive Tutoring Systems Work.............................160

Benefits of Adaptive Tutoring Systems 162

Knowledge Delivery: The Role of Technology.................165

Chapter 16 The Moral Responsibility of Agentic AI 168

Moral Responsibility and Machine Learning....................170

Legal and Regulatory Frameworks......................................171

Ethical Frameworks for Agentic AI 173

Chapter 17 Bias and Fairness in Agentic Systems 176

Chapter 18 Privacy Concerns in Autonomy..........................185

The Rise of Autonomy and Its Promise 185

Privacy Concerns in Autonomous Systems.......................187

Balancing Agency with Data Security..................190

Chapter 19 Employment Disruption........................195

　The Rise of AI and Workforce Disruption........................196

　Job Displacement and Job Creation..................197

　The Transformation of Skills and Workforce Adaptation 199

　Ethical and Social Implications of AI in the Workforce..200

　Navigating the Future: Preparing for an AI-Driven Workforce..................201

Chapter 20 Social Acceptance of Autonomous Agents........204

　The Evolution of Autonomous Agents..................205

　Understanding Public Perception..................205

　Trust in Autonomous Agents..................209

Chapter 21 Scaling Agentic AI Systems..................214

　The Nature of Agentic AI Systems..................215

　Computational Power Challenges..................216

　Efficiency Challenges..................219

　Trade-Offs in Scaling Agentic AI Systems..................222

Chapter 22 Error Propagation in Autonomous Systems.....224

    The Nature of Error Propagation 225

    The Consequences of Error Propagation 227

    Mitigating Risks of Error Propagation 229

Chapter 23 Robustness Against Adversarial Attacks 233

Chapter 24 Real-Time Adaptation..243

    Understanding Real-Time Adaptation 244

    Challenges in Dynamic Environments................................245

    Overcoming the Challenges of Real-Time Adaptation ...249

Chapter 25 Energy and Resource Optimization 253

Chapter 26 Agentic AI in Space Exploration 262

    The Evolution of Autonomous Rovers and Probes.........263

    Autonomous Rovers in Space Exploration........................265

    Hazard Detection and Avoidance...266

    Scientific Exploration 267

    Autonomous Probes in Space Exploration.......................268

    Challenges and Limitations of Agentic AI in Space Exploration..269

    The Future of Agentic AI in Space Exploration 270

Chapter 27 Creative AI and Artistic Agency 272

The Rise of Creative AI 272

The Concept of Creativity: Human or Machine? 274

Artistic Agency and the Role of the Creator 275

The Impact of AI on Human Creativity 277

Ethical and Philosophical Considerations 279

Chapter 28 Agentic AI in Environmental Protection 281

Understanding Agentic AI 281

AI in Climate Change Monitoring 282

AI in Climate Change Mitigation 284

Ethical and Governance Issues 288

Chapter 29 Autonomous Transportation................................290

The Rise of Autonomous Cars..290

Technologies Behind Autonomous Cars..........................291

Challenges in Autonomous Car Development................294

Autonomous Trucks 296

Chapter 30 Agentic AI in Law and Governance...................300

Understanding Agentic AI 301

The Potential Benefits of Agentic AI in Law and
Governance 302

Challenges and Risks of Agentic AI in Law and Governance 305

The Future of Agentic AI in Law and Governance..........308

Chapter 31 The Next Generation of Agentic AI 310

Trends Shaping the Future of Agentic AI........................311

Chapter 32 Collaborative Multi-Agent Systems 319

What is a Collaborative Multi-Agent System?....................320

Agent Interactions in Collaborative Multi-Agent Systems 321

Applications of Collaborative Multi-Agent Systems.........324

Future Trends in Collaborative Multi-Agent Systems 327

Chapter 33 Quantum Computing and Agentic AI 329

Quantum Computing: A New Paradigm 330

The Intersection of Quantum Computing and AI...........331

Chapter 34 AI Ethics in a Global Context..............................339

The Global Nature of AI Development............................340

Ethical Concerns in Autonomous Systems 341

The Need for Global AI Ethics Guidelines 343

Challenges to Harmonizing Global AI Ethics 345

Chapter 35 The Role of Agentic AI in Space Colonization 348

    The Role of Agentic AI in Space Colonization 351

Chapter 36 Overcoming Technological Hurdles 358

Chapter 37 Ensuring Human Oversight 367

    The Challenge of Autonomous Systems........................367

    The Importance of Human Oversight..............................368

    Mechanisms for Ensuring Accountability 370

    The Role of Public Trust...374

Chapter 38 Interfacing Agentic AI with Humans..................376

Chapter 39 Mitigating Environmental Impact 386

Chapter 40 Preparing Society for Agentic AI.......................396

Chapter 41 Philosophical Reflections on Agency.................405

Chapter 42 The Future of Work with Agentic AI 414

    The Impact of Agentic AI on the Workforce...................415

    The Creation of New Roles 417

    Transformation of Workplaces 417

    AI in Industry Transformation..418

    Healthcare and Medicine...419

Financial Services and Insurance 420

Chapter 43 Ethical Dilemmas and Moral Questions............423

    Understanding Ethical Dilemmas 423

    The Role of Ethics in Decision Making..............................424

    Unresolved Ethical Challenges in Modern Society 425

Chapter 44 Collaboration Between AI and Humanity..........433

    The Role of AI in Shaping the Future 434

    The Power of Human Creativity and Judgment...............435

    Building Partnerships for a Better Future.........................441

Chapter 45 Beyond Agency: The Next Frontier in AI.........443

    The Role of AI in Shaping the Future 443

    The Power of Human Creativity and Judgment...............444

    Overcoming Challenges in AI-Human Collaboration.....449

    Early Concepts and Foundations...460

    The Rise of Computing and Robotics................................461

    From Automation to Autonomy 462

    Current Trends and Future Directions 462

    Future Directions 464

Integration with Emerging Technologies 465

Manufacturing 465

Transportation and Logistics 466

Healthcare 466

Agriculture 466

Energy 467

Defense and Security 467

Entertainment and Media 468

About the Author 501

Bibliography 506

Glossary 510

Summary

This book provides an in-depth exploration of Agentic AI, a groundbreaking field in artificial intelligence characterized by systems capable of autonomous decision-making, adaptability, and goal-oriented behavior. With over 40 chapters, it presents a holistic view of this transformative technology, charting its evolution from theoretical concepts to practical applications shaping industries and societies worldwide.

The journey begins by tracing the historical roots of Agentic AI, detailing how advancements in computing power, neural networks, and machine learning algorithms have paved the way for autonomous systems. Foundational principles such as agency, autonomy, and reinforcement learning are explored to provide readers with a clear understanding of the mechanisms enabling these systems to operate independently within defined environments.

The book delves into diverse applications of Agentic AI, highlighting its impact across sectors. In healthcare, autonomous AI systems revolutionize diagnostics, treatment planning, and patient care by leveraging real-time data and personalized algorithms. Autonomous mobility features prominently, with self-driving vehicles and drones representing the forefront of innovation. In finance, AI-driven trading agents demonstrate the ability to analyze market trends and execute decisions faster and more accurately than human counterparts. Creative industries are also transformed, as AI systems generate art, music, and narratives that challenge traditional notions of authorship and creativity. Meanwhile, defense and security sectors benefit from intelligent systems capable of real-time threat detection and response.

Ethical considerations and societal implications form a critical part of the discourse. The book tackles pressing questions about accountability, particularly in scenarios where autonomous decisions lead to significant consequences. It also addresses the risks of bias in AI systems, emphasizing the need for fairness and inclusivity in their design and deployment. Governance and control mechanisms are discussed extensively, underscoring the importance of regulatory frameworks to ensure safe and ethical use.

The human-AI relationship is another focal point, as the book examines how Agentic AI reshapes traditional roles and collaborations. From augmenting human capabilities to raising concerns about job displacement, the interplay between humans and autonomous systems presents both opportunities and challenges.

Looking ahead, the book envisions a future where Agentic AI continues to evolve, driving innovation while reshaping global industries and societal structures. Emerging trends, such as hybrid human-AI teams and AI-enhanced decision-making in governance, are explored alongside speculative scenarios about the potential risks and benefits of superintelligent systems. The book emphasizes the need for proactive policymaking and international cooperation to harness the benefits of Agentic AI while mitigating its risks.

This comprehensive guide serves as a resource for professionals, policymakers, and enthusiasts alike, offering both theoretical insights and practical perspectives. It is a call to action for embracing the possibilities of Agentic AI responsibly and ethically, ensuring that its development aligns with the values and needs of humanity. By providing a thorough understanding of Agentic AI's capabilities, challenges, and future potential, this book equips readers to navigate the complexities of an increasingly AI-driven world.

Chapter 1 The Concept of Agency in AI

Artificial Intelligence (AI) has rapidly evolved, not just in its technical capabilities but also in its conceptual foundations. One of the most pivotal aspects of AI research and development is the concept of agency. Agency in AI refers to the capacity of systems to perceive, decide, and act within their environment, often autonomously and with minimal human intervention. Understanding this concept is crucial for advancing AI technologies and addressing their ethical, practical, and philosophical implications.

Agentic AI embodies three interrelated attributes: autonomy, decision-making, and self-directed goals. These elements work in harmony to create systems capable of operating in dynamic and complex environments.

Autonomy

Autonomy in AI refers to the ability of a system to operate independently of direct human control. An autonomous system can analyze its environment, interpret data, and execute tasks without requiring constant oversight. For example, self-driving cars must navigate traffic, respond to obstacles, and make route decisions autonomously.

Autonomy is a spectrum rather than a binary attribute. On one end, systems exhibit low autonomy, functioning primarily as tools that execute predefined instructions. On the other end are highly autonomous systems capable of learning, adapting, and even evolving their behaviors over time. Autonomy in AI raises critical questions about control, accountability, and trust. For instance, who bears responsibility when an autonomous system makes an error?

Decision-Making

Decision-making is at the core of agentic AI. It involves selecting a course of action from multiple alternatives based on input data, learned experiences, or preprogrammed rules. Decision-making can range from simple binary choices, such as a thermostat deciding to turn on or off, to complex scenarios, such as AI diagnosing diseases or managing stock portfolios.

Advanced AI systems leverage algorithms, neural networks, and probabilistic reasoning to make informed decisions. Reinforcement learning, for instance, allows AI to learn optimal decision-making strategies through trial and error. Systems like AlphaGo, which defeated human champions in the game of Go, showcase how sophisticated decision-making capabilities enable AI to excel in specialized domains.

Self-Directed Goals

Self-directed goals distinguish agentic AI from purely reactive systems. An agentic AI system is not merely responding to stimuli but also pursuing objectives that it prioritizes based on its programming or learned behavior. For instance, a robotic vacuum cleaner might optimize its cleaning pattern to cover the entire floor efficiently, while a language model might refine its answers to align with user preferences.

Self-directed goals can be predefined by developers or emergent, arising from the system's interactions with its environment. This aspect of agency brings AI closer to mimicking human-like intentionality, which raises philosophical and ethical debates about the nature of machine intelligence and its potential alignment with human values.

Historical Context and Evolution

The concept of agency in AI has roots in early artificial intelligence research, where the goal was to create systems that could emulate human problem-solving and decision-making. Early programs, like the Logic Theorist (1956) and ELIZA (1966), exhibited rudimentary forms of agency by performing tasks like proving theorems or simulating conversation.

The development of intelligent agents gained momentum in the 1980s and 1990s with advancements in distributed systems, robotics, and cognitive science. These agents were designed to operate in specific environments, such as monitoring network traffic or managing supply chains. The emergence of multi-agent systems further expanded the concept of agency, emphasizing collaboration and competition among multiple AI entities to achieve shared or individual goals.

Today, agentic AI is integral to various applications, from virtual assistants like Siri and Alexa to autonomous drones and industrial robots. The increasing sophistication of these systems reflects the rapid progress in machine learning, natural language processing, and computer vision.

Applications of Agentic AI

Agentic AI finds applications across diverse domains, enhancing efficiency, productivity, and innovation. Some prominent examples include:

Healthcare

AI agents in healthcare assist in diagnostics, treatment planning, and patient monitoring. Systems like IBM Watson analyze medical records and research to recommend personalized treatment plans. Autonomous surgical robots enhance precision and reduce human error.

Finance

In the financial sector, agentic AI is used for algorithmic trading, fraud detection, and credit scoring. Autonomous agents analyze market trends and execute trades with minimal human intervention, often outperforming traditional strategies.

Transportation

Autonomous vehicles exemplify agentic AI, combining autonomy, decision-making, and goal-directed behavior to navigate complex road conditions. These systems integrate data from sensors, cameras, and maps to make real-time decisions.

Customer Service

Chatbots and virtual assistants leverage natural language processing to understand and respond to customer queries. These systems adapt to user preferences over time, improving their ability to address concerns effectively.

Robotics

Robotic systems in manufacturing and logistics demonstrate agentic behavior by performing tasks like assembling products or managing inventory autonomously. Collaborative robots, or cobots, work alongside humans to enhance efficiency and safety.

Ethical and Philosophical Implications

The rise of agentic AI brings several ethical and philosophical challenges to the forefront.

Responsibility and Accountability

When an AI system makes a decision or takes an action, determining who is responsible can be complex. Is it the developer, the user, or the system itself? This question becomes critical in scenarios involving accidents or unintended consequences.

Bias and Fairness

Agentic AI systems rely on data for training, which can embed existing biases into their decision-making processes. Ensuring fairness and preventing discrimination requires careful design, testing, and oversight.

Alignment with Human Values

As AI systems become more autonomous, ensuring their goals align with human values becomes increasingly important. Misaligned goals can lead to unintended and potentially harmful outcomes.

Agency and Personhood

The notion of agency in AI raises philosophical questions about personhood and consciousness. If an AI system exhibits decision-making and goal-directed behavior, does it warrant moral consideration? While current AI lacks consciousness, future advancements may blur these distinctions.

The Future of Agentic AI

The evolution of agentic AI is poised to transform society further, with both opportunities and risks. Emerging trends include:

Generalized Agency

Future AI systems may move beyond domain-specific capabilities to exhibit generalized agency, handling diverse tasks with minimal retraining. This shift would enable more adaptable and versatile systems.

Human-AI Collaboration

Advances in agentic AI will enhance collaboration between humans and machines, combining the strengths of both to solve complex problems. For example, AI agents could assist researchers in scientific discovery or aid policymakers in addressing global challenges.

Regulatory Frameworks

As agentic AI becomes more prevalent, developing robust regulatory frameworks will be essential to address issues of safety, accountability, and ethical considerations. Policymakers and stakeholders must work together to ensure responsible development and deployment.

The concept of agency in AI is a cornerstone of its potential to transform industries, enhance human capabilities, and address societal challenges. By defining agentic AI through the lenses of autonomy, decision-making, and self-directed goals, we gain a deeper understanding of its capabilities and limitations. As the field continues to evolve, fostering interdisciplinary collaboration and ethical foresight will be crucial to harnessing the power of agentic AI for the greater good.

Chapter 2 Historical Roots of Agentic Systems

The concept of agentic systems, referring to entities capable of independent action and decision-making, has fascinated humanity for centuries. The journey from early automata to modern artificial intelligence (AI) developments provides a rich tapestry of innovation, cultural significance, and technological breakthroughs. This exploration reveals not only the evolution of technology but also humanity's unrelenting quest to replicate and extend its cognitive and mechanical capabilities.

Early Automata: The Seeds of Agentic Thought

The roots of agentic systems can be traced back to ancient civilizations. Early myths and legends frequently featured self-operating machines and intelligent constructs. For example, in Greek mythology, Hephaestus, the god of blacksmithing, was said to have crafted automata—mechanical servants that could move and act independently. Similarly, the Golem of Jewish folklore symbolized the idea of an artificial entity created to perform tasks or protect its creator.

Ancient Mechanical Marvels

The first tangible evidence of automata appeared in ancient Egypt, Greece, and China. One notable example is the Greek engineer Hero of Alexandria (10–70 CE), whose designs included mechanical birds, puppets, and even a steam-powered device called the aeolipile. These creations were driven by principles of hydraulics, pneumatics, and mechanics, showcasing a rudimentary understanding of automated systems.

In China, inventors like Su Song in the 11th century constructed elaborate water clocks with mechanical figurines that could move and interact. Such devices were not merely functional; they also embodied the human fascination with mimicking life's dynamics, setting the stage for more advanced pursuits.

The Islamic Golden Age

During the Islamic Golden Age (8th to 14th centuries), engineers like Al-Jazari expanded the boundaries of automata.

His "Book of Knowledge of Ingenious Mechanical Devices" (1206) described numerous machines, including programmable humanoid automata and automated water clocks. These inventions emphasized practical applications and introduced early forms of programmability—a foundational concept in modern agentic systems.

Renaissance and Enlightenment: Mechanizing Intelligence

The Renaissance saw a resurgence of interest in automata, spurred by advances in mechanics and an intensified curiosity about human anatomy and cognition. Philosophers, artists, and engineers began envisioning machines that not only performed tasks but also simulated aspects of human intelligence.

Leonardo da Vinci's Automata

Leonardo da Vinci, a polymath of the Renaissance, designed several mechanical devices, including a knight automaton capable of mimicking human movements. Though his creations were not realized during his lifetime, da Vinci's detailed schematics revealed an intricate understanding of mechanics and human physiology.

Cartesian Philosophy and Mechanistic Views

The Enlightenment era introduced philosophical underpinnings for the study of intelligence and agency. René Descartes famously compared animals to machines, positing that their behaviors could be explained entirely through mechanical principles. This mechanistic view encouraged thinkers to approach intelligence as a system of processes, inspiring early explorations into artificial cognition.

The Industrial Revolution: Precision and Automation

The Industrial Revolution (18th to 19th centuries) marked a turning point in the development of agentic systems. The rise of manufacturing technologies and precision engineering enabled the construction of more sophisticated machines, many of which performed tasks autonomously.

Automata as Entertainment

The 18th century saw a surge in intricate automata created for entertainment. Jacques de Vaucanson's "Digesting Duck" and Pierre Jaquet-Droz's "The Writer" demonstrated remarkable ingenuity. These devices could mimic complex actions, such as writing or playing musical instruments, sparking both wonder and debate about the potential for artificial intelligence.

Early Computational Machines

Simultaneously, inventors began exploring mechanical computation. Charles Babbage's Analytical Engine (1837) and Ada Lovelace's conceptualization of programming it marked the dawn of programmable systems. Lovelace's insights, particularly her assertion that machines could manipulate symbols to create patterns and even music, laid the groundwork for future AI research.

The 20th Century: The Birth of Artificial Intelligence

The 20th century witnessed rapid advancements in mathematics, computer science, and engineering, culminating in the formal emergence of artificial intelligence as a discipline. Researchers sought to build systems capable of reasoning, learning, and interacting with their environments.

Theoretical Foundations

In 1936, Alan Turing introduced the concept of a "Universal Machine," capable of simulating any algorithmic process. This idea became the theoretical cornerstone of computer science and AI. Turing later posed the question, "Can machines think?" in his seminal 1950 chapter, proposing the Turing Test as a criterion for evaluating machine intelligence.

Simultaneously, Norbert Wiener's work on cybernetics explored feedback mechanisms in machines, drawing parallels between biological and mechanical systems. These ideas influenced early AI research, emphasizing the importance of adaptive and self-regulating behaviors.

Early AI Programs

The first AI programs emerged in the mid-20th century, with notable examples including the Logic Theorist (1955) and the General Problem Solver (1957). These systems attempted to replicate human reasoning and problem-solving, albeit within limited domains. The development of Lisp in 1958 by John McCarthy provided a powerful programming language for AI applications, accelerating progress in the field.

Robotics and Perception

Parallel to theoretical AI research, robotics advanced significantly during this era. Shakey the Robot (1966) was one of the earliest examples of a mobile robot capable of perceiving and interacting with its environment. Combining AI algorithms with sensors and actuators, Shakey demonstrated rudimentary agentic behavior, paving the way for modern autonomous systems.

Modern AI Developments: Toward Autonomous Agents

The 21st century has seen an explosion of AI applications, driven by exponential increases in computational power, data availability, and algorithmic sophistication. Today's agentic systems span a diverse range of domains, from robotics and natural language processing to autonomous vehicles and smart assistants.

Machine Learning and Neural Networks

Machine learning, particularly deep learning, has revolutionized AI. Inspired by the structure of biological neurons, artificial neural networks enable systems to learn patterns and make decisions from vast datasets. Breakthroughs in image recognition, natural language understanding, and game-playing AI exemplify the power of these techniques. For instance, AlphaGo's victory over a human world champion in 2016 highlighted the potential for AI to master complex strategic reasoning.

Robotics and Autonomy

Modern robotics integrates AI to create systems capable of navigating and manipulating complex environments. Boston Dynamics' robots, such as Atlas and Spot, exhibit remarkable agility and adaptability, demonstrating how far agentic systems have come since the days of mechanical automata. Autonomous vehicles, driven by AI technologies like computer vision and reinforcement learning, are poised to revolutionize transportation.

Ethical and Societal Implications

As AI systems become more autonomous, ethical considerations have gained prominence. Issues such as algorithmic bias, privacy, and the potential displacement of human labor challenge researchers and policymakers. The development of explainable AI (XAI) and frameworks for responsible AI seeks to address these concerns, ensuring that agentic systems align with human values.

The Rise of Multi-Agent Systems

Multi-agent systems, where multiple autonomous entities interact and collaborate, represent a cutting-edge area of research. These systems are crucial for applications such as swarm robotics, distributed problem-solving, and smart city infrastructure. By modeling interactions between agents, researchers aim to create more robust and scalable solutions to complex challenges.

Future Directions: Beyond Human Cognition

The trajectory of agentic systems suggests an ongoing evolution toward greater autonomy, intelligence, and integration with human society. Emerging technologies, such as quantum computing and brain-computer interfaces, hold the potential to transform AI further, enabling systems that surpass human cognitive capabilities in specific domains.

Artificial General Intelligence (AGI)

While current AI systems excel at specialized tasks, the quest for AGI—a system capable of general, human-like intelligence—remains a grand challenge. Advances in cognitive architectures, meta-learning, and neuro-symbolic AI are key areas of focus for achieving this milestone.

Human-AI Collaboration

Rather than replacing humans, future agentic systems may enhance human capabilities. From collaborative robots (cobots) in manufacturing to AI-driven medical diagnostics, the emphasis is shifting toward symbiotic relationships between humans and intelligent agents.

The historical roots of agentic systems reveal humanity's enduring fascination with creating entities that can think, act, and learn. From the early automata of ancient civilizations to the sophisticated AI systems of today, this journey underscores the interplay between technological ingenuity and philosophical inquiry. As we continue to push the boundaries of what machines can do, the lessons of history remind us to balance innovation with responsibility, ensuring that agentic systems serve the greater good of humanity.

Chapter 3 Philosophy of Agency in Machines

The concept of agency has traditionally been a cornerstone of philosophical inquiry, rooted in questions about human autonomy, intentionality, and moral responsibility. However, the rise of artificial intelligence (AI) and increasingly autonomous systems has introduced a new dimension to the discourse: Can machines possess agency, and if so, what does that imply for society, ethics, and human-machine interaction? Examining agency through the combined lens of philosophy and cognitive science offers a nuanced understanding of this question, providing insights into the nature of machine autonomy and its implications.

Defining Agency: Philosophical Foundations

At its core, agency refers to the capacity of an entity to act intentionally and autonomously within a given environment. Philosophical traditions, from Aristotelian ethics to Kantian deontology, have explored the prerequisites for agency, often emphasizing characteristics like rationality, intentionality, and moral responsibility.

Intentionality and Autonomy

Intentionality is the directedness of mental states toward objects, events, or states of affairs. For an entity to have agency, it must act with intent—a deliberative quality that distinguishes goal-directed behavior from mere reaction.

Autonomy refers to the ability to make independent decisions, free from external coercion. Philosophers like Kant argue that autonomy is foundational to moral agency, as it allows an entity to act according to principles rather than external influences.

Responsibility and Moral Agency

Responsibility is a hallmark of agency. Human agents are held accountable for their actions because they are presumed to act intentionally and autonomously.

The attribution of moral agency to an entity depends on its capacity to understand the consequences of its actions and align them with ethical principles.

Agency in Machines: A Cognitive Science Perspective

While traditional philosophy often limits agency to humans (and sometimes higher animals), advances in cognitive science challenge this view by exploring how agency might manifest in artificial systems.

Cognitive Architecture and Machine Autonomy

Modern AI systems, such as reinforcement learning agents, exhibit goal-directed behavior. By optimizing for specific outcomes based on feedback from their environment, these systems demonstrate a form of pseudo-intentionality.

Autonomy in machines is often defined in terms of self-sufficiency in decision-making. Autonomous vehicles, for instance, must navigate complex environments without direct human intervention, mimicking human-like decision-making processes.

Simulation of Intentionality

AI systems simulate intentionality through algorithms that prioritize goals, assess probabilities, and make decisions. However, these processes lack the subjective experience that characterizes human intentionality.

Cognitive scientists debate whether this simulated intentionality constitutes genuine agency or merely an illusion of agency engineered by human designers.

Embodiment and Situatedness

Embodiment theory suggests that agency arises from the interaction of an entity with its physical environment. Robots equipped with sensory and motor capabilities demonstrate a form of embodied agency, adapting their behavior based on environmental stimuli.

Situated cognition emphasizes the importance of context in shaping agency. Machines designed to operate in dynamic environments, such as drones or robotic assistants, embody this principle by modifying their actions in response to real-world conditions.

Philosophical Challenges to Machine Agency

Despite the advancements in AI and robotics, the attribution of agency to machines raises significant philosophical challenges.

The Problem of Consciousness

Agency in humans is deeply tied to consciousness, the subjective awareness of one's existence and actions. Critics argue that without consciousness, machines cannot possess true agency.

While some AI systems can mimic decision-making processes, they lack qualia—the subjective experiences that underpin human intentionality.

Free Will and Determinism

The debate over free will versus determinism complicates discussions of machine agency. If human actions can be reduced to deterministic processes, then machines operating under deterministic algorithms might be said to possess a comparable form of agency.

However, this deterministic view undermines traditional notions of moral responsibility, raising questions about whether machines should be held accountable for their actions.

Ethical Implications

If machines possess agency, they may also bear moral responsibility for their actions. Autonomous weapons systems, for example, challenge ethical frameworks by operating without direct human oversight.

Assigning agency to machines could blur the lines of accountability, shifting blame from human operators to systems that lack genuine moral understanding.

Cognitive Science Contributions to Understanding Machine Agency

Cognitive science provides a framework for analyzing the mechanisms underlying machine behavior, offering insights into whether such behavior qualifies as agency.

Neural Networks and Learning

Deep learning models replicate certain aspects of human cognition, such as pattern recognition and decision-making. By learning from data, these systems exhibit adaptive behavior akin to human learning.

However, the opacity of neural networks, often referred to as the "black box" problem, raises questions about the intentionality behind machine decisions.

Cognitive Models and Artificial Minds

Cognitive models simulate human thought processes, providing a basis for designing AI systems with agency-like qualities. Projects like cognitive architectures (e.g., ACT-R or Soar) aim to emulate human reasoning in machines.

These models, while sophisticated, remain limited in their ability to replicate the depth and richness of human cognition.

Ethological Approaches

Ethology, the study of animal behavior, informs the design of autonomous systems by emphasizing adaptive behavior in response to environmental cues.

By modeling machine behavior on biological systems, researchers create robots and AI agents capable of exhibiting goal-directed actions, further blurring the lines between human and machine agency.

Practical Implications of Machine Agency

The attribution of agency to machines has far-reaching implications for technology, society, and ethics.

Human-Machine Collaboration

Machines with agency-like properties can serve as collaborators in fields such as medicine, engineering, and education. Autonomous surgical robots, for example, perform precise procedures while responding to real-time data.

Effective collaboration requires trust, which hinges on understanding the limits of machine agency and ensuring transparency in decision-making processes.

Legal and Ethical Frameworks

As machines take on more autonomous roles, legal systems must adapt to address questions of liability and accountability. Should an autonomous vehicle be held responsible for an accident, or should liability rest with its designers?

Ethical guidelines, such as the EU's AI Ethics Guidelines, emphasize the importance of ensuring that machines operate transparently and align with human values.

Cultural and Social Impact

The perception of machine agency influences societal attitudes toward AI. Anthropomorphizing machines, as seen with virtual assistants like Siri or Alexa, fosters a sense of agency that may not reflect the underlying reality.

This anthropomorphism can have both positive and negative effects, enhancing user engagement while potentially obscuring the limitations of machine capabilities.

Toward a Unified Theory of Agency

Reconciling philosophical and cognitive science perspectives on agency requires a unified theory that accommodates both human and machine forms of agency.

Gradations of Agency

Agency may exist on a spectrum, with humans occupying one end and simpler systems like thermostats occupying the other. Machines, depending on their complexity, fall somewhere in between.

This gradient model acknowledges the varying degrees of autonomy, intentionality, and responsibility across entities.

Emergent Agency

Emergent agency arises from the interaction of simpler components within a complex system. Swarm robotics, for instance, demonstrates collective behavior that mimics agency despite the absence of centralized control.

Philosophical inquiry into emergent phenomena can shed light on how agency manifests in systems that lack individual consciousness.

Interdisciplinary Collaboration

Bridging philosophy and cognitive science requires collaboration between disciplines. Philosophers can provide conceptual clarity, while cognitive scientists offer empirical data to test hypotheses about agency.

This interdisciplinary approach ensures a holistic understanding of agency, encompassing both theoretical and practical dimensions.

Conclusion

The philosophy of agency in machines is a dynamic and evolving field that challenges traditional notions of autonomy, intentionality, and responsibility. By integrating insights from philosophy and cognitive science, researchers can develop a more comprehensive understanding of what it means for machines to act with agency. As AI and robotics continue to advance, this dialogue will become increasingly important, shaping the ethical and societal frameworks that govern human-machine interaction.

Chapter 4 Components of Agentic AI

Artificial Intelligence (AI) has evolved into a transformative technology, reshaping industries and our daily lives. Among its many branches, agentic AI stands out as a domain focused on developing autonomous systems capable of perceiving their environment, reasoning about their goals, learning from experience, and acting purposefully. These core components—perception, reasoning, learning, and action—form the foundation of agentic AI, enabling systems to function effectively in complex, dynamic environments. In this discussion, we delve into these components, exploring their significance, interconnections, and the challenges they present.

1. Perception: Sensing and Understanding the Environment

Perception is the process by which an AI system gathers and interprets data from its environment. This capability mimics the human sensory system, allowing agents to create a meaningful representation of the world around them. Perception typically involves sensors (hardware) and algorithms (software) that process raw data into actionable information.

Key Aspects of Perception:

Sensors and Data Acquisition:

Sensors capture raw data from various modalities such as vision (cameras), sound (microphones), touch (haptic sensors), and more. Advanced systems may also use LIDAR, RADAR, or thermal imaging for specific applications.

Data Processing:

Raw sensor data is often noisy and unstructured. Preprocessing techniques like filtering, noise reduction, and feature extraction are applied to make the data usable.

Recognition and Interpretation:

Using machine learning models, particularly convolutional neural networks (CNNs) for image data or recurrent neural networks (RNNs) for temporal data, AI systems recognize patterns, objects, and events. For instance, a self-driving car must identify pedestrians, traffic lights, and road signs.

Challenges in Perception:

Ambiguity: Interpreting ambiguous data, such as distinguishing shadows from physical obstacles.

Dynamic Environments: Handling rapidly changing scenarios, like moving objects in a crowded space.

Multimodal Fusion: Integrating information from multiple sensors seamlessly to improve accuracy.

Perception is foundational for the other components of agentic AI because it provides the input that reasoning and learning processes rely on.

2. Reasoning: Making Informed Decisions

Reasoning allows AI systems to process information, draw conclusions, and make decisions. This capability mirrors human cognitive processes, where logic, inference, and problem-solving play central roles. Reasoning can be deductive, inductive, or abductive, each serving different problem-solving contexts.

Types of Reasoning:

Deductive Reasoning:

Involves deriving specific conclusions from general principles. For example, if an AI knows all vehicles stop at red lights, it can deduce that a nearby car will halt when the light turns red.

Inductive Reasoning:

Involves generalizing from specific observations. For instance, if an AI notices that heavy traffic consistently occurs during rain, it might infer a correlation between rain and traffic congestion.

Abductive Reasoning:

Involves forming the best explanation for observed phenomena. If an AI detects smoke, it might infer the possibility of a fire.

Reasoning Frameworks:

Rule-Based Systems:

Use predefined rules for decision-making. While efficient for well-defined tasks, they lack flexibility in dynamic scenarios.

Probabilistic Reasoning:

Models uncertainty using probability distributions, enabling systems to make informed decisions despite incomplete information. Bayesian networks are a common tool in this approach.

Logic-Based Reasoning:

Employs formal logic systems, such as propositional or predicate logic, for precise reasoning.

Challenges in Reasoning:

Scalability: Handling large-scale, complex reasoning problems.

Uncertainty: Making decisions with incomplete or ambiguous data.

Dynamic Adaptation: Adjusting reasoning strategies based on real-time feedback.

3. Learning: Improving Over Time

Learning enables AI systems to adapt and improve their performance based on experience. This capability is essential for handling novel situations and achieving long-term autonomy. Machine learning (ML), the core mechanism for AI learning, spans supervised, unsupervised, and reinforcement learning paradigms.

Learning Paradigms:

Supervised Learning:

Involves training models on labeled datasets where input-output pairs are provided. This approach is common in tasks like image classification and speech recognition.

Unsupervised Learning:

Deals with unlabeled data, focusing on discovering hidden structures or patterns. Clustering and dimensionality reduction are key techniques.

Reinforcement Learning (RL):

Trains agents through interaction with their environment. Agents receive rewards or penalties based on their actions, learning optimal strategies through trial and error. RL is crucial for applications like game-playing AI and robotic control.

Transfer and Meta-Learning:

Transfer Learning: Leveraging knowledge from one domain to improve performance in another. For example, an AI trained to recognize cats might adapt to recognize dogs with minimal additional training.

Meta-Learning: Often referred to as "learning to learn," this approach enables models to adapt rapidly to new tasks with limited data.

Challenges in Learning:

Overfitting: Models that perform well on training data but poorly on unseen data.

Data Quality: Reliance on high-quality, diverse datasets.

Continual Learning: Maintaining performance while learning new tasks without forgetting previously learned ones (the catastrophic forgetting problem).

Learning is vital for enabling agentic AI systems to operate effectively in environments that are too complex or unpredictable to be fully specified in advance.

4. Action: Executing Purposeful Behavior

Action involves translating decisions into physical or virtual outcomes. This component enables agentic AI to interact with the world, completing the perception-reasoning-action loop. Actions can range from robotic movements to generating text or making transactions.

Action Planning and Execution:

Motion Planning:

In robotics, this involves determining the optimal path for movement, considering constraints like obstacles and energy efficiency. Algorithms like Rapidly-exploring Random Trees (RRT) and A* are common.

Policy Execution:

In reinforcement learning, actions are chosen based on a policy that maps states to actions. Policies can be deterministic or stochastic.

Feedback Control:

Ensures actions achieve desired outcomes by continuously monitoring and adjusting performance. For example, a robotic arm might use feedback to grasp an object securely.

Challenges in Action:

Latency: Ensuring timely responses, particularly in safety-critical systems like autonomous vehicles.

Precision: Achieving high accuracy in physical tasks, such as surgical robotics.

Coordination: Managing multiple actions simultaneously, especially in multi-agent systems.

Interplay Among Components

The true power of agentic AI lies in the seamless integration of perception, reasoning, learning, and action. Each component feeds into and depends on the others:

Perception provides the data for reasoning and learning.

Reasoning uses this data to make decisions and informs learning processes about relevant features.

Learning refines the models used in perception and reasoning, improving performance over time.

Action generates new interactions with the environment, creating additional data for perception and learning.

For example, in autonomous driving, perception identifies road conditions, reasoning determines the safest route, learning adapts to new driving scenarios, and action executes the driving commands. A failure in any component can compromise the entire system.

Challenges and Future Directions

Despite significant progress, agentic AI faces several challenges:

Generalization:

Developing systems that perform well across diverse tasks and environments without extensive retraining.

Ethical Considerations:

Ensuring AI actions align with human values and do not cause harm.

Robustness:

Building systems resilient to errors, adversarial attacks, and unforeseen circumstances.

Explainability:

Making AI decisions and actions interpretable to humans, especially in high-stakes domains like healthcare.

Future Directions:

Neuro-symbolic AI:

Combining symbolic reasoning with neural networks to leverage the strengths of both approaches.

Lifelong Learning:

Developing AI systems capable of continuous learning without catastrophic forgetting.

Human-AI Collaboration:

Enhancing interaction between humans and AI systems to create synergistic workflows.

Embodied AI:

Integrating AI with physical systems like robots to enable more intuitive and effective interactions with the physical world.

Agentic AI represents a frontier in artificial intelligence, aiming to create systems that perceive, reason, learn, and act autonomously. These capabilities enable AI to tackle complex, real-world problems, from autonomous vehicles to personalized healthcare. However, the challenges of integrating these components, ensuring ethical alignment, and achieving robustness and generalization remain significant. Continued advancements in this field promise transformative impacts across industries and society, bringing us closer to realizing the full potential of intelligent, autonomous agents.

Chapter 5 Agentic AI vs Other AI Models

In the field of artificial intelligence (AI), various models are designed with different purposes and capabilities. From narrow AI systems that are specialized in a single task, to the theoretical ideal of general AI, these models differ greatly in scope and function. Among these, the concept of *agentic AI* has emerged as a novel and dynamic approach. But what exactly is agentic AI, and how does it compare to other prevalent AI models such as narrow, general, and hybrid systems? In this chapter, we will explore these distinctions, examining their characteristics, strengths, limitations, and implications.

What is Agentic AI?

Agentic AI refers to artificial intelligence systems that exhibit autonomous decision-making capabilities. These systems are designed to function as "agents" that act in the world based on certain goals, preferences, and reasoning processes.

Agentic AI is often associated with goal-directed behavior, where the AI makes decisions to achieve certain outcomes, sometimes with minimal human intervention. It can adjust its strategies, learn from its environment, and potentially optimize its actions to fulfill long-term goals.

Unlike traditional AI systems, which are typically programmed with specific, predefined tasks in mind, agentic AI possesses a level of flexibility and adaptability, which enables it to function in dynamic environments. This autonomy is what sets agentic AI apart from many other models, as it behaves not merely as a tool, but as an independent entity capable of interacting with and influencing the world in complex ways.

Agentic AI is often linked to concepts such as reinforcement learning (RL), where agents learn through trial and error, receiving feedback that shapes their future actions. For instance, an agentic AI might be tasked with navigating a dynamic environment or performing a sequence of operations without the need for constant human supervision.

Narrow AI (Weak AI)

Narrow AI, also known as *weak AI*, is perhaps the most prevalent form of artificial intelligence today. Narrow AI systems are designed to perform a specific task or a set of closely related tasks. These systems can achieve remarkable results within their designated domain but are limited in their capacity to handle tasks outside that scope.

Examples of narrow AI include image recognition software, natural language processing (NLP) applications, voice assistants like Siri or Alexa, and recommendation algorithms used by streaming services. These systems excel in the tasks they are programmed to perform but lack the ability to generalize or learn beyond their designated domain.

Key Characteristics of Narrow AI:

Specialization: Narrow AI excels in specific tasks but is not designed for general problem-solving.

Limited Autonomy: While narrow AI can make decisions within its task, it is still heavily dependent on human input and programming for its operation.

Task-Specific: These systems cannot adapt to or operate in situations outside their specific area of expertise.

Comparison to Agentic AI:

Narrow AI is fundamentally different from agentic AI in that it lacks autonomy and general problem-solving capabilities. While agentic AI is designed to act as an independent agent making decisions to achieve broader goals, narrow AI is constrained by its domain-specific design. Narrow AI is typically task-bound, and its abilities are limited to the tasks for which it has been programmed, without the flexibility seen in agentic AI.

For example, a narrow AI used in a customer service chatbot can answer a set of pre-determined queries but would be unable to engage in a more complex or open-ended conversation about unrelated topics. In contrast, agentic AI could potentially learn new ways to respond to unforeseen queries by adapting its strategies and problem-solving techniques.

General AI (Strong AI)

General AI, also known as *strong AI*, is an idealized form of artificial intelligence that would have the capacity to understand, learn, and apply intelligence across a broad range of tasks—similar to human cognition. Unlike narrow AI, which is restricted to a single domain, general AI is designed to function with a level of versatility and adaptability that would allow it to perform any intellectual task that a human can do.

General AI would be able to integrate knowledge from diverse fields, reason abstractly, and make decisions based on complex understanding. In theory, general AI would not only be capable of tasks like image recognition and language processing but would also possess the flexibility to navigate new challenges, devise strategies, and transfer knowledge from one domain to another.

Key Characteristics of General AI:

Broad Applicability: General AI can solve problems in a wide variety of fields, not limited to a narrow domain.

Human-like Flexibility: It can adapt and learn from experience, applying knowledge in ways similar to human intelligence.

Reasoning and Understanding: General AI can reason through complex situations, abstractly process information, and make decisions based on a high-level understanding.

Comparison to Agentic AI:

While agentic AI is designed to autonomously achieve specific goals through intelligent decision-making, general AI focuses more on broad cognitive abilities and the capability to solve a wide range of problems. Both share a certain level of flexibility, but the distinction lies in their purpose. Agentic AI is typically goal-oriented, making it ideal for autonomous systems, while general AI's purpose is more about replicating human-like intelligence across various domains.

General AI, in theory, could encompass agentic AI's autonomous decision-making abilities, but it would also incorporate broader cognitive abilities, such as emotional understanding, reasoning, and abstract thought. As a result, agentic AI could be seen as a subset of general AI, focusing on autonomy and goal-driven behavior rather than the entirety of human intelligence.

Hybrid AI Systems

Hybrid AI systems combine elements of different types of artificial intelligence models to achieve greater flexibility and problem-solving capability. These systems integrate techniques from narrow AI, general AI, machine learning, and other approaches to create more robust and adaptable AI solutions.

For instance, a hybrid AI system might combine rule-based logic (typically seen in narrow AI) with machine learning (often used in general AI) to create a system that can handle both structured and unstructured data. Hybrid systems are particularly useful when a single AI model would be insufficient to address the complexity of a task.

Key Characteristics of Hybrid AI:

Integration of Multiple Approaches: Hybrid AI combines strengths from different AI methodologies to create a more capable system.

Adaptability: These systems can leverage the best attributes of narrow and general AI models, offering both task-specific optimization and greater versatility.

Scalability: Hybrid AI systems can scale to handle various types of tasks, making them useful in industries like healthcare, finance, and robotics.

Comparison to Agentic AI:

While hybrid AI systems are designed to leverage a variety of AI approaches, agentic AI focuses primarily on autonomous decision-making to achieve specific goals. In a sense, hybrid systems could incorporate agentic AI as one of their components, benefiting from its goal-driven capabilities. However, hybrid AI also encompasses a broader set of functionalities and is not limited to the decision-making autonomy seen in agentic AI.

For example, in a hybrid system used for medical diagnosis, narrow AI techniques might handle data processing and pattern recognition, while agentic AI could make autonomous decisions on treatment options based on the patient's medical history. This blending of approaches results in a system that is both adaptable and goal-directed.

Summary of Key Differences

Model	Core Focus	Strengths	Limitations
Agentic AI	Goal-driven, autonomous decision-making	High flexibility, adaptability, autonomy	May lack broader cognitive understanding like general AI
Narrow AI	Task-specific expertise	Excellent performance in specific domains	Limited to predefined tasks, cannot generalize
General AI	Broad, human-like intelligence	Can solve diverse problems, human-like reasoning	Theoretical and not yet achieved in practice
Hybrid AI	Integration of multiple AI approaches	Combines strengths of various AI models	Complex to design and maintain

Agentic AI represents a unique approach in the AI landscape by emphasizing autonomy, goal-directed behavior, and adaptability. While it shares similarities with narrow AI, such as its specialized functionality, it surpasses it in its ability to act independently and make decisions without human oversight. Compared to general AI, agentic AI is more focused on achieving specific goals, whereas general AI aims to emulate the full range of human intelligence. Hybrid AI systems, on the other hand, combine various approaches, including agentic AI, to create more versatile and capable systems.

As AI continues to evolve, understanding the distinctions between these models will help guide the development of more sophisticated, efficient, and ethical artificial intelligence systems.

Chapter 6 Building Autonomy in AI Systems

Artificial Intelligence (AI) has rapidly evolved from a theoretical concept into a powerful tool that is increasingly integrated into various industries and domains. One of the key areas where AI systems are making significant strides is in their ability to become autonomous—systems that can operate independently, make decisions, and pursue goals without human intervention. The development of autonomy in AI is essential for enabling systems to perform complex tasks in dynamic environments, adapt to new challenges, and provide scalable solutions. This chapter will explore how AI systems can be designed to enable decision-making and goal orientation, focusing on key concepts such as decision theory, reinforcement learning, multi-agent systems, and ethical considerations in autonomous AI design.

The Foundation of Autonomy in AI Systems

Autonomy in AI systems refers to the ability of an AI to make decisions and take actions based on its internal models and environment, without requiring constant human oversight. The goal is to create systems that can perform tasks, solve problems, and achieve objectives in a way that is independent and adaptive. The development of autonomous systems is grounded in several core principles, including decision-making, learning, and goal-setting. To enable these capabilities, AI systems must have the following elements:

6.1.1. Decision-Making

Decision-making is the process through which an AI system evaluates its environment, considers available options, and selects an action that aligns with its objectives. The decision-making framework used in AI systems can be categorized into several types, such as deterministic decision-making (where outcomes are known and predictable) and probabilistic decision-making (where outcomes are uncertain and depend on probabilities). AI systems that exhibit high autonomy must be capable of making decisions in both static and dynamic environments, where uncertainty and complexity are common.

6.1.2. Learning and Adaptation

A key feature of autonomous AI systems is their ability to learn from experiences and adapt to new situations. Learning enables AI systems to improve their decision-making over time, even in the face of new or unexpected challenges. Reinforcement learning (RL), for instance, is a popular framework for training autonomous agents by allowing them to interact with their environment, receive feedback in the form of rewards or penalties, and adjust their actions accordingly. This process allows the system to learn optimal behaviors and improve its decision-making in future scenarios.

6.1.3. Goal Orientation

For AI systems to be autonomous, they must be able to define and pursue goals. These goals can be set by the system itself (in a self-directed manner) or defined by external entities, such as users or other systems. Goal-oriented AI systems are designed to focus their efforts on achieving specific outcomes, and they adjust their strategies in response to changing conditions and obstacles. Goal-setting in AI systems involves defining clear objectives, determining the resources and actions needed to reach those objectives, and assessing progress over time.

6.2. Enabling Decision-Making in Autonomous AI Systems

Effective decision-making is crucial for enabling autonomy in AI systems. AI systems must be able to weigh different alternatives, consider long-term consequences, and make trade-offs between competing objectives. Several approaches have been developed to enable decision-making in autonomous AI systems:

6.2.1. Classical Decision Theory

Classical decision theory is a well-established framework for understanding how decisions are made under conditions of certainty and uncertainty. It provides a foundation for AI decision-making models by focusing on maximizing utility or expected outcomes. In classical decision theory, an agent selects the action that maximizes its expected utility, given the available information. While this approach is effective in structured environments, real-world situations often involve high levels of uncertainty, which require more advanced decision-making techniques.

6.2.2. Reinforcement Learning (RL)

Reinforcement learning (RL) is one of the most powerful techniques for enabling autonomous decision-making in AI systems. In RL, an agent interacts with an environment and learns from the feedback it receives in the form of rewards and punishments. The agent seeks to maximize cumulative reward over time by learning the optimal policy, which is a mapping from states of the environment to actions. RL is particularly useful for tasks where the decision-making process is sequential, and there is no clear or immediate solution. Over time, RL agents can adapt to new situations, learn from failures, and improve their decision-making abilities.

RL has been successfully applied in various domains, including robotics, gaming, and autonomous vehicles. For example, RL algorithms have enabled AI systems to master complex games such as Go and chess, where the agent must evaluate a wide range of possible moves and select the best strategy over multiple turns.

6.2.3. Decision Trees and Markov Decision Processes (MDPs)

Decision trees and Markov decision processes (MDPs) are mathematical models used to represent decision-making in uncertain environments. A decision tree is a flowchart-like structure that captures a sequence of decisions and their possible outcomes. By evaluating the expected utility of each branch, an AI system can select the most promising path.

Markov decision processes (MDPs) extend decision trees by incorporating probabilities and rewards. In an MDP, an agent transitions between different states based on its actions, and the outcome of each action is probabilistic. By modeling an environment as an MDP, AI systems can compute optimal strategies for decision-making in dynamic settings. Techniques such as value iteration and policy iteration are commonly used to solve MDPs and guide autonomous agents' actions.

6.2.4. Multi-Agent Systems

In some scenarios, autonomous decision-making must occur within a system of interacting agents. Multi-agent systems (MAS) are a powerful framework for enabling autonomy in situations where multiple agents must cooperate or compete to achieve their goals. These systems model interactions between agents, which can be either cooperative, competitive, or neutral, depending on the context.

MAS can be used to solve problems in various domains, such as distributed problem-solving, resource allocation, and coordination of autonomous vehicles. In such systems, agents must make decisions not only based on their individual goals but also considering the goals and actions of other agents. This introduces additional complexity, as agents must reason about the actions of others and adapt their strategies accordingly.

6.3. Goal-Oriented Behavior in Autonomous AI Systems

In addition to making decisions, autonomous AI systems must also be able to set and pursue goals. Goal-oriented behavior is essential for AI systems to direct their efforts toward achieving specific outcomes. To achieve goal orientation, AI systems must be able to:

6.3.1. Define and Represent Goals

Goal representation is a critical aspect of goal-oriented behavior. AI systems must be capable of representing goals in a way that is both interpretable and actionable. Goals can be represented as specific tasks, objectives, or states that the system seeks to achieve. For example, a goal for an autonomous vehicle could be to reach a particular destination, while the goal of a robot could be to complete a manufacturing task.

Goal representation can be static or dynamic. In static goal systems, the goal remains fixed, while in dynamic goal systems, goals may evolve over time based on new information or changes in the environment. For example, an autonomous robot may initially be tasked with cleaning a specific area, but if the area becomes cluttered during the task, the robot may update its goal to clean up the newly added mess.

6.3.2. Decompose Goals into Subgoals

Complex goals often need to be broken down into smaller, manageable subgoals. This decomposition process enables AI systems to focus on smaller tasks that contribute to the overall objective. For instance, a robot tasked with assembling a product may first need to acquire the necessary parts, then assemble those parts into a subcomponent, and finally assemble the entire product.

Goal decomposition is essential for managing complexity and enabling efficient planning. Techniques such as hierarchical task networks (HTNs) and means-ends analysis are used to structure and organize goals into hierarchical layers of subgoals. By decomposing goals into manageable components, autonomous systems can focus their efforts on achieving the larger objective without becoming overwhelmed by complexity.

6.3.3. Monitor Progress and Adjust Strategies

For goal-oriented behavior to be effective, AI systems must continuously monitor their progress toward achieving their goals. This requires the ability to track outcomes, evaluate performance, and adjust strategies when necessary. If an AI system encounters obstacles or realizes that its current approach is inefficient, it must be capable of modifying its plan to stay on course.

Progress monitoring can be accomplished using feedback mechanisms that provide real-time information on the system's performance. These mechanisms allow the system to adjust its actions dynamically and make course corrections as needed. In more complex scenarios, reinforcement learning can be used to continually refine the AI's strategies based on past experiences.

6.4. Ethical Considerations in Autonomous AI Systems

As AI systems become more autonomous, ethical considerations must play a central role in their design. Ensuring that autonomous systems make decisions that align with human values and societal norms is crucial to their successful integration into real-world applications. Several key ethical issues must be addressed:

6.4.1. Transparency and Accountability

Autonomous AI systems must be transparent in their decision-making processes, allowing users and stakeholders to understand how decisions are made. This is particularly important in high-stakes environments, such as healthcare, autonomous vehicles, and law enforcement. Accountability mechanisms must be in place to ensure that AI systems can be held responsible for their actions, especially when they make decisions that have significant consequences.

6.4.2. Fairness and Bias

Autonomous AI systems must be designed to avoid bias and ensure fairness in their decision-making. AI systems can inadvertently reinforce existing biases present in the data they are trained on, leading to unfair or discriminatory outcomes. It is essential to implement mechanisms that detect and mitigate biases, ensuring that AI systems treat all individuals and groups equitably.

6.4.3. Safety and Security

Autonomous AI systems must be designed with safety and security in mind to prevent harm to individuals, society, or the environment. AI systems must be able to make decisions that prioritize human safety and security, especially in contexts where their actions could have life-threatening consequences, such as autonomous driving or healthcare.

Building autonomy in AI systems is a complex and multi-faceted challenge that involves enabling decision-making, goal orientation, and adaptation. By leveraging decision theory, reinforcement learning, and multi-agent systems, AI developers can create systems that operate autonomously and pursue goals in dynamic and uncertain environments. As AI continues to evolve, addressing ethical concerns related to transparency, fairness, and safety will be essential for ensuring that autonomous systems are deployed responsibly and in alignment with human values. The future of AI autonomy holds great promise for solving complex problems and enhancing the e

fficiency and effectiveness of a wide range of applications.

Chapter 7 The Role of Reinforcement Learning in Agency

Reinforcement learning (RL) is a type of machine learning that emphasizes how agents should take actions within an environment in order to maximize cumulative rewards. Rooted in the principles of behavioral psychology and inspired by how organisms learn through trial and error, RL has emerged as a powerful framework for developing autonomous systems capable of adapting to complex, dynamic environments. This adaptive learning process, driven by feedback and decision-making, mirrors the behavior of human beings and animals, offering insights into both artificial intelligence (AI) and cognitive science.

Defining Reinforcement Learning

At its core, reinforcement learning revolves around the concept of an agent making decisions to maximize rewards over time by interacting with its environment. The RL process involves four key components:

Agent: The learner or decision maker, which interacts with the environment.

Environment: The external system that the agent interacts with, often described through states.

Actions: The set of possible moves or decisions the agent can make at any given state.

Rewards: Feedback from the environment after the agent takes an action, which is either positive or negative, helping the agent learn what is good or bad.

The agent's goal in RL is to learn a strategy or policy that will allow it to make optimal decisions by balancing exploration (trying new things) and exploitation (choosing the best-known option based on prior experience). The process typically involves trial and error, where the agent makes decisions, receives feedback, and uses that feedback to refine its behavior in future interactions.

Trial and Error Learning: The Basis of Adaptive Agency

Trial and error is a fundamental concept in reinforcement learning and serves as the driving force behind adaptive behavior. This learning method is rooted in the observation that individuals—whether human, animal, or artificial agent—improve their performance by repeatedly testing different strategies and adjusting their actions based on the feedback received.

In the context of RL, trial and error takes place as the agent makes decisions and receives rewards (or penalties) based on those decisions. Initially, the agent may make random or suboptimal choices, but over time, through repeated interactions with the environment, the agent learns to associate certain actions with positive rewards. This leads to the development of a policy—a mapping from states of the environment to the best possible actions.

The process of learning through trial and error in RL typically unfolds through three key stages:

Exploration: The agent tries new actions, even if they are not guaranteed to yield high rewards. This phase is crucial for discovering the optimal actions in unfamiliar situations.

Exploitation: Once the agent has gained some understanding of the environment, it shifts toward exploiting the knowledge it has acquired to maximize rewards.

Balancing Exploration and Exploitation: A central challenge in RL is determining the right balance between exploring new actions and exploiting known actions. Too much exploration can lead to inefficiency, while too little exploration can prevent the agent from discovering better strategies.

Reinforcement learning thus serves as a powerful model for adaptive agency because it reflects how real-world agents adjust their behavior in response to changing conditions, risks, and rewards.

Reinforcement Learning and Decision-Making in Complex Environments

In many real-world applications, agents must make decisions in environments that are uncertain, dynamic, and partially observable. The challenge for these agents is to navigate these complexities, learning to make optimal decisions even when complete information is unavailable. RL provides a framework for handling such complexities by allowing agents to learn from partial feedback.

For instance, in robotics, an autonomous robot may need to perform a task like picking up an object or navigating through an obstacle-filled environment. Initially, the robot may lack the necessary information about how its actions affect the world. By using trial and error, the robot can gradually learn which actions lead to successful outcomes and which ones result in failure. Over time, the robot becomes more skilled at performing its task, adapting to the environment based on the rewards it receives.

Similarly, in video games or self-driving cars, RL allows agents to adapt to the environment's ever-changing conditions. For example, in a racing game, an agent learns to avoid obstacles while racing at high speeds by adjusting its actions based on feedback such as time penalties for crashes or rewards for completing laps quickly. The trial-and-error nature of this process is crucial because the agent does not have a complete model of the game's physics or the track layout at the outset.

The Exploration-Exploitation Dilemma: A Key Aspect of Adaptive Learning

One of the most challenging aspects of reinforcement learning is managing the exploration-exploitation dilemma. This dilemma arises because agents need to explore new strategies (exploration) while also exploiting known strategies that maximize rewards (exploitation). Finding the right balance is essential for ensuring long-term success in adaptive learning.

When an agent explores too much, it may not make enough progress toward optimizing its behavior, as it wastes time trying out suboptimal actions. On the other hand, if an agent exploits too early, it might miss better strategies that could lead to higher long-term rewards. In real-world systems, this dilemma often reflects how human decision-making is shaped by both the desire for certainty and the need to explore new opportunities.

In reinforcement learning, methods such as epsilon-greedy algorithms (which balance exploration and exploitation) and Upper Confidence Bounds (UCB) (which focus on choosing actions with the highest potential for improvement) are used to address this dilemma. These methods help agents find equilibrium where they both explore the environment for better strategies and exploit known successful actions to maximize rewards.

The Role of Reward Signals in Shaping Agency

In reinforcement learning, rewards play a critical role in shaping the agent's behavior. Positive rewards reinforce actions that lead to desirable outcomes, while negative rewards (or penalties) discourage actions that lead to undesirable results. The structure of the reward system—how rewards are distributed and whether they are immediate or delayed—greatly influences how an agent learns and adapts.

The concept of delayed rewards is particularly significant in environments where actions do not immediately result in consequences. In such cases, agents need to develop the ability to associate long-term outcomes with their actions. This is especially important in complex environments like finance, healthcare, or multi-step games, where an agent's actions today may lead to consequences far in the future. Reinforcement learning algorithms such as temporal difference learning (TD learning) or Q-learning are designed to handle such situations, allowing agents to learn long-term strategies despite delayed feedback.

Additionally, the design of the reward function itself can influence how agents behave. If the reward function is poorly defined or overly simplistic, the agent might learn suboptimal or unintended behaviors. For instance, if an RL agent in a game is rewarded solely for speed, it might learn to ignore other important aspects of the game, such as avoiding hazards, resulting in poor overall performance. Thus, the careful design of reward signals is crucial for ensuring that the agent's learning aligns with its goals and desired outcomes.

Real-World Applications of Reinforcement Learning

Reinforcement learning has been successfully applied in numerous real-world applications, demonstrating its capacity for adaptive learning through trial and error. Some prominent examples include:

Autonomous Vehicles: Self-driving cars use RL to learn how to navigate complex environments, deal with traffic, and make safe driving decisions. Through trial and error, these vehicles can optimize their routes and improve their ability to make split-second decisions in dynamic settings.

Robotics: Robots, especially in manufacturing or surgery, use RL to improve their dexterity and decision-making. These robots learn from experience to improve the precision and efficiency of their actions.

Healthcare: RL is used in personalized medicine to optimize treatment plans based on patient data. By experimenting with different therapies and measuring patient responses, RL systems can help doctors find the most effective treatments over time.

Finance: In the financial sector, RL is used for portfolio optimization and algorithmic trading. Agents learn to make decisions based on market conditions, balancing risk and reward to maximize investment returns.

These examples demonstrate how RL can create adaptive agents that learn and improve over time through continuous interaction with their environments, making it a transformative technology in fields ranging from healthcare to transportation.

Reinforcement learning is a powerful paradigm for enabling adaptive agency through trial and error. By allowing agents to learn from feedback and adjust their actions to maximize rewards, RL mimics a fundamental aspect of human learning and decision-making. The process of exploration, exploitation, and refining policies makes RL particularly effective in complex and dynamic environments. Its applications span diverse industries, including robotics, healthcare, and autonomous systems, showing the profound impact it has on the development of intelligent agents. As RL continues to evolve, it holds the potential to revolutionize not only how machines learn but also how they collaborate with humans to solve complex problems.

Chapter 8 Behavioral Modeling in Agentic AI

Behavioral modeling in Agentic Artificial Intelligence (AI) represents a dynamic frontier in both AI development and our understanding of complex systems. Agentic AI refers to systems that exhibit autonomous decision-making capabilities, often resembling the intentionality and agency that we associate with human-like behaviors. When such systems are tasked with mimicking human or natural systems, the approach combines insights from cognitive science, behavioral psychology, and computational theory. This exploration aims to examine the various methodologies involved in behavioral modeling, how it aligns with the complex, adaptive behaviors of humans and nature, and the challenges associated with creating truly autonomous, agentic AI systems.

Agentic AI is a concept that describes machines capable of independent action, based on their learned experiences and decisions. Unlike traditional AI systems, which perform tasks based on fixed algorithms or predetermined rules, agentic AI possesses the ability to self-direct, adapt to new information, and learn from interactions with their environment.

These systems generally operate under certain constraints or goals but are not explicitly programmed with a static set of responses. They embody aspects of agency, where decisions are made based on a mix of intrinsic values, experiences, and external stimuli, much like a human being navigating a complex environment. This makes them well-suited for tasks that require creativity, unpredictability, and flexibility—traits often attributed to living organisms and humans.

The Role of Behavioral Modeling

Behavioral modeling in Agentic AI refers to the process of simulating the behavior of agents—whether they are humans, animals, or other systems—through computational models. In this context, the objective is not only to replicate behaviors in a statistical or deterministic manner but to create systems that can mimic the rich, dynamic, and often unpredictable nature of biological processes.

In human contexts, this means developing AI that can simulate cognition, emotion, social interaction, and other human-like processes. In natural systems, it refers to mimicking ecological dynamics, evolutionary principles, or even the behavior of natural elements like weather patterns, the flow of rivers, or the spread of diseases.

Behavioral modeling is essential in creating Agentic AI because it provides a framework for developing systems that are not simply reactive but exhibit a level of agency—capacity for self-driven action that aligns with a given set of goals or ethical guidelines. Furthermore, these models help AI systems respond more naturally to new stimuli, enabling more human-like decision-making and adaptability.

Mimicking Human Behavior in AI

One of the most ambitious goals of Agentic AI is to mimic human behavior, which encompasses a broad spectrum of activities, including reasoning, problem-solving, learning, emotional responses, and social interactions. Behavioral models aimed at replicating human-like behavior often integrate findings from various disciplines such as psychology, cognitive science, and neurobiology.

Cognitive Modeling

Cognitive modeling is a key component in behavioral modeling for agentic AI. The field aims to replicate human thought processes, allowing AI systems to reason, plan, and make decisions in a manner similar to humans. Cognitive architectures, such as ACT-R (Adaptive Control of Thought—Rational) and Soar, attempt to represent and simulate how humans process information, make decisions, and learn.

These models are rooted in the idea that human cognition operates according to certain rules and patterns that can be captured computationally. By modeling attention, memory, perception, and learning, cognitive systems allow AI to simulate behaviors such as problem-solving, creative thinking, and social interaction.

Emotional and Social Behavior

Humans do not make decisions in a vacuum; emotions, social dynamics, and interpersonal relationships are significant factors in behavior. Emotions like fear, happiness, anger, and sadness often guide human choices, shaping responses in ways that are hard to predict purely from rational deliberation. In AI, this behavioral complexity is addressed through emotional models, where the AI is designed to recognize and react to emotions in humans and other agents.

Affective computing, a subset of AI that focuses on emotion recognition and simulation, plays a central role in enabling agentic AI to behave in socially appropriate and emotionally sensitive ways. For instance, a chatbot designed to help users through stressful situations may recognize when a user is frustrated and adjust its responses to convey empathy or encouragement.

Learning and Adaptation

For agentic AI to effectively mimic human behavior, it must be able to learn from experience. Humans are not born with all of their behavioral patterns pre-programmed; rather, they learn through interactions with their environment. Similarly, agentic AI systems, particularly those based on reinforcement learning, are trained through trial and error, where positive or negative outcomes shape future decisions.

Deep reinforcement learning (DRL) is particularly valuable here, as it allows an AI system to optimize its decision-making process over time. DRL-based agents can learn to perform tasks through exploration, trial, and reward feedback, simulating how humans adapt to new information and develop expertise in various domains.

Mimicking Natural Systems in AI

Beyond human-like behavior, agentic AI can also be tasked with mimicking broader natural systems. Natural systems, such as ecosystems, weather patterns, or the behavior of populations, exhibit self-organizing properties that can provide valuable insights into creating more robust and adaptive AI systems.

Evolutionary and Ecological Models

In nature, systems evolve over time to adapt to changing environments. This principle can be adopted in AI systems through evolutionary algorithms, which simulate the process of natural selection. These algorithms generate a population of potential solutions to a problem, select the best-performing ones, and then mutate or recombine them to create new solutions. Over generations, the system adapts to increasingly complex challenges.

Ecological modeling, which focuses on the interactions between organisms and their environment, offers insights into how agents in an AI system can cooperate or compete to achieve their goals. Just as in an ecosystem, AI agents can develop behaviors that are interdependent, such as collaboration in multi-agent systems or competitive strategies in adversarial scenarios.

Mimicking the Natural World

Agentic AI systems can also model non-living, natural systems, such as the behavior of rivers, weather patterns, or tectonic movements. These systems are often modeled using fluid dynamics, thermodynamics, or chaos theory to simulate their unpredictable and complex behaviors.

For instance, in the context of climate modeling, AI agents can replicate natural processes to predict climate changes or develop new environmental policies. These systems allow for a deeper understanding of how natural systems evolve and how AI might assist in making decisions related to conservation, sustainability, or disaster management.

Challenges in Behavioral Modeling for Agentic AI

Despite the potential of behavioral modeling to create more intelligent and autonomous AI systems, significant challenges remain in replicating the complexity of human and natural behaviors.

Uncertainty and Complexity

Human and natural systems are inherently unpredictable. While statistical models and machine learning algorithms can make accurate predictions based on historical data, there are many factors, particularly in dynamic environments, that make modeling human or natural behavior extremely complex.

AI systems often struggle to predict the long-term consequences of their actions, especially in environments where changes occur rapidly or feedback loops are involved. This issue is particularly relevant in complex agent-based models where multiple agents with differing goals interact. Maintaining stability and minimizing errors in these environments is a challenging aspect of developing reliable agentic AI.

Ethical and Social Concerns

As agentic AI mimics human and natural systems, ethical considerations become increasingly important. For instance, if AI systems exhibit human-like decision-making capabilities, how do we ensure they align with human values? Should we model AI behavior after only the best aspects of human nature, or include more challenging, darker traits?

Further, the impact of AI behavior on societal systems must be considered. When mimicking social dynamics, AI systems may unintentionally reinforce biases or perpetuate harmful behaviors. Developers must ensure that these systems are transparent and can be audited to avoid unintended consequences.

Behavioral modeling is a critical aspect of Agentic AI that aims to replicate human or natural systems to create more intelligent, adaptable, and autonomous agents. By combining insights from cognitive science, emotional modeling, and evolutionary theory, behavioral models can help AI agents navigate complex environments, learn from experience, and make decisions that resemble human or ecological processes. However, the challenges of uncertainty, complexity, and ethical concerns highlight the need for responsible development and ongoing research in this exciting field. As Agentic AI continues to evolve, the potential to transform industries and address global challenges becomes more tangible, offering exciting possibilities for both scientific progress and societal benefit.

Chapter 9 Integrating Ethics into AI Agency

One of the most complex issues in AI ethics lies in embedding moral frameworks into autonomous decision-making systems, ensuring that these systems not only perform tasks effectively but also make decisions that are morally sound and in accordance with societal expectations.

Understanding AI Agency and Ethical Decision-Making

AI systems are designed to perform tasks autonomously, often without direct human intervention. The more advanced these systems become, the more they gain the capability to make decisions on behalf of humans. This raises the question: can AI systems be considered autonomous agents? If so, how should they behave when faced with ethical dilemmas?

AI agency refers to the capacity of an AI system to act autonomously, make decisions, and influence outcomes in a given context. This is closely related to the concept of autonomy in ethics, which involves acting independently and making decisions based on reasoning. For AI systems, autonomous decision-making can lead to scenarios where they must weigh competing interests, prioritize actions, and choose between various outcomes, often without human oversight in real-time.

In this context, embedding ethical decision-making frameworks into AI is not simply about programming a system to follow rules; it is about making those systems capable of reasoning through complex ethical questions. For instance, in a healthcare setting, an AI system might have to decide how to allocate limited resources like ventilators during a crisis. The system must consider multiple factors—such as the likelihood of recovery, age, and quality of life—while adhering to ethical principles like fairness, justice, and respect for human dignity.

Challenges of Embedding Ethics into AI Systems

The task of integrating ethics into AI decision-making is fraught with challenges. One of the main difficulties is the inherent complexity and diversity of ethical theories. Ethics itself is not a one-size-fits-all discipline; different cultures, societies, and individuals have varying moral standards.

Consequently, it is difficult to define a universal ethical framework that can guide all AI systems in all contexts. The ethical frameworks that are embedded into AI systems must be carefully considered to reflect both universal moral principles and the contextual needs of specific applications.

Furthermore, AI systems are often trained on data that may contain inherent biases, inaccuracies, or ethically questionable content. These biases can influence the AI's decision-making, potentially leading to unjust outcomes. For example, if an AI system is trained on historical data from a biased judicial system, it may perpetuate those biases in its decision-making processes. This highlights the need for both ethical oversight during the training of AI systems and continuous monitoring and auditing to ensure that the systems remain aligned with evolving ethical standards.

Another challenge is the potential conflict between efficiency and ethics. AI systems are often designed to maximize utility, minimize costs, or achieve a specific goal as efficiently as possible. In many cases, these goals might conflict with ethical considerations. For instance, an AI used for law enforcement might prioritize preventing crime, but this could come at the expense of privacy, fairness, and individual freedoms. Balancing these competing priorities is a central concern in the integration of ethics into AI.

The Role of Moral Frameworks in AI Decision-Making

Moral frameworks serve as the foundation for ethical decision-making, providing AI systems with a set of rules or guidelines to follow when making choices. There are several key moral frameworks that can be considered for integration into AI systems, each offering a different approach to ethical decision-making.

Deontological Ethics: Deontological ethics focuses on the adherence to rules and duties. In the context of AI, this would mean programming the system to follow strict moral guidelines regardless of the consequences. For example, an AI system might be programmed to prioritize individual rights and fairness, such as the principle that no person should be discriminated against based on race, gender, or other factors.

Deontological approaches are appealing because they provide clear and unambiguous rules for AI systems to follow. However, they also come with limitations. In real-world scenarios, ethical dilemmas are rarely clear-cut, and rigid adherence to rules can lead to outcomes that are not desirable. For instance, an AI system that prioritizes fairness might choose to allocate resources equally, even if doing so leads to a suboptimal outcome, such as denying life-saving treatment to those with a higher chance of survival.

Utilitarianism: Utilitarianism is a consequentialist moral theory that focuses on maximizing overall happiness or well-being. When applying this to AI systems, a utilitarian approach would involve programming the AI to make decisions that result in the greatest good for the greatest number of people. For example, an AI system in healthcare might prioritize saving the lives of those with the highest likelihood of recovery, even if this means not providing care to individuals with lower survival chances.

Utilitarianism offers flexibility and the ability to adapt to complex situations, but it also raises concerns about how to measure and compare different forms of well-being. Additionally, it can justify actions that may seem morally objectionable if they lead to a greater overall benefit. For example, sacrificing the well-being of a few individuals for the benefit of many can lead to morally questionable decisions, such as disregarding the rights of minorities.

Virtue Ethics: Virtue ethics emphasizes the development of good character traits and moral virtues, rather than focusing solely on the adherence to rules or the outcomes of actions. An AI system based on virtue ethics would strive to make decisions that reflect virtuous qualities such as compassion, honesty, and fairness. For example, an AI in a customer service role might prioritize treating individuals with respect and empathy, even if doing so requires going beyond the strict requirements of the job.

Virtue ethics is appealing because it encourages AI systems to develop a more nuanced understanding of human values and emotions. However, it is difficult to program an AI to recognize and embody virtues in the same way that humans do, as virtue ethics requires a level of emotional intelligence and moral reasoning that AI systems may struggle to replicate.

Practical Approaches to Integrating Ethics into AI Systems

Integrating ethical decision-making frameworks into AI requires both technical and philosophical approaches. Below are some practical strategies that can help ensure ethical decision-making is embedded into AI systems:

Ethical AI Design: The design of AI systems should begin with a clear ethical framework in mind. This includes identifying the ethical principles that the system should adhere to and ensuring that the system is designed to make decisions that align with these principles. This may involve defining clear rules, developing algorithms that can reason through ethical dilemmas, and establishing guidelines for how the AI should respond in ethically complex situations.

Bias Detection and Mitigation: AI systems must be regularly audited for biases and inaccuracies in their decision-making. This includes ensuring that the training data used to develop AI systems is free from harmful biases, as well as designing algorithms that can identify and correct for biases during the decision-making process. Transparency and accountability in the AI development process are crucial to preventing discrimination and injustice.

Human-in-the-Loop Systems: In some contexts, it may not be feasible to fully entrust decision-making to AI systems. In these cases, a human-in-the-loop approach can be used, where humans remain involved in the decision-making process, either to oversee the AI's decisions or to make final judgments in cases where ethical dilemmas arise. This ensures that there is an accountability mechanism and that AI systems are not left to make complex ethical decisions without human oversight.

Continuous Monitoring and Feedback: Ethical decision-making in AI is not a one-time process; it requires ongoing monitoring and feedback. AI systems should be continuously evaluated to ensure they are making ethical decisions in practice. This may involve using performance metrics to assess the ethical impact of AI decisions and adjusting the system as needed to align with evolving ethical standards.

Integrating ethics into AI agency is an ongoing challenge that requires careful consideration of both moral theory and practical application. AI systems have the potential to make decisions that profoundly impact individuals and society, which means it is crucial to ensure that these systems adhere to ethical principles. By embedding moral frameworks into autonomous decision-making, we can ensure that AI systems not only perform their tasks efficiently but also make decisions that are just, fair, and aligned with human values. Ultimately, the goal is to create AI systems that are not only intelligent but also morally responsible agents, capable of contributing positively to the well-being of society.

Chapter 10 Balancing Control and Independence

Artificial Intelligence (AI) is transforming industries, enhancing productivity, and offering new opportunities for problem-solving across a wide spectrum of fields, from healthcare and finance to entertainment and robotics. However, as AI systems become more integrated into our daily lives, the need to balance control and independence within these systems becomes increasingly critical. The challenge lies in ensuring that AI can operate effectively, making decisions and performing tasks with autonomy, while still remaining under human oversight and operating within ethical, legal, and social boundaries.

The key to achieving this balance involves addressing several fundamental questions: How much control should humans exert over AI systems? To what extent should AI have the ability to act independently? And how can we ensure that AI's autonomy does not lead to unintended consequences or harm? This chapter explores these questions, offering insights into how control and independence can be balanced to ensure AI operates within acceptable parameters.

The Rise of Autonomous AI Systems

Autonomous AI systems are capable of performing tasks with little to no human intervention. This ability to act independently is what makes AI systems highly valuable in fields like autonomous driving, robotics, and AI-powered decision-making platforms. These systems can learn from experience, adapt to changing conditions, and even make decisions in complex environments that would be difficult or impossible for humans to manage manually.

For example, self-driving cars rely on AI to process data from sensors and cameras, make decisions in real-time, and navigate through traffic without human input. Similarly, AI-powered medical diagnostic tools are designed to analyze medical data, detect patterns, and provide recommendations to doctors, all without the need for direct oversight in each individual case.

As these systems become more sophisticated, the degree of autonomy they possess increases. This raises concerns about how much control should be retained by humans, particularly in areas where decisions made by AI could have significant consequences. For instance, the use of AI in military drones or surveillance systems raises ethical questions about the potential for AI to make life-and-death decisions without human oversight.

The Need for Control

While the autonomy of AI systems can offer tremendous benefits, it is essential to retain control over certain aspects of their functioning. This ensures that AI does not operate outside of the boundaries established by human values, laws, and ethical principles. The need for control can be broken down into several key considerations:

Accountability: One of the primary reasons for retaining control over AI is accountability. If AI systems are allowed to operate independently without human oversight, it can become difficult to assign responsibility in the event of a failure or undesirable outcome. For example, if a self-driving car causes an accident, it is important to determine whether the fault lies with the AI, the vehicle's manufacturer, or the human who programmed or supervised the system. Ensuring that humans remain in control of AI's actions can help to clarify accountability and establish clear lines of responsibility.

Ethical Boundaries: AI systems must operate within ethical guidelines to prevent harm to individuals or society at large. For instance, an AI system in a healthcare setting must prioritize patient safety and privacy while avoiding biases in decision-making. Without control, AI systems may inadvertently perpetuate biases, discriminate against certain groups, or violate ethical norms. In financial sectors, AI systems need to ensure fairness, transparency, and compliance with regulations to avoid unethical practices like market manipulation or fraud.

Safety and Security: AI systems that operate with high levels of independence, particularly in fields like defense or critical infrastructure, must be carefully monitored to prevent misuse or malfunction. Autonomous weapons or cyberattacks orchestrated by AI could have catastrophic consequences if not properly controlled. Ensuring that AI systems can be shut down or overridden in case of emergency is essential for safeguarding human lives and national security.

Legal Compliance: AI systems must operate within the framework of existing laws and regulations. This includes respecting privacy laws, intellectual property rights, and consumer protection laws. By maintaining human control over AI systems, organizations can ensure that AI adheres to legal requirements, preventing legal violations and the potential for costly litigation.

The Case for Independence

On the other side of the equation is the argument for granting AI a degree of independence. The autonomy of AI systems allows for greater efficiency, faster decision-making, and the ability to perform tasks in dynamic and unpredictable environments. The advantages of AI independence include:

Improved Efficiency: Autonomous AI systems can process vast amounts of data and make decisions faster than human operators. In industries like finance, where AI can analyze market trends in real-time and execute trades with high precision, this speed can lead to better outcomes and reduced operational costs. Similarly, in healthcare, AI can quickly analyze medical data to identify potential health risks, facilitating faster diagnoses and treatments.

Learning and Adaptation: AI systems, particularly those based on machine learning, are capable of learning from data and experiences. By allowing AI to operate independently, these systems can continuously improve over time. In environments where rapid adaptation is required, such as emergency response or disaster management, autonomous AI systems can react more quickly and effectively than human-controlled systems.

Reduction of Human Error: AI systems are not prone to the cognitive biases, fatigue, or emotional influences that often affect human decision-making. In fields like aviation, where AI assists with navigation and flight control, AI systems can help reduce human error, leading to safer outcomes. The autonomy of AI ensures that decisions are based on data and algorithms, rather than human fallibility.

Exploration of New Frontiers: In areas like space exploration, deep-sea research, or hazardous material handling, AI systems must operate independently in environments where human presence is impractical or dangerous. Autonomous robots and AI-powered drones have the potential to explore new frontiers, gather valuable data, and complete tasks that would otherwise be impossible for humans to undertake.

Striking a Balance

The key to ensuring that AI operates within acceptable parameters is striking the right balance between control and independence. This balance involves setting clear boundaries for AI's autonomy while ensuring that humans retain the ability to intervene when necessary. Several strategies can help achieve this balance:

Human-in-the-Loop Systems: One approach to balancing control and independence is the human-in-the-loop (HITL) model. In HITL systems, AI performs tasks autonomously but requires human oversight at critical junctures. This allows for quick intervention if the AI encounters an unfamiliar situation or makes a questionable decision. For example, in autonomous vehicles, AI can handle routine driving tasks, but a human driver is always present and can take control if necessary.

Transparency and Explainability: To ensure that AI operates within acceptable boundaries, it is essential for AI systems to be transparent and explainable. This means that AI decisions should be understandable to humans, and the reasoning behind those decisions should be accessible for review. By making AI's processes more transparent, it becomes easier for humans to spot errors, biases, or unintended behaviors and correct them before they lead to undesirable outcomes.

Ethical Guidelines and Oversight: Establishing ethical guidelines for AI development and implementation is crucial for ensuring that AI operates within socially acceptable boundaries. These guidelines should address issues like fairness, privacy, transparency, and accountability. Additionally, AI systems should be subject to regular audits by external organizations to ensure compliance with ethical standards.

Adaptive Regulation: AI technology is rapidly evolving, and regulatory frameworks must be flexible enough to keep pace with these changes. Governments and regulatory bodies should adopt adaptive regulations that allow for continuous monitoring and updating of AI standards. This ensures that as AI becomes more capable, regulations can evolve to account for new risks and challenges.

Fail-Safe Mechanisms: Implementing fail-safe mechanisms in AI systems is essential for ensuring that AI can be deactivated or overridden in the event of malfunction or dangerous behavior. This could include features like emergency stop buttons, kill switches, or automatic safety protocols that activate in critical situations.

As AI systems continue to grow in capability and complexity, ensuring that they operate within acceptable parameters becomes an increasingly important concern. The challenge lies in balancing control and independence to ensure that AI can perform tasks autonomously while remaining aligned with human values, ethical guidelines, and legal requirements.

Retaining human oversight is crucial for accountability, ethical compliance, safety, and legal adherence. At the same time, allowing AI systems to operate independently offers significant advantages in terms of efficiency, adaptability, and the ability to handle complex tasks. By adopting strategies like human-in-the-loop systems, transparency, ethical guidelines, adaptive regulation, and fail-safe mechanisms, we can create an environment where AI operates responsibly, safely, and effectively, benefiting society as a whole.

Ultimately, the goal is not to stifle the potential of AI but to ensure that it serves humanity in ways that are responsible, ethical, and aligned with the greater good. By balancing control and independence, we can harness the full potential of AI while mitigating the risks and challenges associated with its use.

Chapter 11 Agentic AI in Healthcare

The healthcare sector is undergoing a profound transformation, driven by technological advancements and the evolving landscape of artificial intelligence (AI). Among the many promising applications of AI, agentic AI stands out as a revolutionary approach, particularly in the domains of autonomous diagnostics and personalized treatment. Agentic AI refers to systems that not only assist but also take independent actions based on data, learning, and context, thereby becoming decision-makers that interact with their environments in real-time. This type of AI can autonomously analyze complex data, diagnose conditions, and even prescribe personalized treatment plans for patients, making it a crucial innovation for the future of medicine.

The Rise of Agentic AI in Healthcare

AI has already made significant strides in healthcare, from assisting doctors with decision-making to providing predictive insights into patient outcomes. However, agentic AI goes a step further by enhancing the role of AI systems as autonomous agents capable of making decisions and taking actions based on their understanding of a given scenario. Unlike traditional AI tools that rely on human intervention to act on their insights, agentic AI can autonomously initiate actions, such as alerting medical personnel, recommending treatments, or even adjusting medication dosages in real time.

This shift towards autonomy is particularly important in healthcare, where timely decisions and interventions can significantly impact patient outcomes. The integration of agentic AI into healthcare systems has the potential to reduce human error, improve operational efficiency, and offer highly tailored care plans for patients, addressing one of the most significant challenges in modern medicine: personalization.

Autonomous Diagnostics: Changing the Way Diseases Are Identified

Autonomous diagnostics powered by agentic AI can revolutionize how healthcare professionals identify and diagnose diseases. In traditional settings, diagnosing complex conditions often relies on a doctor's experience, intuition, and knowledge. However, these methods can be prone to human error, especially when faced with complex, multi-faceted health conditions. With the vast amount of data generated by medical imaging, lab results, and patient history, it becomes increasingly difficult for human doctors to keep up with every nuance.

Agentic AI systems are capable of processing massive datasets quickly, identifying patterns, and recognizing abnormalities that may go unnoticed by human doctors. Machine learning (ML) algorithms, especially deep learning models, have shown remarkable success in analyzing medical images such as X-rays, MRIs, and CT scans. These systems can identify the subtle signs of conditions like cancer, heart disease, and neurological disorders, often with accuracy surpassing that of experienced physicians.

For instance, a well-trained agentic AI system can analyze thousands of mammograms to identify early signs of breast cancer, improving early detection rates and allowing for more effective interventions. Moreover, because AI systems can process data without fatigue, they have the potential to provide faster diagnoses, ensuring that patients receive timely care.

AI-driven diagnostics are also advancing into the realm of genomics. By analyzing a patient's genetic makeup, agentic AI can predict susceptibility to certain diseases and tailor diagnostic protocols accordingly. This personalized diagnostic approach enables more precise identification of conditions based on the individual's genetic predisposition, making the process of diagnosis not only more efficient but also highly personalized.

Personalized Treatment: Customizing Care for Every Patient

One of the most compelling advantages of agentic AI in healthcare is its ability to deliver personalized treatment plans. Personalized medicine, which takes into account an individual's genetic makeup, lifestyle, and environmental factors, is becoming more feasible thanks to AI's capacity to process large amounts of data and identify relevant patterns.

Historically, treatment regimens have been designed based on population-level data, meaning they may not work equally well for all patients. However, agentic AI systems can evaluate a vast array of variables, including genetic data, medical history, and even environmental influences, to design treatments that are more precisely tailored to individual patients. This allows for highly customized healthcare that accounts for the unique biology and circumstances of each patient.

For example, in oncology, agentic AI can analyze a patient's tumor at the molecular level and compare it with a global database of genetic markers to determine the most effective therapies. With AI systems being able to predict how a patient might respond to a particular drug, they can suggest personalized drug combinations or even identify novel therapies that may not be part of standard treatment protocols.

In the realm of chronic diseases like diabetes or cardiovascular disease, agentic AI can monitor a patient's progress in real-time, making recommendations for lifestyle changes or adjustments in medication. By continuously analyzing data from wearable devices, sensors, or medical records, AI can autonomously adjust treatment plans in response to changes in the patient's condition, ensuring that care remains optimized.

Another exciting development in personalized treatment is the use of AI in pharmacogenomics, which examines how genes affect a person's response to drugs. AI systems can analyze genetic data and predict how different drugs will interact with a patient's body, ensuring that the most effective drug is prescribed, with the least amount of trial and error. This ability to predict adverse reactions or identify the best therapeutic options can dramatically reduce complications and side effects, leading to safer and more effective treatments.

Ethical and Practical Considerations

While the potential benefits of agentic AI in healthcare are enormous, there are also significant ethical and practical considerations that must be addressed. Autonomous diagnostics and treatment recommendations introduce concerns related to accountability, patient privacy, and the trustworthiness of AI systems.

Accountability and Trust: Who is responsible if an AI system makes an incorrect diagnosis or treatment recommendation? Although AI systems may make decisions autonomously, human oversight remains essential. It is crucial to ensure that there is a clear line of accountability in case something goes wrong. Additionally, patients must trust that AI systems are acting in their best interests, which requires transparency in how these systems make decisions.

Data Privacy and Security: Healthcare data is among the most sensitive information, and AI systems require access to vast amounts of personal data to function effectively. Ensuring that patient data is protected and kept secure is paramount. AI systems must adhere to strict data privacy regulations, such as the General Data Protection Regulation (GDPR) in the EU or the Health Insurance Portability and Accountability Act (HIPAA) in the US, to prevent data breaches and misuse.

Bias and Equity: AI systems are only as good as the data they are trained on. If the data used to train these systems is biased—whether due to underrepresentation of certain populations or outdated information—the AI can inadvertently perpetuate these biases in its decision-making. For example, if an AI system is primarily trained on data from one demographic group, it may not perform as well for others, leading to unequal care. Ensuring diversity in training datasets and ongoing monitoring of AI systems is necessary to prevent such biases from affecting healthcare outcomes.

Interdisciplinary Collaboration: The integration of agentic AI in healthcare requires close collaboration between AI specialists, medical professionals, and ethicists. AI systems should not operate in isolation; they should complement and enhance human expertise. Doctors and healthcare providers will still play a crucial role in patient care, as they bring the human touch, empathy, and experience that AI cannot replicate. The successful implementation of agentic AI relies on striking the right balance between human expertise and autonomous decision-making.

The Future of Agentic AI in Healthcare

As technology advances, the role of agentic AI in healthcare will only expand. With ongoing improvements in AI algorithms, computing power, and data availability, agentic AI will become increasingly adept at providing more accurate diagnoses, optimizing treatment plans, and enhancing patient care.

We can expect to see AI systems that integrate seamlessly into healthcare workflows, acting as an extension of medical teams rather than replacements. The future may bring fully autonomous diagnostic and treatment systems that allow patients to receive personalized care quickly and accurately, even in remote or underserved areas where access to healthcare professionals is limited.

Moreover, with the growing adoption of telemedicine and wearable health technologies, agentic AI systems could monitor patients' health continuously, providing real-time updates and interventions. The potential to diagnose and treat diseases before they reach advanced stages is within reach, and the use of AI to predict health trends could help prevent illnesses from developing in the first place.

Ultimately, agentic AI promises to usher in a new era of healthcare—one that is more efficient, personalized, and patient-centric. While there are challenges to overcome, the benefits of agentic AI in autonomous diagnostics and personalized treatment hold the potential to redefine how healthcare is delivered, leading to better outcomes for patients around the world.

Chapter 12 The Rise of Agentic AI in Healthcare

The healthcare sector is undergoing a profound transformation, driven by technological advancements and the evolving landscape of artificial intelligence (AI). Among the many promising applications of AI, agentic AI stands out as a revolutionary approach, particularly in the domains of autonomous diagnostics and personalized treatment. Agentic AI refers to systems that not only assist but also take independent actions based on data, learning, and context, thereby becoming decision-makers that interact with their environments in real-time. This type of AI can autonomously analyze complex data, diagnose conditions, and even prescribe personalized treatment plans for patients, making it a crucial innovation for the future of medicine.

AI has already made significant strides in healthcare, from assisting doctors with decision-making to providing predictive insights into patient outcomes. However, agentic AI goes a step further by enhancing the role of AI systems as autonomous agents capable of making decisions and taking actions based on their understanding of a given scenario. Unlike traditional AI tools that rely on human intervention to act on their insights, agentic AI can autonomously initiate actions, such as alerting medical personnel, recommending treatments, or even adjusting medication dosages in real time.

This shift towards autonomy is particularly important in healthcare, where timely decisions and interventions can significantly impact patient outcomes. The integration of agentic AI into healthcare systems has the potential to reduce human error, improve operational efficiency, and offer highly tailored care plans for patients, addressing one of the most significant challenges in modern medicine: personalization.

Autonomous Diagnostics: Changing the Way Diseases Are Identified

Autonomous diagnostics powered by agentic AI can revolutionize how healthcare professionals identify and diagnose diseases. In traditional settings, diagnosing complex conditions often relies on a doctor's experience, intuition, and knowledge. However, these methods can be prone to human error, especially when faced with complex, multi-faceted health conditions. With the vast amount of data generated by medical imaging, lab results, and patient history, it becomes increasingly difficult for human doctors to keep up with every nuance.

Agentic AI systems are capable of processing massive datasets quickly, identifying patterns, and recognizing abnormalities that may go unnoticed by human doctors. Machine learning (ML) algorithms, especially deep learning models, have shown remarkable success in analyzing medical images such as X-rays, MRIs, and CT scans. These systems can identify the subtle signs of conditions like cancer, heart disease, and neurological disorders, often with accuracy surpassing that of experienced physicians.

For instance, a well-trained agentic AI system can analyze thousands of mammograms to identify early signs of breast cancer, improving early detection rates and allowing for more effective interventions. Moreover, because AI systems can process data without fatigue, they have the potential to provide faster diagnoses, ensuring that patients receive timely care.

AI-driven diagnostics are also advancing into the realm of genomics. By analyzing a patient's genetic makeup, agentic AI can predict susceptibility to certain diseases and tailor diagnostic protocols accordingly. This personalized diagnostic approach enables more precise identification of conditions based on the individual's genetic predisposition, making the process of diagnosis not only more efficient but also highly personalized.

Personalized Treatment: Customizing Care for Every Patient

One of the most compelling advantages of agentic AI in healthcare is its ability to deliver personalized treatment plans. Personalized medicine, which takes into account an individual's genetic makeup, lifestyle, and environmental factors, is becoming more feasible thanks to AI's capacity to process large amounts of data and identify relevant patterns.

Historically, treatment regimens have been designed based on population-level data, meaning they may not work equally well for all patients. However, agentic AI systems can evaluate a vast array of variables, including genetic data, medical history, and even environmental influences, to design treatments that are more precisely tailored to individual patients. This allows for highly customized healthcare that accounts for the unique biology and circumstances of each patient.

For example, in oncology, agentic AI can analyze a patient's tumor at the molecular level and compare it with a global database of genetic markers to determine the most effective therapies. With AI systems being able to predict how a patient might respond to a particular drug, they can suggest personalized drug combinations or even identify novel therapies that may not be part of standard treatment protocols.

In the realm of chronic diseases like diabetes or cardiovascular disease, agentic AI can monitor a patient's progress in real-time, making recommendations for lifestyle changes or adjustments in medication. By continuously analyzing data from wearable devices, sensors, or medical records, AI can autonomously adjust treatment plans in response to changes in the patient's condition, ensuring that care remains optimized.

Another exciting development in personalized treatment is the use of AI in pharmacogenomics, which examines how genes affect a person's response to drugs. AI systems can analyze genetic data and predict how different drugs will interact with a patient's body, ensuring that the most effective drug is prescribed, with the least amount of trial and error. This ability to predict adverse reactions or identify the best therapeutic options can dramatically reduce complications and side effects, leading to safer and more effective treatments.

Ethical and Practical Considerations

While the potential benefits of agentic AI in healthcare are enormous, there are also significant ethical and practical considerations that must be addressed. Autonomous diagnostics and treatment recommendations introduce concerns related to accountability, patient privacy, and the trustworthiness of AI systems.

Accountability and Trust: Who is responsible if an AI system makes an incorrect diagnosis or treatment recommendation? Although AI systems may make decisions autonomously, human oversight remains essential. It is crucial to ensure that there is a clear line of accountability in case something goes wrong. Additionally, patients must trust that AI systems are acting in their best interests, which requires transparency in how these systems make decisions.

Data Privacy and Security: Healthcare data is among the most sensitive information, and AI systems require access to vast amounts of personal data to function effectively. Ensuring that patient data is protected and kept secure is paramount. AI systems must adhere to strict data privacy regulations, such as the General Data Protection Regulation (GDPR) in the EU or the Health Insurance Portability and Accountability Act (HIPAA) in the US, to prevent data breaches and misuse.

Bias and Equity: AI systems are only as good as the data they are trained on. If the data used to train these systems is biased—whether due to underrepresentation of certain populations or outdated information—the AI can inadvertently perpetuate these biases in its decision-making. For example, if an AI system is primarily trained on data from one demographic group, it may not perform as well for others, leading to unequal care. Ensuring diversity in training datasets and ongoing monitoring of AI systems is necessary to prevent such biases from affecting healthcare outcomes.

Interdisciplinary Collaboration: The integration of agentic AI in healthcare requires close collaboration between AI specialists, medical professionals, and ethicists. AI systems should not operate in isolation; they should complement and enhance human expertise. Doctors and healthcare providers will still play a crucial role in patient care, as they bring the human touch, empathy, and experience that AI cannot replicate. The successful implementation of agentic AI relies on striking the right balance between human expertise and autonomous decision-making.

The Future of Agentic AI in Healthcare

As technology advances, the role of agentic AI in healthcare will only expand. With ongoing improvements in AI algorithms, computing power, and data availability, agentic AI will become increasingly adept at providing more accurate diagnoses, optimizing treatment plans, and enhancing patient care.

We can expect to see AI systems that integrate seamlessly into healthcare workflows, acting as an extension of medical teams rather than replacements. The future may bring fully autonomous diagnostic and treatment systems that allow patients to receive personalized care quickly and accurately, even in remote or underserved areas where access to healthcare professionals is limited.

Moreover, with the growing adoption of telemedicine and wearable health technologies, agentic AI systems could monitor patients' health continuously, providing real-time updates and interventions. The potential to diagnose and treat diseases before they reach advanced stages is within reach, and the use of AI to predict health trends could help prevent illnesses from developing in the first place.

Ultimately, agentic AI promises to usher in a new era of healthcare—one that is more efficient, personalized, and patient-centric. While there are challenges to overcome, the benefits of agentic AI in autonomous diagnostics and personalized treatment hold the potential to redefine how healthcare is delivered, leading to better outcomes for patients around the world.

Chapter 13 Smart Cities and Infrastructure

In the rapidly evolving landscape of modern cities, the concept of smart cities is emerging as a transformative force. A smart city integrates digital technologies, particularly the Internet of Things (IoT), artificial intelligence (AI), and big data analytics, to improve urban living conditions, increase efficiency, and reduce environmental impact. The use of AI-driven urban planning and management is at the core of this transformation. By harnessing the power of AI, cities can optimize infrastructure, streamline services, enhance sustainability, and provide citizens with a higher quality of life.

What Makes a City "Smart"?

A smart city is one that uses technology and data to enhance the quality of life for its inhabitants, streamline urban operations, and make better use of resources. Key components of a smart city include:

Connected Infrastructure: Buildings, roads, and utilities are embedded with sensors and IoT devices that collect and transmit real-time data about their condition and usage. This data can be analyzed to predict maintenance needs, optimize energy consumption, and improve traffic flow.

Sustainable Environment: Smart cities focus on sustainability by integrating renewable energy sources, reducing waste, promoting green spaces, and optimizing water and energy usage through smart meters and sensors.

Data-Driven Decision Making: By collecting large volumes of data through IoT devices and sensors, cities can make data-driven decisions that are more efficient, responsive, and proactive in addressing urban challenges.

Enhanced Mobility and Transport: A smart city's transportation system incorporates AI to optimize traffic flow, reduce congestion, and improve public transportation. Autonomous vehicles, smart traffic lights, and AI-powered route planning are some examples of how transportation is integrated into the smart city framework.

Citizen Engagement: Smart cities prioritize improving the lives of their citizens by creating platforms for interaction. These include mobile apps that allow citizens to report issues like potholes, broken streetlights, or waste management problems, and access information about city services and initiatives.

AI-driven urban planning and management are essential for achieving the vision of a smart city. Through machine learning, deep learning, and advanced data analytics, AI technologies are increasingly being applied to optimize infrastructure, enhance mobility, and address a wide range of urban challenges.

AI-Driven Urban Planning

Urban planning involves designing and organizing the use of land and resources to create functional and sustainable communities. Traditional urban planning methods often rely on historical data and human expertise, but they can be slow, reactive, and sometimes inefficient. AI-driven urban planning takes a more proactive approach by leveraging vast amounts of real-time data to forecast needs, evaluate scenarios, and suggest solutions.

AI can assist urban planners in a variety of ways:

Predictive Analysis for Infrastructure Needs: One of the most significant benefits of AI in urban planning is its ability to predict future infrastructure needs. By analyzing current patterns in traffic, population growth, building occupancy, energy consumption, and waste generation, AI algorithms can forecast future demands and help city planners make informed decisions about where to build new roads, schools, hospitals, or housing projects. This predictive capability allows cities to address potential issues before they become problems.

Optimizing Land Use: AI can help planners identify the most efficient use of available land. By analyzing zoning regulations, environmental factors, and demographic data, AI algorithms can suggest the most suitable land-use strategies that balance residential, commercial, and recreational spaces. This ensures that cities are designed to accommodate growth while maintaining a high quality of life for residents.

Sustainable Urban Design: Sustainable cities are those that minimize environmental impact and maximize resource efficiency. AI can aid in designing energy-efficient buildings, optimizing waste management systems, and planning green spaces. Through simulations, AI can model the environmental impact of different urban designs and recommend solutions that reduce carbon footprints and enhance sustainability.

Smart Building Design: AI is increasingly used in the design and construction of buildings. Through data analysis, AI can optimize energy consumption by controlling heating, cooling, and lighting systems in real-time. Smart buildings equipped with sensors and AI technologies can adjust their environment based on occupancy, weather, and energy prices, making them more energy-efficient and comfortable for residents.

AI-Driven Infrastructure Management

Once a city is designed and constructed, the focus shifts to managing its infrastructure. AI plays a pivotal role in monitoring and maintaining the vast networks of roads, utilities, and public services that keep a city running smoothly. AI-driven infrastructure management offers a wide range of benefits:

Predictive Maintenance: Maintaining the infrastructure of a city—such as bridges, roads, water pipes, and electrical grids—is a complex and costly task. AI can predict when maintenance is required by analyzing data from sensors embedded in infrastructure. For example, AI algorithms can detect small cracks in roads, pipes, or bridges that may indicate potential failure. By predicting these issues in advance, cities can carry out preventive maintenance before costly repairs or catastrophic failures occur.

Energy Optimization: Energy management is a critical aspect of smart cities, and AI can help optimize energy use by analyzing data from energy meters, weather forecasts, and consumption patterns. AI can adjust heating, cooling, and lighting systems in real-time to reduce energy waste. In addition, AI can manage the distribution of energy from renewable sources, ensuring that energy grids remain balanced and efficient.

Traffic and Mobility Management: Traffic congestion is one of the most pressing issues facing urban areas, leading to longer commute times, increased pollution, and reduced economic productivity. AI can optimize traffic flow by analyzing real-time data from traffic cameras, sensors, and GPS devices. AI-powered systems can control traffic lights, adjust public transport schedules, and even predict traffic jams, offering real-time route suggestions to drivers. Autonomous vehicles, guided by AI, could also be integrated into the transportation system, further reducing congestion and enhancing mobility.

Waste Management: AI can also play a significant role in optimizing waste management. Through data analysis, AI can predict waste generation patterns and optimize the collection routes and schedules. Smart trash bins equipped with sensors can notify waste collection services when they are full, reducing unnecessary trips and saving time and fuel. In addition, AI can help in sorting waste, identifying recyclables, and improving recycling efficiency.

Water and Sewer Management: AI can help manage water distribution and wastewater treatment systems more efficiently. Sensors embedded in water pipes can provide real-time data on water pressure, quality, and flow. AI can detect leaks, predict maintenance needs, and optimize water usage, helping cities conserve this precious resource. Additionally, AI-driven systems can monitor and optimize sewer systems, reducing the risk of blockages and contamination.

Disaster Management: AI-driven systems can play a crucial role in managing natural and man-made disasters. For example, AI can analyze meteorological data to predict and respond to extreme weather events, such as hurricanes, floods, or wildfires. During a disaster, AI can assist in coordinating evacuation efforts, managing resources, and providing real-time updates to residents.

Challenges of AI-Driven Urban Planning and Infrastructure Management

While the potential benefits of AI in urban planning and infrastructure management are vast, there are several challenges that cities must address to successfully implement these technologies:

Data Privacy and Security: The use of AI in smart cities requires the collection of large amounts of data from citizens and infrastructure. Ensuring the privacy and security of this data is paramount. Cities must implement strict data protection policies and secure systems to prevent breaches or misuse of personal information.

Integration of Legacy Systems: Many cities have existing infrastructure that is not designed to work with modern AI technologies. Integrating new AI systems with older infrastructure can be complex and costly. Upgrading these legacy systems requires careful planning and significant investment.

Cost and Funding: Implementing AI-driven solutions can be expensive, especially for large cities with outdated infrastructure. Securing funding for AI projects can be challenging, and governments may face resistance from stakeholders who are hesitant to invest in unproven technologies.

Ethical Considerations: The use of AI in smart cities raises ethical concerns about algorithmic biases, decision-making transparency, and the potential displacement of jobs. Policymakers must ensure that AI technologies are deployed in a way that is equitable and transparent, and that the benefits of these technologies are shared fairly among all citizens.

Public Acceptance: Citizens may be wary of the increasing presence of AI in their cities, particularly if they are unsure about how their data is being used. Public awareness and education campaigns are essential to build trust and ensure that citizens understand the benefits of smart city technologies.

The Future of AI-Driven Smart Cities

As AI technology continues to advance, the future of smart cities looks increasingly promising. AI-driven urban planning and management can transform cities into more efficient, sustainable, and livable spaces. By harnessing the power of AI, cities can optimize resource use, enhance mobility, reduce environmental impact, and improve the overall quality of life for their residents.

The integration of AI into urban planning and infrastructure management is still in its early stages, but with continued investment and collaboration between governments, tech companies, and citizens, smart cities will become a reality. The challenges ahead are significant, but the rewards of building smarter, more sustainable cities are too great to ignore.

Chapter 14 Agentic AI in Defense and Security

The rise of artificial intelligence (AI) has significantly impacted various sectors, and defense and security are no exception. In particular, agentic AI—AI that can act autonomously, make decisions, and execute actions in the world without direct human intervention—is revolutionizing the way military and security operations are conducted. From autonomous drones to sophisticated surveillance systems and advanced threat assessment algorithms, agentic AI is reshaping the landscape of defense and security in profound ways. This chapter explores the applications, benefits, challenges, and ethical considerations of agentic AI in defense and security, with a focus on autonomous drones, surveillance systems, and threat assessment technologies.

Understanding Agentic AI

Agentic AI refers to systems that possess the ability to autonomously perceive their environment, make decisions based on those perceptions, and take actions without requiring constant human oversight. These systems can operate in dynamic, uncertain environments, adapting to changing conditions and learning from their experiences. In the context of defense and security, agentic AI is increasingly used for tasks that were once considered too dangerous, complex, or tedious for humans, offering enhanced efficiency, speed, and precision.

The key feature of agentic AI is its ability to act autonomously, often through deep learning, reinforcement learning, and other advanced AI techniques. These systems can be integrated into a variety of platforms, including autonomous drones, surveillance systems, and threat detection technologies, to support military and security operations in real time.

Autonomous Drones in Defense and Security

One of the most prominent applications of agentic AI in defense is in the development of autonomous drones. These drones are capable of conducting a variety of missions, ranging from reconnaissance to combat, without the need for constant human control. Autonomous drones can be deployed for surveillance, intelligence gathering, search and rescue operations, and targeted strikes. By using agentic AI, these drones can make decisions about when and where to act based on the data they gather in real-time, without requiring human intervention.

Surveillance and Reconnaissance

Autonomous drones equipped with agentic AI are particularly valuable in surveillance and reconnaissance missions. These drones can fly for extended periods, monitor large areas, and collect data from a variety of sensors, including cameras, infrared sensors, and radar. Agentic AI enables the drones to analyze the data they collect and identify patterns or anomalies, such as the movement of potential threats or the presence of hostile forces.

For instance, drones can be used to monitor border regions, track the movement of enemy troops, or identify suspicious activity in urban areas. The AI's ability to analyze this data in real time allows military and security agencies to respond quickly to emerging threats. Moreover, autonomous drones can operate in environments where human presence is dangerous, such as conflict zones, disaster areas, or hazardous terrains.

Combat and Targeted Strikes

In combat scenarios, autonomous drones equipped with agentic AI can perform targeted strikes with high precision. By integrating AI with advanced targeting algorithms and sensor fusion techniques, these drones can autonomously identify and engage enemy targets while minimizing collateral damage. The AI enables the drones to make decisions about when and where to strike based on predefined rules of engagement, the status of friendly forces, and the assessment of potential risks.

Autonomous drones have already demonstrated their value in military operations. For example, during conflicts in the Middle East, drone strikes have been used to target key individuals and destroy enemy equipment with remarkable accuracy. The ability of agentic AI to process vast amounts of data in real time and make rapid decisions has made autonomous drones a vital asset in modern warfare.

AI-Enhanced Surveillance Systems

Surveillance is a cornerstone of modern defense and security operations. With the advent of agentic AI, surveillance systems have become more intelligent, efficient, and capable of operating in complex and dynamic environments. AI-powered surveillance systems can autonomously monitor vast areas, analyze incoming data, and detect potential threats with a level of precision and speed that far exceeds human capabilities.

Real-Time Threat Detection

AI-enhanced surveillance systems can analyze video feeds, radar data, and other sensor information to detect and classify potential threats in real time. By using machine learning algorithms, these systems can be trained to recognize various objects, behaviors, or patterns that indicate the presence of a threat. For example, AI systems can differentiate between civilian and military vehicles, detect unusual movements or formations, and identify suspicious behavior in large crowds.

The ability to detect threats in real time is crucial in defense and security operations, where delays in response can have devastating consequences. AI-powered surveillance systems can reduce the time it takes to identify a threat, allowing security forces to act swiftly to neutralize it. Furthermore, these systems can autonomously prioritize threats based on severity, enabling decision-makers to focus on the most critical situations first.

Integration with Other Systems

One of the key advantages of AI-powered surveillance systems is their ability to integrate with other defense and security technologies, creating a comprehensive network of interconnected systems. For example, AI-enhanced surveillance can be integrated with autonomous drones, unmanned ground vehicles, and military command centers to share real-time data and coordinate responses to emerging threats.

This integration allows for a more coordinated and efficient defense strategy, as AI systems can collaborate across different platforms to enhance situational awareness and decision-making. For instance, if an AI-powered surveillance system detects an enemy force moving toward a critical location, it can alert autonomous drones to monitor the area and provide real-time intelligence to ground forces. This level of coordination can significantly improve the effectiveness of military and security operations.

AI-Driven Threat Assessment

Threat assessment is a critical aspect of defense and security operations. AI technologies, particularly agentic AI, are revolutionizing the way threats are assessed, allowing for more accurate, timely, and data-driven decision-making. Traditional threat assessment processes often involve humans manually analyzing large amounts of data, which can be time-consuming and error-prone. Agentic AI, on the other hand, can autonomously process vast quantities of data from multiple sources, such as intelligence reports, surveillance feeds, and satellite imagery, to assess potential threats.

Predictive Analytics

One of the key benefits of AI in threat assessment is its ability to perform predictive analytics. By analyzing historical data and identifying patterns, AI systems can forecast potential threats before they materialize. For example, AI can analyze the movements of hostile forces, detect trends in the behavior of terrorist organizations, or predict the likelihood of cyberattacks based on known indicators. This predictive capability enables defense and security agencies to take proactive measures to prevent or mitigate threats before they escalate.

In addition to detecting and predicting threats, AI-driven threat assessment systems can also provide valuable insights into the intentions of adversaries. By analyzing communication patterns, social media activity, and other data sources, AI systems can assess the likelihood of hostile actions and provide strategic recommendations to military and security agencies.

Situational Awareness

AI-enhanced threat assessment systems contribute to improved situational awareness by providing decision-makers with real-time insights into the evolving security environment. These systems can process data from a wide range of sources, including intelligence reports, satellite imagery, drone surveillance, and social media, to create a comprehensive picture of the current situation. This allows military commanders, security officials, and policymakers to make informed decisions based on the most up-to-date information.

For example, if a conflict is brewing in a particular region, AI systems can analyze a variety of factors—such as troop movements, political developments, and media reports—to assess the likelihood of escalation. This information can be used to develop strategies, allocate resources, and coordinate responses to potential threats.

Challenges and Ethical Considerations

While the potential benefits of agentic AI in defense and security are significant, there are also challenges and ethical concerns that must be addressed. One of the primary concerns is the risk of AI systems making autonomous decisions that could lead to unintended consequences. For example, an autonomous drone might misidentify a target and engage a civilian vehicle, leading to collateral damage. Ensuring that AI systems are programmed with ethical guidelines and are subject to oversight is critical to minimizing these risks.

Accountability and Transparency

As AI systems become more autonomous, questions about accountability and transparency become increasingly important. If an AI-powered system makes a mistake—such as launching an unauthorized strike or failing to detect a threat—who is responsible? Ensuring that there is clear accountability for the actions of AI systems is essential, as is ensuring transparency in how these systems make decisions. This will help build trust in AI technologies and ensure that they are used ethically and responsibly.

Bias and Discrimination

Another challenge is the potential for AI systems to exhibit bias or discrimination. AI algorithms are trained on historical data, and if that data contains biases, the AI system may perpetuate those biases in its decision-making. For example, an AI-powered surveillance system may disproportionately target certain racial or ethnic groups, leading to unfair treatment. Addressing bias in AI systems requires careful attention to the data used to train them and ongoing monitoring to ensure that they operate fairly and impartially.

Agentic AI is transforming the defense and security sectors by enhancing the capabilities of autonomous drones, surveillance systems, and threat assessment technologies. These AI-powered systems are enabling more efficient, accurate, and timely decision-making, ultimately improving the effectiveness of military and security operations. However, the deployment of agentic AI also raises important ethical and practical challenges that must be addressed to ensure that these technologies are used responsibly. As AI continues to evolve, it will play an increasingly critical role in shaping the future of defense and security, providing new opportunities for enhancing global safety and stability.

Chapter 15 Education and Learning Systems

Education is one of the cornerstones of human development, enabling individuals to acquire knowledge, skills, and competencies necessary for personal growth, societal engagement, and professional success. Over the centuries, the methods and systems of delivering education have evolved significantly, shaped by advances in technology, pedagogy, and psychological theories. In recent decades, the integration of technology into education has led to the rise of adaptive tutoring systems and innovative knowledge delivery methods. These systems, powered by artificial intelligence (AI) and machine learning (ML), represent a dynamic shift in how learners engage with educational content, fostering personalized and efficient learning experiences.

Adaptive Tutoring Systems: An Overview

Adaptive tutoring systems are a class of computer-based learning tools designed to personalize the learning experience by tailoring content, feedback, and instruction to the individual needs of each learner. These systems rely on sophisticated algorithms to analyze a learner's performance and adjust the content and pace of instruction accordingly. The goal is to optimize learning outcomes by addressing the unique strengths, weaknesses, and learning styles of each student.

One of the core principles of adaptive tutoring systems is the idea of "individualized instruction." In traditional classroom settings, teachers are often tasked with managing a diverse group of students, each with their own learning needs and abilities. As a result, it can be difficult for teachers to provide the level of attention and customization that every student requires. Adaptive tutoring systems aim to overcome this limitation by providing personalized feedback and content that adjusts in real-time based on student interactions.

For example, in a math tutoring system, the program might detect that a student is struggling with a particular type of algebraic equation. The system would then adjust the difficulty level, offer additional practice problems, or provide hints tailored to the student's specific misconceptions. Similarly, if a student demonstrates proficiency in a certain area, the system can accelerate the pace and present more advanced content. By continuously assessing a student's progress and adapting to their needs, adaptive tutoring systems offer a dynamic and responsive learning environment.

How Adaptive Tutoring Systems Work

Adaptive tutoring systems are powered by a combination of AI, machine learning, and educational theory. These technologies enable the system to collect data on the student's interactions with the platform, analyze this data, and make informed decisions about how to modify the learning experience. Several key components are typically involved in the functioning of adaptive tutoring systems:

User Modeling: The system creates a model of the learner's knowledge, skills, and preferences. This model is updated continuously as the student interacts with the system. The model can include information such as the student's current proficiency in a particular subject, their learning style, and their preferred pace of learning. User modeling enables the system to provide content that aligns with the student's individual needs.

Content Delivery: Based on the user model, the system selects and delivers appropriate content. This content can include instructional material such as text, videos, quizzes, and interactive exercises. The system uses algorithms to determine which type of content is most likely to support the student's learning goals at any given moment. For example, if a student is struggling with a specific concept, the system may deliver additional explanations or examples to reinforce the idea.

Real-Time Feedback: Adaptive tutoring systems provide immediate feedback on the student's performance. This feedback can include hints, corrective suggestions, or encouragement. Timely feedback is essential for reinforcing learning and helping students stay motivated. For example, if a student answers a question incorrectly, the system might provide a hint or guide them through the problem-solving process to ensure they understand the correct approach.

Assessment and Adaptation: Continuous assessment is a key feature of adaptive tutoring systems. The system tracks the student's progress through assessments, such as quizzes, problem-solving exercises, and simulations. Based on the results, the system adapts the content and difficulty level to ensure the student is appropriately challenged. This dynamic adjustment helps maintain an optimal balance between engagement and difficulty, preventing frustration or boredom.

Benefits of Adaptive Tutoring Systems

Personalization: One of the most significant advantages of adaptive tutoring systems is their ability to provide a personalized learning experience. Students can learn at their own pace, receiving tailored content and feedback that meets their unique needs. This level of personalization is difficult to achieve in traditional classroom settings, where teachers must manage the needs of multiple students at once.

Efficiency: Adaptive systems optimize learning by delivering content that is specifically targeted to the student's current level of understanding. This reduces the amount of time spent on material that the student already knows and focuses attention on areas that require improvement. As a result, students can progress more quickly through the material, mastering concepts at a faster rate.

Accessibility: Adaptive tutoring systems can be accessed at any time and from any location, making education more flexible and accessible. This is particularly beneficial for students with different learning schedules, those who need additional support outside of school hours, or those in remote areas without access to traditional educational resources.

Data-Driven Insights: Adaptive systems generate valuable data on student performance, which can be used by educators, administrators, and policymakers to improve the learning process. This data provides insights into common misconceptions, areas where students are struggling, and overall trends in student performance. This information can be used to inform instructional decisions and curriculum development.

Support for Diverse Learners: Adaptive systems can cater to a wide range of learning needs, including students with disabilities or those who require accommodations. For example, the system can adjust the pace of instruction, provide audio or visual support, or offer content in different formats to meet the needs of diverse learners.

Challenges and Limitations of Adaptive Tutoring Systems

Despite the many benefits, adaptive tutoring systems also face challenges and limitations. Some of the most significant issues include:

Technology and Infrastructure: Adaptive tutoring systems rely on technology, including computers, internet access, and software platforms. In areas with limited access to these resources, students may be unable to fully benefit from adaptive systems. Additionally, technological issues such as software glitches or connectivity problems can hinder the effectiveness of the system.

Quality of Content: The quality of content delivered by adaptive systems is crucial to their success. If the content is poorly designed, inaccurate, or lacks engagement, the system may not be effective in promoting learning. Ensuring that adaptive systems have high-quality, evidence-based instructional materials is essential for their success.

Student Engagement: While adaptive systems provide personalized content, they may not always be as engaging or motivating as human teachers. Some students may struggle with the lack of human interaction, and the system's reliance on automated feedback may not provide the same level of emotional support or encouragement as a teacher can offer.

Privacy and Data Security: Adaptive systems collect vast amounts of data on student performance and behavior. This data can be valuable for improving learning outcomes, but it also raises concerns about privacy and data security. It is important for educators and developers to ensure that student data is protected and used ethically.

Scalability: While adaptive tutoring systems are effective for individualized learning, they may not be feasible on a large scale in every educational setting. The costs of developing, maintaining, and deploying adaptive systems may be prohibitive for some schools or districts, particularly those with limited budgets.

Knowledge Delivery: The Role of Technology

In addition to adaptive tutoring systems, advances in technology have revolutionized how knowledge is delivered to learners. Traditional models of education, such as lectures and textbooks, are being supplemented or replaced by digital platforms, online courses, and multimedia content. These innovative methods of knowledge delivery are transforming education by offering new opportunities for engagement, interactivity, and accessibility.

Online Learning Platforms: Online learning platforms such as Coursera, edX, and Khan Academy provide learners with access to courses from top universities and institutions around the world. These platforms offer a wide range of subjects and allow students to learn at their own pace, with the flexibility to study from home or on the go.

Interactive Learning Tools: Digital tools such as simulations, virtual labs, and gamified learning experiences offer students interactive and immersive ways to engage with content. These tools can enhance understanding by allowing students to experiment, visualize concepts, and receive immediate feedback.

Video and Multimedia Content: The use of video, animations, and interactive media has become a standard feature of modern education. Multimedia content can make complex ideas more accessible and engaging, helping students retain information more effectively.

Artificial Intelligence and Machine Learning: AI and machine learning are being integrated into various aspects of knowledge delivery. For example, intelligent tutoring systems, chatbots, and automated feedback mechanisms can provide real-time assistance and guidance to students, enhancing the learning experience.

Adaptive tutoring systems and innovative knowledge delivery methods are reshaping the educational landscape. By leveraging AI, machine learning, and advanced technology, these systems offer personalized, efficient, and accessible learning experiences that can benefit students of all backgrounds and abilities. While challenges remain, particularly in terms of technology access and content quality, the potential for adaptive systems to transform education is immense. As technology continues to advance, adaptive tutoring systems and knowledge delivery methods will play an increasingly important role in shaping the future of education.

Chapter 16 The Moral Responsibility of Agentic AI

One of the core challenges surrounding agentic AI is the issue of accountability. When an AI system takes an autonomous action, such as a self-driving car causing an accident or a medical diagnostic tool misinterpreting a patient's symptoms, it becomes difficult to assign responsibility. Should the blame fall on the AI itself, its creators, or its users? The question of who is ultimately accountable for the actions of an autonomous system is a complex legal and ethical problem.

The principle of accountability for autonomous AI actions requires clear definitions of what constitutes accountability and which entities are morally or legally responsible for the consequences of those actions. Here are three central parties that could be held accountable:

The AI system itself: Some argue that if AI systems are autonomous agents capable of making decisions and taking actions based on their own reasoning, they should be held accountable for their behavior, akin to how humans are held responsible for their actions. However, this argument faces significant opposition, as it presupposes that AI can bear moral responsibility. Most legal and moral frameworks do not grant moral personhood to AI, as these systems lack human consciousness, intent, and understanding of ethics. AI systems, as they currently exist, are tools—albeit advanced ones—created and controlled by humans.

The developers or manufacturers: Another perspective holds that the developers or creators of AI systems should be held accountable for the behavior of their creations. Developers program the system's algorithms, set parameters, and often design the learning mechanisms. If an AI system causes harm due to a design flaw, negligence, or failure to account for certain risks, the developers or manufacturers may bear moral or legal responsibility. This raises questions about the extent of responsibility developers have in predicting the possible outcomes of their systems and mitigating potential harm.

The users: The end-users of AI systems may also be held responsible if their use of the system results in harm. For example, a company that deploys an autonomous delivery drone that crashes into a building may be considered liable for the consequences, depending on the circumstances of the event and the terms under which the drone was operated. This perspective suggests that users must exercise caution, oversight, and diligence when deploying AI systems in real-world scenarios, especially when they are responsible for monitoring the AI's actions.

Moral Responsibility and Machine Learning

A significant factor contributing to the complexity of accountability in AI is the nature of machine learning, which underpins many advanced AI systems. Unlike traditional programming, where every action is explicitly coded by a developer, machine learning allows AI systems to learn from data and adjust their behavior based on past experiences. This means that AI systems can evolve in ways that are not entirely predictable, and their decisions may sometimes reflect biases, errors, or unintended consequences.

The role of machine learning complicates moral responsibility because it is difficult to determine the exact cause of a harmful action. For instance, an AI system may make a decision that leads to harm, but its reasoning may be opaque or difficult to trace due to the complexity of its neural networks or learning processes. This phenomenon, often referred to as the "black box" problem, raises ethical concerns about transparency and explainability in AI systems.

Ethical frameworks for AI must take into account the possibility that AI agents can learn and make decisions in ways that were not anticipated by their creators. This introduces an additional layer of moral responsibility for developers to ensure that systems are designed with mechanisms for transparency, monitoring, and accountability.

Legal and Regulatory Frameworks

Given the rapid advancement of agentic AI, there is a pressing need for legal frameworks to establish accountability for the actions of autonomous systems. Governments and international bodies are beginning to recognize the need for regulations governing AI, but much work remains to be done in establishing legal structures that address the full spectrum of accountability concerns.

One key issue is how laws can assign liability when AI systems cause harm. Should the legal system treat autonomous agents as "tools" that are owned by the creators or operators? Or should AI systems be granted a certain level of legal personhood, enabling them to be held responsible for their actions in a similar manner to individuals? The question of whether AI can be legally classified as an "agent" with independent moral responsibility remains a contentious debate. Most current legal systems, however, focus on human responsibility, with AI acting as a tool or means by which humans perform actions.

Several countries, including the European Union, have taken steps to develop AI-specific regulations that outline the roles and responsibilities of developers, users, and other stakeholders in ensuring the safe and ethical deployment of autonomous systems. The EU's General Data Protection Regulation (GDPR), for instance, addresses concerns related to data privacy and AI, while the European Commission has proposed the Artificial Intelligence Act, which categorizes AI systems based on risk and provides guidelines for their regulation.

As AI technology continues to evolve, there is a need for legislation that can keep pace with advancements in autonomy and machine learning. This includes establishing clear guidelines for transparency, explainability, and oversight mechanisms to ensure that AI systems are used responsibly and that their developers and users can be held accountable when things go wrong.

Ethical Frameworks for Agentic AI

In addition to legal and regulatory measures, the moral responsibility of agentic AI must be considered through an ethical lens. Several ethical frameworks can be employed to guide the development and use of autonomous systems:

Utilitarianism: A utilitarian approach to AI ethics emphasizes maximizing overall well-being and minimizing harm. Under this framework, AI systems should be designed to make decisions that contribute to the greater good, with their actions subject to constant evaluation to ensure that they are aligned with ethical outcomes. Accountability, in this case, would fall on the developers and users who ensure that the AI's objectives are aligned with socially beneficial outcomes.

Deontological Ethics: From a deontological perspective, the moral responsibility of AI would involve adherence to moral rules or duties, such as respecting human rights and dignity. Developers would be accountable for ensuring that AI systems comply with established moral principles, such as fairness, justice, and transparency, and for designing safeguards to prevent unethical outcomes.

Virtue Ethics: Virtue ethics emphasizes the development of good character traits and decision-making processes. In the context of AI, this framework would suggest that developers and users have a moral responsibility to ensure that AI systems embody virtues such as honesty, fairness, and compassion. AI should be designed and deployed with a focus on promoting ethical decision-making and fostering positive human values.

As agentic AI becomes increasingly integrated into society, the moral responsibility for autonomous actions must be addressed through both legal and ethical frameworks. While AI systems themselves may not currently possess the capacity for moral responsibility, the developers and users who create and deploy these systems must bear responsibility for their actions. To ensure the ethical use of AI, it is essential to establish clear accountability mechanisms that hold developers and users responsible for the consequences of AI's actions. Additionally, ethical principles such as transparency, fairness, and the minimization of harm should guide the design, implementation, and regulation of AI technologies. The evolving nature of AI calls for ongoing dialogue and collaboration to establish standards that protect individuals and society from the potential risks of autonomous systems while maximizing their benefits.

Chapter 17 Bias and Fairness in Agentic Systems

Agentic systems, also known as autonomous systems or artificial agents, are rapidly becoming integral components in various sectors, including healthcare, finance, law enforcement, hiring, and even creative industries. These systems, powered by advanced algorithms and artificial intelligence (AI), have the potential to revolutionize the way we make decisions, process information, and perform tasks. However, as these systems become more integrated into critical decision-making processes, concerns over bias and fairness have risen to the forefront.

Bias and fairness in agentic systems are complex and multifaceted issues that touch on ethical, social, and technological dimensions. Bias can manifest in the data, algorithms, and outcomes generated by these systems. Data-driven disparities, which occur when certain groups are disadvantaged or discriminated against based on data patterns, can lead to serious societal consequences. To address these disparities, it is essential to understand the root causes of bias, identify strategies to mitigate it, and ensure that fairness is an integral part of the design and implementation of agentic systems.

The Roots of Bias in Agentic Systems

The primary cause of bias in agentic systems often lies in the data used to train these models. Machine learning algorithms, which power most modern agentic systems, rely on large datasets to identify patterns and make predictions or decisions. These datasets are frequently sourced from historical records, which may contain inherent biases reflecting past societal inequalities. For example, data collected from healthcare systems may reflect historical biases in the treatment of different racial or ethnic groups, or hiring algorithms may replicate existing gender or racial disparities in employment decisions.

1. Historical Bias: Historical bias is one of the most significant sources of bias in data. When datasets are based on historical records, they often inherit the prejudices, stereotypes, and systemic inequalities that have existed in society for generations. For instance, if a hiring algorithm is trained on data from companies with a long history of hiring predominantly men for technical roles, the system may learn to favor male candidates over equally qualified female candidates, perpetuating gender disparities in the workforce.

2. Sampling Bias: Sampling bias occurs when the data collected does not adequately represent the entire population it is intended to reflect. In agentic systems, this can lead to poor predictions for underrepresented groups. For example, facial recognition systems trained primarily on images of lighter-skinned individuals may struggle to accurately identify people with darker skin tones, leading to disproportionately high error rates for these individuals.

3. Label Bias: Label bias arises when the labels assigned to data points are influenced by human judgment or societal biases. This can occur when the labeling process reflects existing stereotypes or prejudices. For instance, in criminal justice systems, risk assessment tools may be trained on data labeled with biased human judgments about the likelihood of reoffending, leading to overestimation of risk for certain racial or ethnic groups.

4. Measurement Bias: Measurement bias occurs when the way data is collected or measured reflects inaccuracies or inconsistencies. For example, if an algorithm relies on biased metrics, such as credit scores, to assess loan eligibility, it may unfairly disadvantage certain communities due to pre-existing inequalities in credit reporting practices.

The Impact of Bias on Agentic Systems

The impact of bias in agentic systems can be far-reaching, particularly when these systems are used in high-stakes decision-making areas. In healthcare, biased algorithms may result in unequal treatment recommendations, leading to worse health outcomes for marginalized populations. In criminal justice, biased risk assessment tools can contribute to unfair sentencing or parole decisions. In finance, biased credit scoring models can exacerbate inequalities in access to financial services.

Bias in agentic systems is not only harmful to individuals but can also undermine public trust in these technologies. If people perceive that agentic systems are making unfair or discriminatory decisions, they may be less likely to adopt or accept these systems, hindering their potential to bring about positive societal changes.

Fairness in Agentic Systems: Defining the Concept

Fairness is a key goal in the development of agentic systems. However, fairness is a nuanced and context-dependent concept that can be interpreted in various ways. In the context of agentic systems, fairness typically refers to the idea that algorithms and decision-making processes should treat individuals and groups equitably, without bias or discrimination. However, achieving fairness is often more challenging than it might initially seem, as there are different ways to define and operationalize fairness.

1. Individual Fairness: Individual fairness is the principle that similar individuals should be treated similarly. In practice, this means that an agentic system should not make arbitrary or discriminatory decisions based on characteristics such as race, gender, or socioeconomic status. For instance, an individual fairness approach would ensure that a hiring algorithm evaluates candidates based on their skills and qualifications rather than irrelevant factors such as their gender or ethnic background.

2. Group Fairness: Group fairness, on the other hand, focuses on ensuring that different groups, such as racial, ethnic, or gender groups, are treated equitably in aggregate. This may involve ensuring that outcomes are distributed fairly across groups, even if the individual treatment of each person is not identical. For example, a criminal justice risk assessment tool may aim to ensure that the risk of false positives (predicting someone will reoffend when they will not) and false negatives (predicting someone will not reoffend when they will) is balanced across racial groups.

3. Fairness as Equal Opportunity: Another approach to fairness is to ensure that individuals have equal opportunity to succeed, regardless of their background or identity. This is particularly relevant in contexts such as hiring or college admissions, where fairness may involve removing barriers that disproportionately disadvantage certain groups and ensuring that all individuals have an equal chance to succeed based on their abilities and qualifications.

4. Procedural Fairness: Procedural fairness emphasizes the fairness of the decision-making process itself. This includes ensuring transparency in how decisions are made, allowing individuals to understand how their data is being used, and providing mechanisms for contesting or appealing decisions. A system that is procedurally fair gives individuals confidence that they are being treated justly, even if they do not always agree with the outcome.

Strategies to Mitigate Bias and Promote Fairness

Addressing data-driven disparities in agentic systems requires a multifaceted approach that involves improving the quality of data, developing fairer algorithms, and implementing transparent decision-making processes. Below are some strategies to mitigate bias and promote fairness in these systems:

1. Diverse and Representative Data: One of the most effective ways to reduce bias is to ensure that the data used to train agentic systems is diverse and representative of the population it serves. This involves actively seeking out data from underrepresented groups and ensuring that the dataset is not skewed toward a particular demographic. For example, in the case of facial recognition systems, ensuring that the training data includes images of people from a wide range of ethnic backgrounds can help improve the system's accuracy for all groups.

2. Bias Detection and Correction Algorithms: Researchers and practitioners are developing algorithms designed to detect and correct bias in machine learning models. These algorithms can identify when a system is disproportionately favoring or disadvantaging certain groups and adjust the decision-making process accordingly. Techniques such as fairness constraints, reweighting data, and adversarial debiasing can be used to reduce bias in agentic systems.

3. Transparent and Explainable AI: Transparency and explainability are crucial for ensuring fairness in agentic systems. By making algorithms more interpretable, it becomes easier to identify and address biases in the decision-making process. Explainable AI (XAI) allows stakeholders to understand how a system arrived at a particular decision, which can be critical for ensuring accountability and fairness.

4. Regular Audits and Monitoring: Regular audits of agentic systems can help identify and address any emerging biases. These audits should assess not only the performance of the system but also its impact on different demographic groups. Monitoring the system's outcomes over time can help identify disparities and provide opportunities for intervention.

5. Stakeholder Involvement and Accountability: Involving diverse stakeholders in the development and deployment of agentic systems is essential for ensuring fairness. This includes input from affected communities, ethicists, legal experts, and other relevant parties. Accountability mechanisms should also be in place to ensure that companies and organizations are held responsible for the impact of their systems on vulnerable populations.

Bias and fairness in agentic systems are critical issues that must be addressed to ensure that these technologies benefit society as a whole. Data-driven disparities can have significant consequences for marginalized communities, and addressing these biases requires concerted effort from researchers, developers, policymakers, and affected groups. By prioritizing fairness, diversity, transparency, and accountability, it is possible to design agentic systems that are more equitable and just, reducing the risk of perpetuating harmful societal inequalities. Ultimately, the goal is to create systems that not only perform well but also treat all individuals and groups with fairness and respect, fostering trust and confidence in these powerful technologies.

Chapter 18 Privacy Concerns in Autonomy

In an increasingly interconnected world, autonomy has become a cornerstone of technological advancements, from self-driving cars to smart homes, wearable devices, and artificial intelligence systems. The push for autonomy in various sectors offers substantial benefits, including greater convenience, efficiency, and personalized experiences. However, as these systems gather more personal data to function effectively, privacy concerns have emerged as a significant challenge. Balancing individual agency and autonomy with the imperative of data security is becoming a complex and pressing issue.

The Rise of Autonomy and Its Promise

Autonomy refers to systems or devices capable of performing tasks or making decisions without human intervention, typically driven by machine learning, artificial intelligence (AI), or automated processes. Autonomous systems are designed to operate independently, making real-time decisions based on pre-programmed algorithms or learned behavior. Examples of autonomous technologies include:

Autonomous Vehicles: Self-driving cars and trucks use a combination of sensors, cameras, and AI to navigate and make decisions on the road.

Smart Home Devices: Technologies like smart thermostats, refrigerators, and voice-activated assistants (e.g., Amazon Alexa, Google Home) collect data to provide personalized services such as adjusting temperature or controlling lights.

Wearable Devices: Fitness trackers, health-monitoring gadgets, and even smartwatches gather personal data to offer insights into physical well-being, sleep patterns, and daily habits.

AI Personal Assistants: Virtual assistants powered by AI, such as Siri, Google Assistant, and chatbots, utilize data to provide personalized responses and improve user interactions.

The advantages of autonomy are significant. Autonomous systems can reduce human error, increase productivity, improve efficiency, and enhance convenience. Self-driving vehicles, for instance, are expected to decrease traffic accidents and ease congestion. Smart home devices offer energy-saving capabilities, while wearable technology can provide individuals with real-time health insights, enabling more proactive and personalized care.

However, the success of autonomous systems hinges on the collection, analysis, and use of vast amounts of personal data. As a result, concerns about the privacy and security of this data have become more pressing, with many questioning how far autonomy should extend without compromising individuals' rights to privacy.

Privacy Concerns in Autonomous Systems

As autonomous technologies rely heavily on data to function, they also pose significant privacy risks. These risks manifest in several key areas:

1. Data Collection and Surveillance

Autonomous systems collect a massive amount of data, ranging from basic information such as location and device usage to more sensitive data, including personal preferences, health metrics, and biometric information. This data collection can be pervasive, often occurring without the explicit consent of the user or without users fully understanding the extent of the data being gathered.

For example, autonomous vehicles continuously collect data about their surroundings, including the driver's behavior, road conditions, traffic patterns, and even facial expressions. While this data is essential for the vehicle to operate safely and efficiently, it also creates potential privacy risks. The data could be accessed by third parties, leading to surveillance concerns and unauthorized tracking of individuals' movements.

Similarly, smart home devices and wearables collect data that can reveal intimate details about an individual's daily life, health, and habits. If such data is not adequately protected, it could be exploited for purposes beyond the user's control, such as targeted advertising, profiling, or even identity theft.

2. Data Security

Data security is another crucial concern, especially given the sensitivity of the data that autonomous systems collect. Hackers or malicious actors may attempt to breach the systems to steal or manipulate personal data. In the case of autonomous vehicles, for example, a breach could result in the vehicle being controlled remotely or a leak of sensitive data, such as the vehicle's location and the driver's identity.

Wearables and health-monitoring devices face similar security risks. Unauthorized access to personal health data, such as heart rate, sleep patterns, and medical history, could have serious consequences. The exposure of such information could lead to discrimination in healthcare, employment, or insurance markets. Even relatively mundane data, such as an individual's location and activity level, could be used to target them with unwanted marketing or political messaging.

The sheer volume of data that autonomous systems generate creates an increasingly complex web of security risks. Protecting this data requires advanced encryption, secure storage methods, and real-time monitoring for potential breaches. Failure to implement strong security measures leaves individuals vulnerable to exploitation, manipulation, or harm.

3. Informed Consent and User Autonomy

The concept of informed consent is central to privacy and data protection. Users must be fully aware of the data being collected, how it will be used, and the risks associated with sharing that data. However, as autonomous systems become more sophisticated, it can be difficult for users to understand the full scope of data collection and how their information is being utilized.

For instance, many smart devices collect data in the background, often without the user's direct input or full understanding. While users may consent to data collection when they first use a device, this consent is often vague, and users may not realize the extent of data gathering or the long-term implications of sharing their information.

The use of autonomous systems may also inadvertently erode personal agency. If users are not fully informed about the potential risks or the ways their data could be exploited, they may be coerced into giving up their privacy in exchange for convenience. The ability to make informed decisions about the collection and use of one's personal data is fundamental to maintaining individual autonomy in a data-driven world.

Balancing Agency with Data Security

While the concerns about privacy in autonomous systems are significant, they are not insurmountable. Achieving a balance between user agency and data security requires a multi-faceted approach that prioritizes transparency, user control, and technological safeguards.

1. Transparency and Clear Communication

One of the most critical steps in addressing privacy concerns is ensuring transparency. Companies that develop autonomous systems must provide clear, easy-to-understand information about data collection practices. This means offering users transparent disclosures about the types of data being collected, how it will be used, and what steps are being taken to protect it.

Furthermore, users should be given the ability to easily review and manage their data. By implementing user-friendly privacy dashboards and consent management tools, users can take control of the information they share and make informed choices about the data they provide. This promotes a sense of agency and allows individuals to maintain greater control over their personal data.

2. Data Minimization and Purpose Limitation

Autonomous systems should adhere to the principles of data minimization and purpose limitation. Data minimization entails collecting only the data necessary to fulfill the specific purpose of the system, while purpose limitation restricts the use of data to the original intent for which it was collected. By focusing on these principles, companies can reduce the volume of data they gather, thereby minimizing the risk of misuse.

For example, autonomous vehicles could be designed to collect only the data essential for navigation, safety, and maintenance, avoiding unnecessary collection of personal data like user preferences or biometric information. Similarly, wearable devices could limit the collection of health data to only what is necessary for the device's core function, such as monitoring heart rate during exercise.

3. Data Security Measures

Robust data security practices are essential in maintaining user privacy in the context of autonomous systems. Companies must implement encryption techniques, secure data storage protocols, and secure communication channels to prevent unauthorized access to sensitive data. Additionally, autonomous systems should include built-in security features that automatically detect and mitigate potential threats in real-time.

Regular security audits and vulnerability assessments should be conducted to ensure that the systems remain secure against emerging threats. Companies must also be transparent about the steps they take to protect user data, providing regular updates on their security practices and any breaches that may occur.

4. User Control and Opt-Out Options

Autonomous systems should empower users with control over their data. This can be achieved through opt-in or opt-out mechanisms that allow users to choose what data they are comfortable sharing. Providing users with the ability to turn off data collection or to delete their data entirely when they choose to stop using a device is crucial to maintaining their autonomy.

Incorporating granular privacy settings enables users to selectively share data with specific services, enhancing their control over what information is shared and how it is used. This ensures that users can enjoy the benefits of autonomy while preserving their privacy.

As autonomous systems continue to proliferate, balancing agency with data security will be one of the most significant challenges of the digital age. While these technologies offer enormous potential for improving convenience, efficiency, and personalization, they also introduce substantial privacy risks. Protecting personal data, ensuring informed consent, and empowering users with control over their information are all vital components of building trust in autonomous systems.

Achieving this balance will require concerted efforts from developers, regulators, and consumers alike. By prioritizing transparency, minimizing data collection, implementing robust security measures, and giving users control over their data, it is possible to safeguard privacy while still reaping the benefits of autonomous technology. Only by striking this balance can we ensure that autonomy does not come at the cost of individual rights and freedoms.

Chapter 19 Employment Disruption

The rise of artificial intelligence (AI) has undoubtedly marked a revolutionary moment in human history, transforming industries, economies, and the way we live. As AI continues to develop, its impact on the workforce is becoming increasingly significant, generating a range of reactions from both fear and excitement. On the one hand, AI promises efficiency, productivity, and new capabilities, but on the other hand, it raises profound concerns about job displacement, automation, and the broader implications for human labor. This chapter explores the various ways in which AI, with its evolving agency, is reshaping the workforce, the economic challenges it presents, and the potential solutions that can mitigate the disruptive effects.

The Rise of AI and Workforce Disruption

AI's integration into the workforce is nothing new. Machine learning algorithms, natural language processing, and robotic automation have already permeated many sectors, from manufacturing and logistics to healthcare and finance. The power of AI lies in its ability to perform complex tasks with speed, accuracy, and consistency—often surpassing human capabilities. However, its potential for widespread disruption lies in its growing ability to act autonomously, increasingly displacing human labor in both blue-collar and white-collar jobs.

In sectors like manufacturing, robots and automation systems have already taken over tasks such as assembly, packaging, and quality control. Jobs once held by humans are now carried out by machines designed to work continuously without the need for rest. Similarly, in the transportation sector, the development of autonomous vehicles is poised to reshape driving professions, potentially displacing millions of drivers globally. Uber, Tesla, and other companies are investing heavily in self-driving technologies, anticipating that these will eventually replace truck drivers, taxi drivers, and delivery drivers.

Beyond manual labor, AI is also making inroads into white-collar professions. Software applications powered by AI are now able to process legal documents, assist with financial planning, and even provide medical diagnoses. Algorithms are capable of sifting through vast amounts of data to generate insights, predictions, and solutions that once required the expertise of professionals in law, finance, medicine, and consulting. With the increasing sophistication of AI-driven technologies, even jobs requiring higher education and specialized skills are at risk of automation.

Job Displacement and Job Creation

The debate surrounding AI and its impact on the workforce often centers on the idea of job displacement. AI has the potential to automate large swaths of labor, displacing millions of workers across various sectors. Studies conducted by organizations like McKinsey & Company suggest that a significant portion of current jobs are at risk of automation. A 2017 report by McKinsey estimated that around 15 percent of the global workforce—or roughly 400 million workers—could be displaced by automation by 2030. While these figures vary depending on the region and industry, the general consensus is clear: automation will disrupt many traditional jobs.

However, this narrative of widespread job loss is not the entire story. While AI may eliminate certain jobs, it also creates new opportunities. History shows us that technological advancements often lead to the creation of new jobs and industries, even as others are displaced. The Industrial Revolution, for example, led to the replacement of manual labor with machines, but it also gave birth to entirely new sectors, such as engineering, factory management, and logistics.

In the case of AI, new roles are already emerging. The development and deployment of AI systems require skilled professionals to design, implement, and maintain them. Data scientists, machine learning engineers, and AI ethicists are just a few examples of new professions that have emerged in response to AI technologies. Additionally, as AI becomes more prevalent in industries like healthcare, education, and entertainment, it will likely lead to the creation of jobs that we cannot yet fully anticipate. For example, the use of AI to personalize education and enhance learning could require new teaching roles or positions that blend technology and pedagogy.

The Transformation of Skills and Workforce Adaptation

One of the central challenges posed by AI in the workforce is the need for workers to adapt and reskill. As automation takes over routine and repetitive tasks, the demand for cognitive, creative, and emotional skills will rise. The jobs that remain will likely require a higher degree of human interaction, problem-solving, and adaptability. For example, AI can analyze vast datasets and provide recommendations, but humans will still be needed to make nuanced decisions based on those recommendations. The ability to work alongside AI and utilize its capabilities effectively will become a critical skill for the future workforce.

To ensure that workers are prepared for this transformation, reskilling and upskilling initiatives are essential. Governments, businesses, and educational institutions must collaborate to provide training programs that equip individuals with the skills needed to thrive in an AI-driven economy. This includes not only technical skills, such as proficiency in programming and data analysis but also soft skills, such as communication, empathy, and creativity—skills that are difficult for AI to replicate.

In addition to technical training, there is a growing need for AI literacy. Understanding how AI works, its limitations, and its ethical implications will be vital for workers across industries. Workers who understand the potential and limitations of AI will be better equipped to leverage its capabilities, ensuring that AI complements human effort rather than replaces it entirely.

Ethical and Social Implications of AI in the Workforce

While the economic and employment implications of AI are significant, there are also ethical and social considerations that must be addressed. One of the most pressing concerns is the potential for AI to exacerbate existing inequalities. The displacement of workers due to automation is likely to disproportionately affect low-income and low-skilled workers, deepening social divides. If AI is not managed properly, it could lead to an erosion of the middle class, further entrenching wealth disparities and reducing social mobility.

Moreover, the ethical implications of AI-driven decision-making are profound. AI systems are only as good as the data they are trained on, and biased or incomplete data can lead to discriminatory outcomes. For example, AI algorithms used in hiring processes, criminal justice, or credit scoring could perpetuate racial, gender, or socio-economic biases. As AI becomes more prevalent in decision-making processes, ensuring that these systems are fair, transparent, and accountable will be crucial.

The question of who benefits from AI is another important issue. While large tech companies are at the forefront of AI development, the benefits of AI are often concentrated in the hands of a few. If AI-driven automation leads to widespread job displacement, there is a risk that the economic benefits of AI will be unevenly distributed, leaving many workers and communities behind.

To address these concerns, policymakers must adopt strategies that ensure the fair distribution of the benefits of AI. This could include introducing policies such as universal basic income (UBI), which provides a guaranteed income to individuals regardless of employment status, or implementing progressive taxation systems that ensure that companies benefiting from automation contribute to the broader economy.

Navigating the Future: Preparing for an AI-Driven Workforce

As AI continues to evolve, it is clear that the workforce will undergo significant transformations. Job displacement will occur, but new opportunities will also arise, especially for those who are able to adapt to the changing landscape. To successfully navigate this transition, there are several key strategies that individuals, businesses, and governments can employ:

Reskilling and Education: Investment in reskilling initiatives is essential for workers to stay relevant in the AI-driven economy. Lifelong learning programs, vocational training, and partnerships between industry and educational institutions will help individuals develop the skills needed to thrive in new roles.

Ethical AI Development: To ensure that AI benefits society as a whole, it is critical to prioritize ethical AI development. This includes promoting transparency, fairness, and accountability in AI systems, as well as addressing issues such as bias and discrimination.

Social Safety Nets: Governments must strengthen social safety nets to protect workers who may be displaced by automation. This could include unemployment benefits, retraining programs, and policies that ensure a smooth transition to new employment opportunities.

Collaboration between Stakeholders: The impact of AI on the workforce cannot be addressed by any one entity alone.

Collaboration between governments, businesses, labor organizations, and educational institutions will be crucial in shaping the future of work and ensuring that the benefits of AI are shared broadly.

AI is undoubtedly reshaping the workforce, bringing both challenges and opportunities. The rise of AI-driven automation will disrupt many industries and lead to job displacement, but it will also create new roles and transform existing ones. To ensure a successful transition, individuals must adapt by reskilling and embracing lifelong learning, while businesses and governments must prioritize ethical AI development and support workers through social safety nets and reskilling initiatives. The future of work will be shaped by how well we navigate these changes, ensuring that AI serves as a tool for progress rather than a force of division.

Chapter 20 Social Acceptance of Autonomous Agents

Autonomous agents, such as self-driving cars, intelligent robots, and artificial intelligence (AI)-driven assistants, have increasingly become a part of everyday life. These technologies are capable of performing tasks that traditionally required human intervention, from driving vehicles to managing household chores and assisting with complex tasks. However, despite the rapid advancements in AI and robotics, public perception and trust in these autonomous systems remain mixed. The acceptance of autonomous agents depends on various factors, including how they are perceived by the public, the degree of trust in their capabilities, their impact on society, and their ethical implications.

The Evolution of Autonomous Agents

The idea of autonomous agents is not new. Early forms of automation can be traced back to the Industrial Revolution, when machines began to take over manual labor in factories. However, modern autonomous agents are fundamentally different due to their ability to learn from data and make decisions without human input. These agents rely on advanced technologies, such as machine learning, computer vision, and natural language processing, to interact with the environment and carry out tasks.

Self-driving cars are perhaps the most prominent example of autonomous agents in current public discourse. Companies like Tesla, Waymo, and Uber have invested heavily in autonomous vehicle technology. Robots designed for personal assistance or industrial automation also present significant potential to improve efficiency and safety in many sectors. From healthcare robots to customer service agents powered by AI, the presence of autonomous systems is expected to grow rapidly.

Understanding Public Perception

Public perception of autonomous agents is shaped by a variety of factors, including individual experiences with technology, cultural attitudes towards innovation, and exposure to the risks associated with new technologies. Understanding these perceptions is critical for the successful integration of autonomous agents into society.

1. The Technology Gap

There exists a technology gap between the creators and the consumers of autonomous agents. Developers and engineers may have a deep understanding of the technology's inner workings, but for most people, the concept of autonomous systems remains abstract. The complexity of algorithms, sensors, and decision-making processes behind autonomous agents can be difficult for the general public to comprehend. This gap can lead to skepticism and resistance, especially when consumers do not fully understand how or why autonomous agents make decisions.

The "black-box" nature of AI decision-making also contributes to this gap. People may trust autonomous agents when they can clearly see how decisions are made, but without transparency in AI processes, individuals may feel disconnected from the technology and unsure of its reliability.

2. Fear of the Unknown

A fundamental aspect of human nature is the fear of the unknown. When it comes to new technologies, this fear is often magnified, particularly when those technologies have the potential to change the way we live, work, and interact with others. The idea of machines making decisions without human oversight raises concerns about accountability, safety, and control.

In the case of self-driving cars, for example, people worry about the potential for accidents. High-profile incidents involving autonomous vehicles, such as crashes and fatalities, have only increased public apprehension. Even if these accidents are statistically rare, they trigger a sense of fear, as people tend to focus on worst-case scenarios.

Similarly, robots and AI-driven systems are often perceived as a threat to human jobs. The fear of unemployment due to automation has been widely discussed in the context of autonomous agents. People may view autonomous agents as competitors in the labor market, creating anxiety about their economic stability and future prospects.

3. Cultural and Societal Factors

Cultural attitudes towards technology play a significant role in shaping public perception of autonomous agents. In societies where innovation is embraced and technological advancement is seen as a sign of progress, people may be more open to the idea of autonomous agents. Conversely, in cultures that are more conservative or resistant to change, the introduction of autonomous agents may be met with skepticism.

For instance, countries like Japan and South Korea, with a long history of technological adoption, tend to be more accepting of robotics and automation. In contrast, in parts of Europe or the United States, where there are concerns about privacy and regulation, people may be more hesitant to trust autonomous systems.

Public perception can also be influenced by media representations of autonomous agents. Movies and TV shows often portray robots and AI as either benevolent helpers or dangerous villains. These portrayals can shape public opinion, either by instilling a sense of excitement or by amplifying fears of malevolent machines. For example, the 2004 film *I, Robot* portrayed AI as a potential danger to humanity, contributing to anxiety about autonomous systems.

Trust in Autonomous Agents

Trust is a cornerstone of social acceptance when it comes to autonomous agents. For any system to be widely adopted, the public must trust that it will perform as expected and that it will not harm people or society.

1. Reliability and Safety

One of the primary concerns when it comes to autonomous agents is their reliability. For people to trust autonomous systems, they must be confident that these agents will function correctly in a variety of situations. In the case of autonomous vehicles, this means ensuring that the vehicles can safely navigate through complex traffic scenarios, respond to unexpected obstacles, and make decisions that prioritize the safety of passengers and pedestrians.

Safety is especially critical when autonomous agents are tasked with performing activities that directly impact human well-being. Robots used in healthcare settings, for example, must be able to accurately diagnose medical conditions, administer treatments, and operate in close proximity to vulnerable individuals. If an autonomous agent were to malfunction or make an error in judgment, the consequences could be severe.

The development of robust testing and validation procedures is essential to fostering trust in autonomous agents. Regulatory bodies, such as the National Highway Traffic Safety Administration (NHTSA) for self-driving cars, play a role in ensuring that autonomous systems meet rigorous safety standards. However, continuous monitoring, real-world testing, and updates to software are necessary to address potential vulnerabilities and ensure that systems remain safe over time.

2. Transparency and Explainability

Transparency and explainability are vital to building trust in autonomous agents. Users must be able to understand why an autonomous agent makes certain decisions, especially in high-stakes situations. If a self-driving car makes an emergency stop, for example, passengers should be able to know the reasoning behind that decision.

Explainable AI (XAI) is an emerging field that seeks to make AI systems more transparent by providing clear and understandable explanations of their decision-making processes. By providing insights into how AI systems arrive at their conclusions, explainable AI can help demystify the technology and build trust with users.

3. Accountability and Responsibility

Another crucial aspect of trust is accountability. If an autonomous agent causes harm or damage, it is essential to establish who is responsible. In the case of a self-driving car accident, should the responsibility fall on the manufacturer, the software developer, or the vehicle owner? Establishing legal frameworks for accountability is a complex but necessary task to ensure that autonomous systems can be trusted.

The introduction of autonomous agents raises questions about liability and insurance as well. In some cases, it may be difficult to determine who is at fault when a machine is involved in an accident. Legal frameworks will need to evolve to address these issues and provide clear guidelines for accountability.

Building Public Trust and Acceptance

To foster public acceptance of autonomous agents, it is essential to address the concerns outlined above. Several steps can be taken to improve public perception and increase trust in these technologies:

Education and Awareness: Public education campaigns can help bridge the technology gap and dispel misconceptions about autonomous agents. By providing accessible information about how these systems work, their benefits, and their safety features, developers can reduce fear and increase trust.

Transparency and Open Dialogue: Open communication between developers, regulators, and the public is essential. Transparent discussions about the capabilities and limitations of autonomous agents can help manage expectations and build confidence in the technology.

Continuous Improvement and Testing: Autonomous agents must be rigorously tested and constantly improved to ensure they meet safety standards. Real-world testing, simulations, and updates to software are necessary to maintain the reliability of these systems.

Ethical Considerations: Addressing the ethical implications of autonomous agents, such as the impact on jobs and privacy, is crucial for fostering trust. Developers must ensure that these technologies are used responsibly and that their benefits are shared equitably across society.

Collaboration with Regulators: Governments and regulatory bodies must collaborate with developers to establish clear guidelines for the safe and ethical use of autonomous agents. Regulations should focus on safety, accountability, and consumer protection to ensure that autonomous systems are introduced in a way that promotes public trust.

The social acceptance of autonomous agents depends on a variety of factors, including public perception, trust, and understanding. While many people are excited about the potential benefits of autonomous agents, others remain hesitant due to concerns about safety, accountability, and the unknown. By addressing these concerns through education, transparency, and continuous improvement, developers and regulators can help foster greater trust in autonomous agents and pave the way for their successful integration into society. Ultimately, the widespread acceptance of autonomous systems will depend on how effectively these technologies can be made safe, reliable, and aligned with the values and needs of the public.

Chapter 21 Scaling Agentic AI Systems

The development of agentic AI systems—intelligent entities that can autonomously act, plan, and make decisions—has emerged as a transformative force across numerous sectors. From healthcare to finance, transportation to entertainment, these systems hold the potential to revolutionize industries by providing unparalleled levels of automation and decision-making capabilities. However, as these systems scale, the challenges related to computational power and efficiency become increasingly prominent. These obstacles can impact the system's ability to process vast amounts of data, make timely decisions, and function in real-world environments. In this chapter, we will explore the challenges in scaling agentic AI systems, focusing on computational power, efficiency, and the trade-offs involved.

The Nature of Agentic AI Systems

Agentic AI systems are designed to operate autonomously within specific environments, taking actions to achieve predefined goals. Unlike narrow AI systems that are typically specialized for a single task (such as image recognition or language translation), agentic AI systems can integrate various functions, making them capable of handling dynamic, complex tasks with adaptability. These systems are often characterized by their ability to:

Perceive the environment: Through sensors, cameras, or other input methods, agentic AI systems gather data that helps them understand the current state of the world.

Plan actions: Using advanced algorithms, these systems generate plans based on their goals and perceived environment.

Execute decisions: Once a plan is devised, the system takes actions, either physically or virtually, to achieve the intended outcome.

Adapt and learn: Over time, agentic AI systems can learn from experience and improve their decision-making through reinforcement learning, supervised learning, or other forms of training.

As these systems grow in capability and complexity, they require increasingly powerful computational resources to handle the enormous amounts of data, perform sophisticated calculations, and ensure that decisions are made in real-time.

Computational Power Challenges

Scaling agentic AI systems requires an exponential increase in computational power. The more sophisticated the AI system becomes, the more processing power is needed to handle complex tasks such as perception, reasoning, planning, and decision-making. The primary challenges in this domain include:

1. Data Processing Requirements

Agentic AI systems generate and process massive amounts of data, particularly when operating in dynamic and unpredictable environments. For instance, self-driving cars rely on a multitude of sensors, cameras, and radars that constantly stream high-resolution data to the AI system. The system must process this data in real-time to make decisions such as when to accelerate, stop, or steer.

The sheer volume of data generated by these sensors can overwhelm traditional processing architectures. AI models like deep neural networks require substantial computational resources to process and interpret this data efficiently. For instance, deep learning models can have millions, if not billions, of parameters, requiring immense amounts of data and computation to train and fine-tune effectively.

2. Real-time Decision-Making

Agentic AI systems must often operate in real-time or near-real-time, making decisions on the fly based on rapidly changing inputs. For example, in a drone surveillance system, the AI must analyze live video feeds, assess the environment, and decide on flight paths without delays. This real-time processing introduces a significant computational burden.

The challenge here is not just the volume of data but the need to process it quickly and efficiently. Many algorithms, particularly those in reinforcement learning and decision theory, can be computationally expensive, requiring significant processing to generate optimal or near-optimal decisions.

3. Complexity of Modeling

As AI systems scale, they need to handle more variables and more intricate models of the world. For instance, a robot designed for industrial automation needs to model the dynamics of its environment, including the movement of objects, the constraints of machinery, and the interaction with humans. More complex environments require more sophisticated models, which in turn require more computational resources to simulate and optimize.

As agentic AI systems grow in their capability to learn from complex, multi-dimensional environments, they must be capable of performing calculations that scale with the complexity of the task at hand. This may involve massive simulation spaces or Monte Carlo methods, both of which require substantial computing resources.

4. Training and Optimization

The training process for agentic AI systems can take an enormous amount of computational power. For instance, training large language models (LLMs) like GPT-3 involves running millions of iterations across billions of parameters on vast datasets. These models require specialized hardware, such as Graphics Processing Units (GPUs) or Tensor Processing Units (TPUs), to accelerate the training process.

However, scaling agentic AI systems requires not only better hardware but also optimization techniques to reduce the training time and resource consumption. Techniques such as model pruning, transfer learning, and distributed training are used to mitigate the burden of training large models. But even with these strategies, training state-of-the-art agentic AI systems remains computationally intensive.

Efficiency Challenges

While increasing computational power allows agentic AI systems to perform more complex tasks, efficiency remains a key challenge in scaling. Computational efficiency directly impacts the ability of these systems to operate effectively in real-world environments. Below are several key challenges associated with achieving efficiency:

1. Energy Consumption

As the complexity of agentic AI systems grows, so does the demand for energy. AI models like deep neural networks require significant amounts of electricity, particularly when they are being trained on large datasets or when operating in real-time environments. Data centers running AI models contribute to a large carbon footprint due to their high energy consumption. This poses a major challenge in scaling agentic AI systems, as the environmental impact of such systems cannot be overlooked.

Energy-efficient hardware and software design are essential for scaling AI systems. Researchers are actively developing specialized AI chips that consume less energy while delivering higher performance. For example, TPUs and FPGAs (Field-Programmable Gate Arrays) are designed to optimize computational workloads for specific types of machine learning tasks, leading to lower energy consumption.

2. Latency and Bandwidth Limitations

In many real-world applications, such as autonomous vehicles or drones, latency can be a significant factor. These systems need to make decisions based on real-time data, but if the communication between the sensors, the central processing unit, and the decision-making algorithms is slow, it can result in delayed or inaccurate decisions.

Bandwidth limitations also contribute to the challenge of scaling agentic AI systems. Real-time decision-making requires high-speed communication between multiple nodes or devices, but data transmission speeds may be constrained, especially in remote or less developed areas where high-speed internet infrastructure is lacking. In these cases, edge computing and distributed architectures may be used to process data locally, reducing the need for large-scale data transmission.

3. Algorithmic Efficiency

Another challenge lies in the efficiency of the algorithms themselves. Many state-of-the-art AI algorithms, especially those in deep learning and reinforcement learning, can be highly computationally expensive. For example, training a deep neural network can involve processing vast amounts of data multiple times, leading to high computational costs. Similarly, reinforcement learning requires multiple simulations to converge on an optimal strategy, further intensifying the computational demand.

Researchers are constantly exploring ways to make algorithms more efficient, such as developing algorithms that require fewer resources or work more effectively with lower-resolution data. Techniques like federated learning, which allows multiple devices to collaboratively train AI models without sharing raw data, are a step towards reducing computational demands.

4. Scalability of Infrastructure

To meet the demands of large-scale AI systems, the underlying infrastructure must be scalable. This includes both hardware (such as processors, memory, and storage) and software (such as distributed computing frameworks). As AI systems scale, they require more processing units, and without the right infrastructure, these systems may become bottlenecked by their limited resources.

Cloud computing platforms and distributed computing frameworks, such as Apache Hadoop and Kubernetes, offer a way to scale AI infrastructure, allowing multiple processors to work in parallel on a single task. However, scaling infrastructure is not without its challenges, including the management of large-scale systems, the allocation of resources, and the need for high availability.

Trade-Offs in Scaling Agentic AI Systems

When scaling agentic AI systems, there are several trade-offs between computational power and efficiency that must be considered:

Performance vs. Energy Consumption: More powerful systems generally consume more energy. Striking a balance between performance and energy efficiency is crucial for scaling AI systems without causing significant environmental impact.

Real-Time Processing vs. Accuracy: Achieving real-time decision-making often comes at the cost of accuracy. In certain applications, such as autonomous driving, a trade-off may be necessary between making decisions in real time and ensuring those decisions are fully optimized.

Centralized vs. Decentralized Models: Centralized models, such as cloud computing, offer vast amounts of computational power but face challenges related to latency and bandwidth. On the other hand, decentralized models, like edge computing, can help reduce latency but may struggle with computational power.

Scaling agentic AI systems presents significant challenges in terms of computational power and efficiency. These systems require immense resources to process data, make real-time decisions, and function autonomously in complex environments. As the demand for more sophisticated AI systems grows, solutions such as energy-efficient hardware, optimization algorithms, and scalable infrastructure will be essential in addressing these challenges. Ultimately, achieving a balance between computational power and efficiency is key to ensuring that agentic AI systems can scale effectively while minimizing their environmental and operational impact.

Chapter 22 Error Propagation in Autonomous Systems

Autonomous systems, such as self-driving cars, drones, and robots, have made significant advancements in recent years. These systems promise to revolutionize industries by reducing human error, improving efficiency, and performing tasks that are dangerous or impossible for humans. However, despite their incredible potential, the propagation of errors in autonomous systems poses a significant challenge. Inaccurate decisions, misinterpretations of sensory data, or faulty algorithms can lead to serious consequences, from minor malfunctions to catastrophic failures. Therefore, understanding and mitigating the risks associated with error propagation is crucial for the safe and reliable deployment of autonomous systems.

The Nature of Error Propagation

In any autonomous system, multiple subsystems work in tandem to perform tasks. These systems rely on sensors, algorithms, and decision-making models to process data, perceive the environment, and execute actions. Each component may introduce errors that propagate through the system, amplifying the impact as they move from one subsystem to another. The problem of error propagation is particularly severe in autonomous systems because decisions made by the system often have real-world consequences.

There are several types of errors that may propagate through autonomous systems:

Sensor Errors: Autonomous systems rely heavily on sensors, such as LiDAR, cameras, GPS, and accelerometers, to perceive their surroundings. Sensor errors can arise from poor calibration, noise in the data, or environmental factors such as fog or low light. These errors, if not properly addressed, can lead to incorrect decisions, such as misidentifying an obstacle or miscalculating the system's location.

Perception Errors: Perception refers to the process of interpreting sensory data and constructing a model of the environment. Errors in perception can occur when the system misidentifies objects, fails to detect obstacles, or incorrectly estimates distances. These errors can lead to wrong decisions, such as moving toward an obstacle or failing to recognize a traffic sign.

Algorithmic Errors: Autonomous systems rely on complex algorithms to process sensor data and make decisions. These algorithms may involve machine learning models, optimization techniques, or control systems. Algorithmic errors can arise from bugs in the code, overfitting of machine learning models, or limitations in the underlying mathematical models. These errors can result in incorrect behavior, such as taking an unsafe route or failing to react to a changing environment.

Decision-Making Errors: Once the system has processed the data and perceived the environment, it must make decisions based on this information. Errors in decision-making can occur when the system fails to weigh different factors appropriately or chooses an action that is not optimal for the given situation. This can be caused by biases in the decision-making process, lack of information, or flaws in the decision-making algorithm.

Actuation Errors: Actuators are responsible for carrying out the decisions made by the autonomous system. These include motors, servos, and other mechanical devices that control movement. Actuation errors can result from faults in the hardware, incorrect commands, or poor coordination between subsystems. These errors can cause the system to behave in ways that are inconsistent with its intended operation, leading to unsafe conditions.

The key challenge in error propagation lies in the interconnectedness of these subsystems. An error in one subsystem can propagate to others, leading to a cascade of failures. For example, a sensor error might lead to incorrect perception, which could then cause an algorithmic error in decision-making, ultimately resulting in an unsafe action by the actuator.

The Consequences of Error Propagation

The impact of error propagation in autonomous systems can range from minor inconveniences to catastrophic failures, depending on the severity of the errors and the context in which they occur. Some of the most concerning consequences of error propagation include:

Accidents and Collisions: In the case of autonomous vehicles, error propagation can lead to accidents and collisions. For example, if a sensor fails to detect an obstacle, the vehicle may continue moving toward it, resulting in a crash. Similarly, errors in decision-making algorithms could lead to poor navigation decisions, such as entering a busy intersection without proper clearance.

Loss of Control: Errors in actuation can result in the loss of control of the autonomous system. For example, a malfunction in a drone's motors could cause it to lose stability and crash. In autonomous robots, errors in movement coordination could lead to the robot veering off course or colliding with objects.

Damage to Equipment and Infrastructure: Even if the system does not cause a human injury, error propagation can lead to significant damage to equipment and infrastructure. For example, a self-driving car might accidentally damage a streetlight or a building if its sensors fail to detect the environment correctly.

Financial Losses: The costs associated with autonomous systems' errors can be substantial. Not only are there direct costs related to repair and compensation, but there may also be indirect costs related to reputation damage, legal liabilities, and regulatory scrutiny. For example, a malfunctioning autonomous delivery drone could lead to damaged goods, legal disputes, and lost customers.

Loss of Trust in Autonomous Technology: Perhaps one of the most significant risks of error propagation is the potential loss of trust in autonomous systems. If errors become widespread or lead to catastrophic consequences, people may lose faith in the technology, delaying or hindering its adoption. This could have long-term effects on industries relying on autonomous systems, such as transportation, healthcare, and logistics.

Mitigating Risks of Error Propagation

To ensure the safety and reliability of autonomous systems, it is essential to mitigate the risks associated with error propagation. Several strategies can be employed to address this challenge:

Redundancy: One of the most effective ways to mitigate the impact of sensor errors and other failures is through redundancy. By incorporating multiple sensors of the same type (e.g., multiple cameras or LiDAR sensors), the system can cross-check data and detect discrepancies. Redundant sensors can help ensure that a failure in one sensor does not lead to incorrect decisions. Redundancy can also be applied at the algorithmic level, where multiple decision-making models can be used to validate each other's outputs.

Error Detection and Correction: Autonomous systems should be equipped with mechanisms to detect and correct errors in real-time. For example, anomaly detection algorithms can monitor sensor data for inconsistencies or outliers, alerting the system to potential sensor malfunctions. Similarly, machine learning models can be trained to identify patterns of incorrect behavior and adjust their predictions accordingly. When an error is detected, the system can take corrective action, such as reinitializing sensors or recalibrating algorithms.

Robustness and Fault Tolerance: Building robust systems that can tolerate faults without catastrophic failure is crucial. This involves designing algorithms and control systems that can handle noisy or incomplete data, adapt to changing environments, and continue operating even in the presence of errors. For instance, autonomous vehicles can be programmed to slow down or stop in case of uncertainty, reducing the risk of accidents when errors occur.

Simulation and Testing: Extensive simulation and testing are critical for identifying potential error propagation issues before deploying autonomous systems in real-world scenarios. By simulating a wide range of scenarios, including rare edge cases, developers can ensure that the system behaves safely under various conditions. Testing should be conducted both in controlled environments (e.g., simulation) and real-world conditions to verify the system's reliability.

Continuous Monitoring and Updates: Autonomous systems should be continuously monitored throughout their lifecycle. This includes monitoring sensor performance, software updates, and system health. Real-time diagnostics can help identify and address potential issues before they cause significant problems. Additionally, over-the-air software updates can be used to fix bugs, improve algorithms, and enhance the system's overall performance.

Explainability and Transparency: One of the challenges with autonomous systems, particularly those that rely on machine learning, is that their decision-making processes can be opaque. To mitigate the risks of incorrect decisions, it is essential to design systems that are interpretable and explainable. This allows developers and users to understand how decisions are made and to identify potential sources of error. Transparency in the decision-making process can also help build trust in autonomous systems.

Human-in-the-Loop: While full autonomy is the goal for many systems, human oversight is essential in many high-stakes applications. By incorporating a "human-in-the-loop" approach, autonomous systems can leverage human expertise to intervene when errors are detected or when the system encounters situations that it cannot handle autonomously. This approach ensures that the human operator can take control if necessary, preventing catastrophic outcomes.

Error propagation is a significant challenge in the development and deployment of autonomous systems. Given the complexity and interdependence of subsystems in these systems, errors in one part can quickly cascade, leading to incorrect decisions and potentially disastrous outcomes. However, through strategies such as redundancy, error detection, robustness, extensive testing, and human oversight, the risks associated with error propagation can be mitigated. By designing autonomous systems with safety, reliability, and transparency in mind, we can unlock the full potential of this transformative technology while ensuring that it remains safe and trustworthy for users.

Chapter 23 Robustness Against Adversarial Attacks

In today's rapidly evolving technological landscape, the security of machine learning (ML) systems has become a critical concern. As these systems are integrated into more applications—from autonomous vehicles to financial services—ensuring their robustness against adversarial attacks is paramount. Adversarial attacks, in which malicious entities manipulate input data to cause incorrect predictions or system failures, can compromise the integrity of these systems, leading to potentially disastrous consequences. This chapter explores the challenges of ensuring robust, secure, and tamper-proof systems, focusing on adversarial machine learning and countermeasures against such threats.

1. Understanding Adversarial Attacks

An adversarial attack refers to a deliberate attempt to fool a machine learning model into making an incorrect prediction or decision by introducing small, carefully crafted perturbations to the input data. These perturbations are often imperceptible to human observers but can significantly impact the model's output. Adversarial attacks exploit the vulnerabilities inherent in the design of ML models, particularly deep neural networks, which learn to map inputs to outputs by optimizing weights and parameters through training on vast datasets.

The nature of adversarial attacks varies across different types of models and applications. For example, in image recognition, an adversary might alter an image in such a way that a neural network misidentifies it. In natural language processing (NLP), adversarial inputs might involve slight changes to text that lead to incorrect sentiment analysis or misclassification of commands. These attacks can be categorized as either white-box or black-box attacks:

White-box attacks: In white-box scenarios, the adversary has full knowledge of the model, including its architecture, parameters, and training data. This allows for more sophisticated manipulation of the inputs to cause misclassifications or errors.

Black-box attacks: In black-box scenarios, the adversary has no direct access to the model but can query the system to observe its responses. Despite limited knowledge, adversaries can still exploit these interactions to generate effective adversarial inputs.

Adversarial attacks are not limited to image recognition tasks; they have been shown to be effective in various domains, including speech recognition, text classification, and even reinforcement learning systems.

2. The Risks of Adversarial Attacks

The risks associated with adversarial attacks are manifold and span across various industries. In autonomous vehicles, for instance, adversarial examples can be crafted to mislead the vehicle's object recognition system, causing it to overlook road signs, pedestrians, or other obstacles. This could result in accidents, injuries, or worse.

In the financial sector, adversarial attacks might be used to deceive fraud detection systems, allowing malicious transactions to slip through unnoticed. Similarly, in the healthcare industry, adversarial attacks on medical imaging systems could lead to misdiagnosis, resulting in severe patient harm.

One of the most alarming aspects of adversarial attacks is their potential to undermine trust in machine learning systems. As these systems become more ingrained in everyday life, their reliability and accuracy are paramount. If adversarial attacks succeed in circumventing security measures or introducing flaws into decision-making, public confidence in the technology could be severely shaken.

3. Methods of Defending Against Adversarial Attacks

Over the past few years, significant research has been dedicated to defending against adversarial attacks and improving the robustness of machine learning models. These defense mechanisms aim to make the model less sensitive to perturbations while maintaining its performance on legitimate tasks.

a. Adversarial Training

Adversarial training is one of the most widely studied methods for increasing model robustness. The approach involves augmenting the training data with adversarial examples so that the model learns to correctly classify perturbed inputs. By repeatedly exposing the model to both clean and adversarial data, it becomes more resilient to attacks. Adversarial training essentially makes the model "aware" of the kinds of perturbations that adversaries might introduce.

However, adversarial training is not without its challenges. It is computationally expensive, as it requires generating adversarial examples during each training iteration. Moreover, the trained model may still exhibit vulnerabilities to more sophisticated or unseen attacks, especially if the adversary employs techniques beyond simple perturbations.

b. Gradient Masking

Gradient masking is a technique aimed at obfuscating the gradient information that adversarial attacks rely on to craft perturbations. This can be achieved by modifying the loss function or adding noise to the gradients during training. By making it difficult for an attacker to compute the gradients, this technique can hinder the success of adversarial attacks.

Despite its potential, gradient masking has been criticized for being a partial solution. Many adversarial attacks, such as the momentum-based iterative method, can bypass gradient masking by using alternative techniques to estimate the gradients indirectly. As such, gradient masking should not be considered a comprehensive defense on its own.

c. Defensive Distillation

Defensive distillation is another technique aimed at improving the robustness of machine learning models. The idea is to train a model (called the "student") to approximate the behavior of a larger, more complex model (the "teacher"). The student model learns from soft labels generated by the teacher, which provide more nuanced information than traditional hard labels (the binary or categorical labels in the dataset). This process helps smooth the decision boundary of the model, making it less sensitive to small input perturbations.

Defensive distillation has shown promise in reducing the success of adversarial attacks, but like other defense strategies, it is not foolproof. Researchers have demonstrated that adversarial examples can still be generated for distilled models, indicating that further research is necessary to improve this technique.

d. Input Preprocessing

Input preprocessing involves transforming the input data before feeding it into the model to remove potential adversarial perturbations. Techniques such as image denoising, feature squeezing, and dimensionality reduction have been proposed as ways to filter out noise or distortions caused by adversarial attacks. For instance, feature squeezing reduces the precision of features to make it harder for adversarial perturbations to have a significant effect.

While input preprocessing can be an effective first line of defense, it is not a guaranteed solution. Sophisticated adversaries can often bypass preprocessing techniques, requiring additional layers of protection to be implemented alongside preprocessing methods.

e. Certified Defenses

Certified defenses are a class of approaches that provide guarantees about the model's robustness in the presence of adversarial attacks. These defenses typically rely on mathematical or theoretical guarantees that ensure the model will behave correctly within a specified region of the input space, even when adversarial perturbations are introduced. One such method is robust optimization, which involves training the model in a way that minimizes the worst-case performance degradation under adversarial attacks.

Certified defenses are still a developing area of research, but they hold significant promise for ensuring the security and reliability of machine learning systems in adversarial environments.

4. The Role of Explainability in Adversarial Robustness

Another crucial aspect of building robust and secure systems is enhancing the explainability of machine learning models.

Explainability refers to the ability of a model to provide human-understandable justifications for its decisions and predictions. By making models more interpretable, we can better identify potential vulnerabilities and understand how adversarial inputs might exploit them.

Techniques such as attention mechanisms and saliency maps have been used to make deep neural networks more transparent, allowing researchers to visualize which parts of the input data contribute most to the model's decision. Such insights can inform the development of stronger defense mechanisms against adversarial attacks.

5. Ensuring Tamper-Proof Systems

While defending against adversarial attacks is vital, ensuring the integrity of machine learning systems also involves safeguarding against tampering and other forms of malicious interference. Tamper-proofing systems requires implementing a combination of cryptographic methods, hardware-based security measures, and rigorous access control policies.

Encryption and Secure Communication: Encrypting data both in transit and at rest can prevent adversaries from tampering with inputs or intercepting communication between the model and external systems.

Hardware Security: Using secure hardware modules such as Trusted Execution Environments (TEEs) or hardware security modules (HSMs) can provide additional layers of protection against tampering by isolating sensitive computations from potential attackers.

Access Control and Auditing: Strict access controls and audit trails are essential for ensuring that only authorized entities can modify or interact with the system. Regular monitoring and logging of model behavior can help detect and mitigate tampering attempts.

As machine learning continues to advance, ensuring that these systems are secure, robust, and resistant to adversarial attacks is crucial for their widespread adoption and success. While various defense strategies, such as adversarial training, gradient masking, and defensive distillation, have been proposed, there is no one-size-fits-all solution. Instead, a combination of approaches, along with ongoing research and innovation, will be necessary to stay ahead of increasingly sophisticated adversaries.

Building tamper-proof systems will require the integration of security measures across all layers of the system, from input preprocessing to model training and deployment. As adversarial attacks evolve, so too must the strategies to mitigate their impact, ensuring that ML models remain reliable, secure, and trustworthy for real-world applications.

In the future, it will be essential for developers and researchers to continue refining these techniques and developing new methodologies to ensure that machine learning models are not only accurate but also resilient against adversarial threats. By taking proactive measures now, we can help safeguard the future of AI and machine learning technologies against malicious attacks, ensuring their safe and effective use across various domains.

Chapter 24 Real-Time Adaptation

In an increasingly complex world, the ability to adapt to dynamic environments in real-time has become a crucial element for success, both in human endeavors and in the technological systems we create. Whether it's an individual making decisions in a fast-paced setting or a machine learning algorithm optimizing operations as new data arrives, real-time adaptation represents the capacity to respond to changes as they unfold, without delay. This adaptive capability is essential in fields ranging from business to robotics, healthcare to environmental monitoring, and even in digital entertainment. The challenges inherent in dynamic environments, such as unpredictability, time constraints, and resource limitations, require sophisticated solutions to ensure that systems remain effective, efficient, and resilient. In this discussion, we will explore the concept of real-time adaptation, the challenges it presents, and the innovative strategies used to overcome these challenges.

Understanding Real-Time Adaptation

At its core, real-time adaptation involves systems, processes, or individuals making adjustments in response to changing conditions or new information as it becomes available. This dynamic capability allows for continuous improvement or course correction, enabling systems to maintain optimal performance even as variables shift. In contrast to static models, where the system's behavior is predetermined, real-time adaptation demands flexibility and agility.

Real-time adaptation can be found in a variety of contexts:

Business and Market Dynamics: Companies must adapt to changing customer preferences, market conditions, and competition, often in real-time, to remain profitable and relevant.

Robotics and Autonomous Systems: Robots and drones must adjust to their environments on the fly, responding to obstacles, weather conditions, and task complexity as they navigate through the world.

Healthcare and Medical Decision-Making: Real-time data from patient monitoring systems allows healthcare providers to adjust treatment plans as a patient's condition evolves.

Financial Trading: High-frequency trading algorithms constantly adjust to market fluctuations, making decisions in milliseconds to maximize profits and minimize risks.

Digital Entertainment and Gaming: Adaptive storytelling or gameplay mechanics respond to player choices and behaviors in real-time, creating a personalized experience.

In all these examples, the core requirement is the ability to process information and make decisions rapidly, ensuring that the system adapts effectively to the dynamic nature of the environment.

Challenges in Dynamic Environments

Real-time adaptation is not without its challenges. The complexity of dynamic environments introduces several barriers to effective adaptation, including unpredictability, data overload, and the need for timely decision-making. The following outlines some of the key challenges faced when attempting real-time adaptation:

1. Uncertainty and Unpredictability

One of the greatest obstacles in dynamic environments is uncertainty. The variables that influence the environment may change unexpectedly, and predicting these changes can be extremely difficult. In business, for instance, market trends might shift due to an unforeseen global event like a natural disaster or a political upheaval. Similarly, in robotics, an autonomous vehicle might face sudden changes in road conditions or encounter obstacles that were not accounted for in its initial programming.

Adapting to unpredictable situations requires systems that can both forecast potential outcomes based on available data and respond to situations that defy expectations. For instance, machine learning algorithms often rely on historical data to predict future trends or behaviors. However, these predictions can be rendered ineffective if the underlying assumptions no longer hold. In such cases, the system must be able to recognize deviations from the expected and adjust accordingly, which requires sophisticated modeling and continuous learning capabilities.

2. Information Overload and Real-Time Processing

Another major challenge in real-time adaptation is the sheer volume of information that must be processed. Dynamic environments generate vast amounts of data in real time, and it can be difficult for systems to sift through this data to extract the most relevant information.

For example, in the financial sector, traders must monitor multiple markets, news sources, and real-time data feeds to make decisions that could impact millions of dollars. Similarly, autonomous systems like self-driving cars need to process data from sensors, cameras, and GPS systems to navigate their environment safely. With so much data coming in simultaneously, there is a risk of information overload, where too much information results in slower decision-making or, worse, errors in judgment.

To address this, adaptive systems need advanced algorithms that can prioritize and filter the incoming data, identifying patterns and anomalies without becoming bogged down by irrelevant information. This often involves the use of artificial intelligence (AI) and machine learning, where algorithms are trained to detect meaningful changes and make real-time decisions based on the most relevant data.

3. Time Constraints and Speed of Response

Real-time adaptation requires making decisions quickly, often under significant time constraints. The speed at which a system can process information and execute changes is critical, especially in high-stakes situations. In healthcare, for example, timely interventions are crucial in saving lives. A patient's condition can deteriorate rapidly, and delays in adjusting treatment protocols can result in severe consequences.

Similarly, in autonomous vehicles, even a fraction of a second can make the difference between avoiding an accident and causing one. In high-frequency trading, algorithms may need to respond to price changes in milliseconds to ensure optimal trading decisions. As the stakes become higher, the speed at which systems can adapt becomes more important, requiring robust, efficient algorithms that can execute decisions quickly without compromising accuracy.

4. Resource Limitations

Adapting to dynamic environments in real time often requires significant computational resources. Systems must be able to process large amounts of data, run complex algorithms, and perform rapid decision-making, all while operating in environments with limited bandwidth, memory, or computational power.

For example, in remote or hazardous environments like space exploration, military operations, or underwater exploration, real-time adaptation may occur with constrained communication and computational resources. In such cases, systems need to be optimized for low-resource environments, ensuring that adaptations can still occur despite limited capacity.

In these cases, researchers are working on distributed computing models and edge computing, where processing occurs closer to the data source (i.e., at the "edge" of the network), minimizing latency and reducing the burden on centralized servers. This enables faster responses and more efficient real-time adaptation in resource-constrained settings.

Overcoming the Challenges of Real-Time Adaptation

Despite these challenges, numerous strategies have been developed to enable systems to adapt to dynamic environments in real-time. Some of the most effective solutions include:

1. Predictive Modeling and Simulation

To address uncertainty and unpredictability, predictive modeling and simulations are widely used to anticipate potential changes in the environment. These models can provide insights into likely future scenarios, helping systems prepare for possible outcomes. For example, in autonomous vehicles, simulations are used to model different driving conditions and obstacles, allowing the system to adapt to unexpected changes in the environment.

Moreover, predictive models can be continually updated as new data becomes available, enhancing their accuracy over time. Machine learning algorithms, for example, can learn from past experiences and apply this knowledge to improve predictions and responses in future situations.

2. Advanced Filtering and Decision Algorithms

To handle information overload and ensure that the most relevant data is processed efficiently, advanced filtering techniques and decision-making algorithms are employed. In complex systems, such as those used in finance or healthcare, algorithms are designed to focus on critical data points and disregard irrelevant information. These systems often rely on AI-driven pattern recognition to detect anomalies and identify important trends in real-time.

By focusing on the most critical factors, systems can make decisions more rapidly and accurately, even in environments filled with massive amounts of data.

3. Real-Time Machine Learning and Continuous Adaptation

Machine learning models that continuously learn and adapt as new data arrives are essential for real-time adaptation. These models can adjust their parameters or strategies based on real-time feedback, ensuring that systems remain flexible and responsive. In the case of autonomous vehicles, for instance, machine learning models can refine their understanding of the environment as they encounter new scenarios, improving their decision-making capabilities over time.

Continuous adaptation can also be enhanced through reinforcement learning, where systems learn by trial and error, adjusting their actions based on rewards or penalties from the environment.

4. Distributed Systems and Edge Computing

To overcome resource limitations and ensure fast, efficient adaptation in real-time, distributed systems and edge computing are becoming increasingly important. By processing data closer to the source, these systems reduce latency and improve decision-making speed. In remote or resource-constrained environments, such as space missions or disaster recovery operations, edge computing allows systems to process information locally and make immediate adjustments without relying on central servers.

In addition to this, distributed systems enable the sharing of computational resources across multiple devices or locations, allowing for scalable, efficient adaptation in dynamic environments.

Real-time adaptation is becoming an essential capability for navigating the complexities of dynamic environments. The ability to respond quickly to change, process vast amounts of data, and make informed decisions in the face of uncertainty is critical for success in fields ranging from business to healthcare to autonomous systems. However, the challenges of unpredictability, information overload, time constraints, and resource limitations make real-time adaptation a daunting task. Overcoming these challenges requires innovative solutions, such as predictive modeling, advanced filtering techniques, real-time machine learning, and distributed systems. As technology continues to evolve, the ability to adapt in real-time will be a key driver of success, resilience, and efficiency in an increasingly dynamic world.

Chapter 25 Energy and Resource Optimization

In an era marked by climate change, resource depletion, and environmental degradation, the necessity of developing sustainable systems has never been more urgent. This urgency is particularly evident in the context of agentic systems, or systems that are capable of autonomously making decisions and taking actions to achieve specific goals. The combination of energy and resource optimization within these systems offers a pathway to ensuring that we not only meet the demands of today but also safeguard the resources necessary for future generations.

Understanding Agentic Systems

An agentic system refers to any system designed to operate autonomously, using a combination of algorithms, sensors, data processing, and decision-making frameworks. These systems can be found in many sectors, including robotics, smart cities, energy management, transportation, and even artificial intelligence (AI). Agentic systems are characterized by their ability to make decisions without constant human intervention, adapt to changing environments, and optimize their actions for efficiency and effectiveness.

Sustainability within this framework hinges on the efficient use of energy and resources. Agentic systems, with their built-in autonomy and optimization capabilities, are uniquely positioned to help us achieve sustainability goals by reducing waste, conserving resources, and making decisions that are better aligned with long-term environmental and societal needs.

The Role of Energy and Resource Optimization

At the core of sustainable agentic systems is energy and resource optimization. Optimization involves the efficient allocation and use of resources to maximize outputs while minimizing waste. In the context of agentic systems, this often means creating systems that can learn from their environment, make data-driven decisions, and autonomously adjust their operations to improve performance in real-time.

Energy Efficiency in Agentic Systems

Energy efficiency is one of the most critical aspects of sustainability. In the realm of agentic systems, energy optimization can be achieved through intelligent algorithms that manage how energy is consumed. For example, in smart buildings, heating, ventilation, and air conditioning (HVAC) systems can be optimized based on real-time occupancy data, weather patterns, and energy usage patterns. An agentic system can autonomously adjust the building's climate control settings to maintain comfort while minimizing energy consumption.

Similarly, in electric grids, smart grids equipped with agentic systems can optimize energy distribution to meet demand while minimizing energy loss during transmission. By leveraging predictive analytics, machine learning, and real-time data, these systems can dynamically adjust energy flow, store surplus energy for future use, and integrate renewable energy sources in a way that maximizes their potential.

Resource Allocation and Management

Sustainable resource management is another pillar of agentic systems. Resources such as water, raw materials, and food need to be used efficiently to prevent overexploitation and depletion. Agentic systems can optimize the extraction, distribution, and consumption of these resources by making decisions based on real-time data and long-term forecasts.

In agriculture, for example, precision farming techniques can be enhanced with agentic systems that monitor soil moisture, crop health, and weather conditions. By adjusting irrigation schedules, fertilizer application, and harvest timing, these systems can significantly reduce water usage, minimize chemical waste, and increase crop yields—all while promoting sustainability.

Similarly, in supply chain management, agentic systems can optimize inventory levels, reduce waste, and minimize the environmental impact of transportation. By automating decision-making processes related to resource use, agentic systems can create supply chains that are both efficient and sustainable, with reduced carbon footprints and less waste.

Building Sustainable Agentic Systems

While the potential of agentic systems for sustainability is immense, building such systems requires careful consideration of their design and operational principles. Several key principles are necessary for ensuring that these systems are not only efficient but also sustainable.

Data-Driven Decision Making

One of the hallmarks of agentic systems is their reliance on data for decision-making. To optimize energy and resource usage, these systems must be capable of collecting, processing, and analyzing vast amounts of data from their environment. Sensors, cameras, and IoT devices provide continuous streams of information that can be used to monitor everything from energy consumption to environmental conditions.

For these systems to be effective, however, they must not only collect data but also interpret it in meaningful ways. Machine learning and AI algorithms are often employed to identify patterns, make predictions, and adjust operations accordingly. For instance, an agentic system in a smart city might analyze traffic flow data to optimize traffic light timings, reducing fuel consumption and emissions while improving transportation efficiency.

Integration of Renewable Resources

Sustainability can only be achieved if agentic systems are designed with renewable resources in mind. Whether it's energy production, resource extraction, or consumption, integrating renewable sources such as solar, wind, and hydropower into the decision-making process is essential for long-term sustainability.

In energy management, agentic systems can be designed to seamlessly integrate renewable energy sources into existing grids. They can optimize the distribution of electricity based on real-time production data from renewable sources and adjust usage patterns accordingly. For example, when the sun is shining, an agentic system might shift energy consumption to non-essential services, allowing for the storage of solar power in batteries for use during nighttime hours.

Lifecycle Optimization

Sustainability is not only about minimizing energy consumption but also about optimizing the entire lifecycle of a product or service. Agentic systems can be employed to monitor and manage the lifecycle of products, from raw material extraction to manufacturing, distribution, use, and end-of-life disposal or recycling.

In manufacturing, agentic systems can optimize production processes by ensuring that materials are used efficiently, waste is minimized, and energy consumption is optimized. These systems can also monitor the use of products and encourage repair or recycling instead of disposal. By continuously analyzing product performance and usage patterns, agentic systems can prolong the life of goods and reduce their environmental impact.

Ethical and Social Considerations

Sustainability extends beyond environmental factors to include social and ethical considerations. Agentic systems that are designed with sustainability in mind must also prioritize social equity, fairness, and inclusivity. This can involve ensuring that the benefits of optimization are distributed equitably, preventing the exacerbation of social inequalities.

For example, in the context of smart cities, agentic systems should be designed to improve the quality of life for all citizens, not just those who can afford to invest in smart technologies. This could mean ensuring that energy efficiency measures, such as subsidized smart thermostats or energy-efficient public transportation, are accessible to low-income communities.

Challenges and Future Directions

Despite their potential, there are several challenges in developing sustainable agentic systems. The most prominent challenges include:

Data Privacy and Security: As agentic systems collect vast amounts of personal and environmental data, ensuring privacy and security is crucial. Sensitive data must be handled carefully to prevent misuse or unauthorized access.

Complexity of Integration: Integrating diverse energy and resource systems into a cohesive agentic framework requires significant technological development and collaboration across sectors. This can be particularly challenging in legacy systems where outdated infrastructure and protocols may limit the adoption of agentic technologies.

Unintended Consequences: While agentic systems are designed to optimize resource use, there is a risk of unintended consequences. For example, an algorithm designed to reduce energy consumption might inadvertently prioritize certain sectors over others, leading to imbalances. Ensuring that agentic systems consider long-term, holistic impacts is essential.

Looking forward, the development of sustainable agentic systems will likely involve further advancements in AI and machine learning, better integration with renewable energy sources, and increased collaboration across industries. By continuing to push the boundaries of what's possible, agentic systems can play a central role in addressing the world's most pressing environmental challenges.

Energy and resource optimization in agentic systems offers an exciting opportunity to build sustainable systems that can adapt to and address the challenges posed by climate change, resource depletion, and environmental degradation. By leveraging autonomous decision-making, data-driven insights, and real-time resource management, these systems have the potential to significantly reduce waste, conserve resources, and ensure a sustainable future.

To realize this potential, it is crucial to design agentic systems that are efficient, equitable, and mindful of their long-term impact on both the environment and society. With continued innovation, collaboration, and ethical consideration, agentic systems can help pave the way toward a sustainable future—one where energy and resources are optimized for the benefit of all.

Chapter 26 Agentic AI in Space Exploration

Space exploration has always been an arena where the boundaries of human ingenuity and technological advancement are tested. From the first successful moon landing to the ongoing exploration of distant planets and moons, the need for cutting-edge tools and technologies has been integral to advancing our understanding of the cosmos. One of the most significant breakthroughs in this domain has been the development of autonomous systems powered by Artificial Intelligence (AI), particularly agentic AI. These AI systems are capable of acting independently, making decisions in real-time, and operating in environments where human intervention is limited or impractical.

Autonomous rovers and probes are among the most notable examples of agentic AI in space exploration. These devices have revolutionized how we explore distant celestial bodies, including Mars, the Moon, and beyond. Through the use of agentic AI, these machines can carry out complex tasks without the need for constant human supervision, enabling more efficient and effective exploration of the cosmos. This chapter delves into the role of agentic AI in space exploration, with a particular focus on autonomous rovers and probes, their capabilities, challenges, and potential future developments.

The Evolution of Autonomous Rovers and Probes

The concept of autonomous machines in space is not new. Early space missions relied heavily on human control and remote operations, with astronauts on board spacecraft or ground control teams managing robotic systems via radio signals. However, the vast distances involved in space travel, coupled with the time delays in communication (especially for missions to distant planets like Mars), make real-time human intervention impossible. This led to the development of autonomous systems capable of acting independently and adapting to changing environments.

The first major breakthrough came with the development of robotic spacecraft like the Voyager probes, which were launched in the 1970s. While these early probes were not fully autonomous, they were designed to perform pre-programmed tasks with minimal input from Earth. As technology advanced, so did the capabilities of autonomous systems, leading to the creation of more sophisticated rovers and probes capable of operating in complex environments without human intervention.

NASA's Mars rovers, particularly Spirit, Opportunity, Curiosity, and Perseverance, are prime examples of autonomous vehicles that have revolutionized planetary exploration. These rovers are equipped with highly advanced AI systems that allow them to navigate the harsh Martian terrain, make decisions about where to go, and conduct scientific experiments—all while transmitting valuable data back to Earth.

At the core of these autonomous systems lies agentic AI, a form of artificial intelligence designed to operate as an independent agent capable of making decisions and taking actions based on its environment. Agentic AI differs from traditional AI systems, which often rely on predefined rules or human oversight. Instead, agentic AI is characterized by its ability to assess situations in real-time, weigh different options, and make decisions based on a combination of logic, learned knowledge, and environmental inputs.

The key feature of agentic AI is autonomy. In the context of space exploration, this means that the AI system within a rover or probe can carry out tasks such as navigation, hazard detection, scientific analysis, and even communication with Earth with minimal or no intervention from mission controllers. This autonomy is crucial for operating in remote and hostile environments where human intervention is impractical or impossible.

Autonomous Rovers in Space Exploration

Autonomous rovers, like those used on Mars, are designed to perform a range of tasks, from basic navigation to complex scientific experiments. These rovers are equipped with a suite of sensors and cameras that provide a wealth of data about the environment. AI systems analyze this data in real-time, allowing the rover to adapt to its surroundings and make decisions that help it fulfill its mission.

Navigation and Terrain Mapping

One of the most important tasks for an autonomous rover is navigation. Spacecraft must be able to traverse challenging terrains, whether that involves rocky surfaces, deep craters, or dust storms. Traditional rovers were manually controlled from Earth, but this became less feasible as missions progressed. For example, Mars missions can experience communication delays of up to 20 minutes, making real-time remote control of rovers impractical.

Agentic AI systems are now integral to the navigation and mapping functions of rovers. These systems rely on advanced machine learning algorithms to process images and sensor data, which allows the rover to build a 3D map of its environment. The rover can then use this map to plan a safe path forward, avoiding obstacles and identifying areas of interest for further exploration.

For example, NASA's Curiosity rover employs a system called AEGIS (Autonomous Exploration for Gathering Increased Science), which allows it to autonomously select targets for scientific study without waiting for instructions from Earth. This AI-driven system enables Curiosity to spend more time conducting experiments rather than waiting for commands.

Hazard Detection and Avoidance

The Martian surface presents numerous hazards, from loose rocks and sand dunes to sudden drops and cliffs. Agentic AI plays a crucial role in detecting these hazards and ensuring the rover remains safe. Using advanced computer vision algorithms, the rover can identify potential dangers in its path, assess the severity of those risks, and take action to avoid them.

Autonomous hazard detection is vital not only for the rover's safety but also for mission success. For instance, if the rover detects a cliff or a particularly rocky area, it can adjust its trajectory or halt its movement to prevent damage. This decision-making process requires the rover to balance its need to explore with the need to stay safe, all without human intervention.

Scientific Exploration

Autonomous rovers are not just tools for navigation; they are also sophisticated laboratories on wheels. They are equipped with various scientific instruments to analyze soil samples, search for signs of water, study atmospheric conditions, and more. AI plays a pivotal role in helping rovers prioritize tasks, interpret scientific data, and even make decisions about which experiments to conduct based on the rover's observations.

For example, Perseverance, the most recent Mars rover, is equipped with a suite of advanced instruments, including a drill for core sampling and a spectrometer for analyzing chemical compositions. The rover uses AI to assess the results of these instruments, identify potential sites for drilling, and choose the most promising locations for further study.

In addition, AI-driven systems enable the rover to adapt to new scientific objectives as it encounters new phenomena on the surface. As the rover gathers data and learns more about its environment, it can modify its behavior and adjust its exploration strategies to maximize the scientific return of the mission.

Autonomous Probes in Space Exploration

Autonomous probes extend the capabilities of agentic AI beyond planetary surfaces, enabling exploration of distant moons, comets, and asteroids. While the challenges faced by probes differ from those of rovers, the principles of autonomy remain the same. Probes, like the Voyager and New Horizons missions, operate over vast distances where real-time communication is not feasible. These probes are equipped with AI systems that allow them to make decisions regarding navigation, data collection, and even anomaly detection, all without human intervention.

For example, the European Space Agency's Rosetta mission involved a probe that traveled to the comet

67P/Churyumov–Gerasimenko and deployed the Philae lander. Although the mission involved significant human oversight, much of the decision-making, particularly regarding the probe's trajectory and the execution of scientific experiments, was driven by autonomous systems.

In the future, autonomous probes could explore other planets or moons, such as the icy moons of Jupiter and Saturn, where conditions are too extreme for human-operated missions. These probes will need to navigate complex environments, make scientific observations, and return valuable data—all while operating independently.

Challenges and Limitations of Agentic AI in Space Exploration

While the benefits of agentic AI in space exploration are clear, there are still significant challenges to overcome. One of the main difficulties is the reliability of AI systems in harsh and unpredictable environments. Space missions often involve long durations, extreme temperatures, radiation, and other unpredictable factors that can challenge the robustness of AI systems.

Another limitation is the reliance on pre-programmed algorithms. Although agentic AI systems are designed to make decisions in real-time, their behavior is still based on the data and algorithms they are trained on. This means that if the AI encounters a situation that it has not been specifically programmed or trained to handle, it may struggle to make the right decisions.

Additionally, there are ethical and safety concerns related to autonomous systems. As AI systems become more autonomous, questions arise about accountability, control, and decision-making. If a rover or probe encounters an unforeseen situation that leads to a failure or accident, who is responsible? And how can we ensure that AI systems are designed to act in a way that aligns with human values and mission objectives?

The Future of Agentic AI in Space Exploration

The future of agentic AI in space exploration is incredibly promising. As AI technology continues to evolve, we can expect even more sophisticated autonomous systems capable of taking on increasingly complex tasks. These systems will be able to explore deeper into space, undertake more ambitious missions, and perhaps even make decisions that will shape the course of humanity's exploration of the cosmos.

For example, future missions to the outer planets or beyond may involve AI-driven spacecraft capable of operating independently for years at a time. These missions could explore distant exoplanets, collect samples from asteroids, or even investigate the possibility of life on distant moons like Europa or Enceladus. With the increasing capabilities of AI, the scope for space exploration is expanding, and the possibilities seem limitless.

In conclusion, agentic AI is revolutionizing space exploration by enabling autonomous rovers and probes to carry out complex tasks without the need for constant human supervision. These systems are critical for navigating the challenges of space, from exploring distant planets and moons to conducting scientific research and hazard detection. While there are still challenges to address, the future of agentic AI in space exploration holds immense potential, opening up new frontiers in our understanding of the universe.

Chapter 27 Creative AI and Artistic Agency

The integration of Artificial Intelligence (AI) into creative fields has stirred profound discussions around the nature of art, authorship, and creativity. AI's growing capability to autonomously generate music, art, and literature prompts crucial questions about the role of human agency in artistic endeavors. As AI-driven systems develop sophisticated abilities to create pieces that resonate with emotional depth, intricacy, and originality, the lines between human and machine authorship blur. This chapter explores the implications of creative AI for artistic agency, examining how autonomous systems challenge our understanding of creativity and artistic expression.

The Rise of Creative AI

In my book on Generative AI, I explained about many aspects of Generative AI. Over the last few years, AI technologies have made significant strides in mimicking human-like creativity. Machine learning, a subfield of AI, allows algorithms to learn from vast datasets and apply this knowledge to produce new works of art, music, and literature. These algorithms can analyze patterns in pre-existing works, from melodies and brush strokes to narrative styles and structures, and generate outputs that are comparable to those created by human artists.

In music, AI systems like OpenAI's MuseNet and Jukedeck can compose complex, multi-instrumental pieces in a variety of genres, from classical symphonies to contemporary pop songs. In visual art, AI programs such as DeepArt and DALL·E have demonstrated an ability to generate striking and original visual works based on textual prompts or predefined artistic styles. In literature, GPT-based models, including OpenAI's GPT-3, can generate prose, poetry, and even full-length novels, drawing on vast corpora of texts.

The autonomy of AI in creative industries raises important philosophical and ethical questions about the role of human agency in the creative process. Can AI be considered truly creative, or is it merely a tool that reflects the creativity of its human programmers and the datasets it is trained on? To answer this, it is essential to explore the concepts of creativity, agency, and authorship in the context of AI-generated works.

The Concept of Creativity: Human or Machine?

Creativity is traditionally viewed as a uniquely human trait, tied to consciousness, emotion, and subjective experience. Artists, musicians, and writers are often seen as individuals who draw on their personal perspectives, emotions, and experiences to create something new and meaningful. However, AI challenges this view by demonstrating that creativity can emerge from systems devoid of consciousness and subjective experience.

AI-driven systems operate through algorithms that process large datasets and generate outputs based on statistical analysis and pattern recognition. Unlike humans, AI does not draw from lived experiences, emotions, or personal reflections. Instead, it synthesizes patterns from the data it is trained on to produce works that may appear creative on the surface. Some argue that this process lacks the depth and intentionality that human creativity entails, while others believe that the results can be just as innovative and emotionally compelling as those produced by humans.

The notion that creativity stems from human experience and consciousness is deeply ingrained in how we view art and artistic expression. However, when AI systems generate art, music, or literature that resonates with audiences, the question arises: can we still call it creativity if the process lacks the intentionality and consciousness of a human creator? Moreover, can we define creativity as the ability to produce novel and meaningful outputs, regardless of whether the creator is human or machine?

Artistic Agency and the Role of the Creator

Artistic agency refers to the capacity of an artist to make intentional decisions about their work and to shape it according to their vision, emotions, and personal perspective. In human artistry, agency is deeply tied to the individual's experiences, intentions, and expressions. However, in the context of AI-generated art, the question of agency becomes more complex.

AI lacks intention, self-awareness, and emotional engagement with its outputs. While it can produce works that mimic human creativity, its "decisions" are based on statistical patterns rather than conscious deliberation. For instance, an AI might generate a song that sounds emotionally moving or visually captivating, but it does not have the capacity to understand or intend the emotional impact of its work. The role of the creator in AI-generated art becomes a matter of interpretation. Some argue that the human programmer or user of the AI system holds artistic agency, as they guide the AI by providing input, setting parameters, or curating the final output. Others contend that the AI itself exercises a form of agency in its autonomous creation.

The debate around artistic agency in AI also extends to questions of authorship. Who owns the rights to a piece of art created by AI? Is it the human who programmed the AI, the person who prompted the system, or the machine itself? The concept of authorship traditionally involves a creator who can claim personal ownership over their work, but AI complicates this understanding. Legal frameworks surrounding intellectual property are still grappling with how to attribute ownership and responsibility for works created by autonomous systems. As AI systems become more sophisticated, the question of artistic agency will continue to evolve.

The Impact of AI on Human Creativity

Despite the debates about AI's creativity and agency, it is clear that AI tools are significantly impacting human artistic practices. AI-driven technologies offer new avenues for exploration, enabling artists to push the boundaries of their creativity in ways that were previously unimaginable.

In music, AI systems can help composers experiment with new sounds, structures, and harmonies, serving as collaborative tools rather than replacements for human creativity. AI can generate new musical ideas, but it is up to the human composer to shape and refine these ideas into a cohesive work. This symbiotic relationship between human creativity and AI's computational power opens up exciting possibilities for innovation. For example, AI can assist in exploring genres or styles that the artist may not have considered, enabling them to experiment with novel approaches to composition.

In the visual arts, AI tools are transforming the way artists approach creation. AI-generated art can be used as inspiration, a draft, or a jumping-off point for further exploration. Many contemporary artists use AI as a medium for creating experimental works that combine human intuition with machine-generated patterns. Far from replacing the artist, AI is becoming an essential tool in the creative process, providing new techniques and perspectives for those willing to engage with it.

In literature, AI-generated texts are being used in various ways, from generating plot ideas to creating complete works of fiction. Writers can input prompts or keywords into AI systems, which then generate narratives based on these inputs. While some writers use AI to assist in the drafting process, others are experimenting with AI as a co-creator, using its outputs as raw material for further development. AI can help writers break through creative blocks or explore unfamiliar genres, but it is ultimately the human writer who gives meaning, context, and emotional depth to the generated text.

Through collaboration with AI, human artists retain creative agency while benefiting from the unique strengths of AI, such as speed, data processing, and pattern recognition. In this sense, AI does not diminish human creativity but rather enhances it, offering new tools and perspectives for creative expression.

Ethical and Philosophical Considerations

The rise of creative AI also raises several ethical and philosophical issues. One major concern is the potential for AI to exacerbate inequalities in the creative industries. If AI systems become capable of producing high-quality art, music, and literature, there is a risk that human artists may be displaced by machines, particularly in commercial contexts where cost-efficiency is a priority. This could lead to a devaluation of human creativity and a shift in the definition of what constitutes art.

Another ethical consideration is the question of authenticity. When AI generates art, music, or literature, it often draws on existing works, remixing and reinterpreting them in novel ways. This raises questions about originality and plagiarism. While human artists have long drawn inspiration from existing works, AI systems may inadvertently reproduce patterns from the datasets they are trained on, leading to concerns about copyright infringement and the protection of intellectual property.

Moreover, as AI-generated works become more prevalent, it becomes increasingly difficult to distinguish between human-created and machine-created art. This challenges our assumptions about the nature of authenticity and the value of art. Can a piece of art or music created by AI have the same emotional impact and cultural significance as one created by a human artist? How do we define originality in an age where machines can produce seemingly unique works?

Creative AI is transforming the landscape of music, art, and literature, challenging our traditional notions of creativity, authorship, and artistic agency. While AI lacks consciousness, intention, and emotional experience, its ability to autonomously generate art raises profound questions about the nature of creativity itself. Human agency in the creative process remains essential, but AI serves as a powerful tool that enhances, rather than replaces, human creativity.

As AI continues to evolve, it is likely that the boundaries between human and machine-generated art will become increasingly fluid. Rather than replacing human artists, AI will offer new ways of creating, experimenting, and collaborating. The future of artistic creation lies in a symbiotic relationship between humans and AI, where both contribute to the production of meaningful and innovative works. The key challenge will be to navigate the ethical, philosophical, and legal implications of this new creative landscape, ensuring that AI serves as a force for positive transformation in the arts.

Chapter 28 Agentic AI in Environmental Protection

As the world faces mounting environmental challenges, the urgency for innovative solutions to protect the planet and mitigate climate change is becoming increasingly evident. Artificial Intelligence (AI) has emerged as a transformative force in various industries, and its potential in environmental protection, particularly in climate change monitoring and mitigation, is profound. The integration of agentic AI—intelligent systems capable of making autonomous decisions and acting to achieve specific goals—has the potential to revolutionize how we address environmental issues. In this chapter, we explore the role of agentic AI in monitoring and mitigating climate change, highlighting its applications, benefits, challenges, and future prospects.

Understanding Agentic AI

Agentic AI refers to systems that are not merely tools for processing data or performing specific tasks but are designed to take autonomous actions aimed at achieving predetermined objectives. These AI systems can perceive their environment, process information, make decisions, and act based on those decisions with minimal human intervention. Unlike traditional AI systems that operate under strict human oversight, agentic AI is capable of adapting to dynamic conditions, learning from its experiences, and improving its decision-making processes over time.

In the context of environmental protection and climate change, agentic AI systems can be employed to monitor environmental variables, predict climate trends, optimize resource use, and implement mitigation strategies. The agentic aspect of these AI systems allows them to not only gather data but also take real-time actions to prevent or reduce environmental harm.

AI in Climate Change Monitoring

Monitoring climate change requires the collection and analysis of vast amounts of data from multiple sources, such as weather stations, satellite imagery, ocean sensors, and atmospheric measurements. Traditional monitoring methods can be resource-intensive and slow, limiting the ability to respond to environmental changes in real-time. Agentic AI, however, offers a powerful solution for continuous and scalable climate monitoring.

Real-Time Data Collection and Analysis

Agentic AI systems can collect and analyze real-time data from various sensors and satellites to track changes in environmental parameters. For example, AI-powered systems can monitor air quality, deforestation, ocean temperatures, and greenhouse gas emissions. These systems can autonomously process large datasets, identifying patterns and anomalies that would otherwise go unnoticed. This enables more accurate and timely detection of environmental changes, which is crucial for responding to climate change threats.

Predictive Modeling

Predicting the future impacts of climate change is a complex task that requires the integration of diverse data sources, including historical climate data, real-time environmental measurements, and socio-economic factors. Agentic AI can significantly improve the accuracy of predictive models by processing this data autonomously and learning from past patterns. These AI systems can generate high-resolution climate models that simulate future climate scenarios, helping policymakers and researchers understand potential risks and take proactive steps.

For instance, AI systems can model the effects of rising temperatures on agriculture, sea-level rise on coastal cities, or extreme weather events like hurricanes and droughts. By predicting such events with greater precision, agentic AI can assist governments, businesses, and communities in preparing for and mitigating the impacts of climate change.

Automated Environmental Monitoring

AI-powered drones, robots, and sensors can be deployed to monitor hard-to-reach areas such as the deep ocean, dense forests, or remote mountain regions. These systems can operate autonomously, gathering data on biodiversity, pollution levels, and environmental degradation without the need for human intervention. The use of autonomous monitoring agents can significantly increase the spatial and temporal resolution of climate change observations, enabling more comprehensive and detailed assessments of environmental health.

AI in Climate Change Mitigation

Mitigating climate change involves reducing the emission of greenhouse gases (GHGs), transitioning to renewable energy sources, and adopting sustainable practices across various sectors. Agentic AI can play a crucial role in these efforts by optimizing processes, reducing waste, and driving the adoption of low-carbon technologies.

Energy Optimization

The energy sector is one of the largest contributors to greenhouse gas emissions. Agentic AI can help mitigate climate change by optimizing energy consumption and promoting the transition to renewable energy sources. AI systems can autonomously manage energy grids, balancing supply and demand, predicting energy needs, and integrating renewable energy sources like solar and wind into existing infrastructures. By optimizing energy distribution and minimizing waste, agentic AI can reduce emissions and enhance the efficiency of energy systems.

AI can also be used in smart buildings, where autonomous systems regulate heating, cooling, and lighting based on real-time occupancy and environmental conditions. This not only reduces energy consumption but also improves the overall sustainability of urban environments.

Carbon Capture and Storage

Carbon capture and storage (CCS) technologies are critical in the fight against climate change. These technologies aim to capture carbon dioxide (CO_2) emissions from industrial processes and store them underground or use them in other applications. Agentic AI can enhance the efficiency and effectiveness of CCS by monitoring CO2 emissions in real-time, detecting leaks or inefficiencies, and optimizing the storage process.

AI-driven robots and drones can be deployed to inspect CCS facilities, identify potential risks, and suggest corrective actions. Additionally, agentic AI can help design more efficient CCS systems by analyzing vast amounts of geological and engineering data, optimizing the selection of storage sites, and improving the scalability of these technologies.

Sustainable Agriculture

Agriculture is both a victim and a contributor to climate change. On one hand, agriculture contributes significantly to greenhouse gas emissions, deforestation, and land degradation. On the other hand, climate change poses a threat to crop yields, water availability, and soil health. Agentic AI can play a key role in promoting sustainable agricultural practices that reduce emissions and adapt to changing environmental conditions.

AI systems can optimize irrigation systems, monitor soil health, and predict pest outbreaks, all while minimizing the use of water, fertilizers, and pesticides. By autonomously managing these processes, agentic AI can help farmers adopt more sustainable and efficient practices, leading to lower emissions and enhanced food security. Additionally, AI-powered systems can assist in the development of climate-resilient crops that are better suited to changing environmental conditions.

Waste Reduction and Circular Economy

The global waste crisis is another significant environmental challenge. Agentic AI can help reduce waste by optimizing supply chains, predicting demand, and ensuring that resources are used efficiently. AI systems can monitor production processes to identify opportunities for reducing material waste, improving recycling, and promoting the circular economy.

In a circular economy, products are designed for longevity, repairability, and recyclability, minimizing waste and reducing the need for raw materials. Agentic AI can assist in designing products and systems that align with these principles, ensuring that materials are reused and waste is minimized. Autonomous systems can also play a role in waste sorting and recycling, increasing the efficiency of these processes and reducing the environmental impact of landfills.

While the potential of agentic AI in environmental protection is vast, several challenges must be addressed to ensure its effective deployment.

Ethical and Governance Issues

The autonomy of agentic AI systems raises important ethical and governance concerns. Who is responsible for the decisions made by these systems, especially when they have the power to take actions that impact the environment or society? There needs to be a clear framework for accountability, transparency, and oversight to ensure that AI systems are acting in the public's best interest.

Data Privacy and Security

Agentic AI systems rely on vast amounts of data to function effectively. This data must be collected, stored, and processed securely to protect privacy and prevent misuse. Ensuring that data governance frameworks are in place to protect individuals' privacy and the integrity of environmental data is essential.

Scalability and Cost

Implementing agentic AI solutions at a large scale can be costly, particularly in developing countries or regions with limited resources. The cost of developing, deploying, and maintaining AI systems may be a barrier to widespread adoption. However, as technology advances and costs decrease, agentic AI could become more accessible to a broader range of stakeholders.

Integration with Existing Systems

To be effective, agentic AI systems must be integrated into existing environmental monitoring and management frameworks. This requires collaboration across sectors, including government, business, and academia, as well as the development of standardized data formats and communication protocols.

Agentic AI offers a powerful tool for monitoring and mitigating climate change. Its ability to autonomously gather data, make decisions, and take action positions it as a key player in environmental protection. From real-time climate monitoring to energy optimization and sustainable agriculture, agentic AI has the potential to address many of the challenges posed by climate change. However, to fully harness its capabilities, we must address ethical, data privacy, scalability, and integration challenges. With continued research and collaboration, agentic AI could become a cornerstone of our efforts to protect the planet for future generations.

Chapter 29 Autonomous Transportation

In recent years, the evolution of autonomous transportation has captured the imagination of industries and consumers alike. Self-driving cars, trucks, and other forms of autonomous vehicles are not just technological marvels; they represent a profound shift in how people, goods, and services will move in the future. This transformation has the potential to revolutionize industries, reduce costs, enhance safety, and improve the overall efficiency of transportation systems. As autonomous technologies continue to develop, self-driving cars and logistics systems are poised to reshape how we understand mobility and commerce.

The Rise of Autonomous Cars

Autonomous vehicles, commonly referred to as self-driving cars, are at the forefront of this transportation revolution. These vehicles utilize a combination of sensors, artificial intelligence (AI), machine learning algorithms, and real-time data processing to navigate and make decisions without the need for human intervention. While fully autonomous vehicles (Level 5) are still in the testing and regulatory stages, significant strides have been made in developing semi-autonomous (Level 2 and Level 3) and highly autonomous (Level 4) vehicles.

Technologies Behind Autonomous Cars

Self-driving cars rely on a variety of technologies that work together to enable the vehicle to understand and interact with its environment. The key components of these systems include:

LIDAR (Light Detection and Ranging): LIDAR is a sensor that uses laser beams to create a detailed 3D map of the car's surroundings. It provides critical data about the environment, such as the distance to objects, road markings, and obstacles, which helps the vehicle understand its position on the road and detect hazards.

Cameras and Computer Vision: Cameras are mounted around the vehicle to capture visual information. Computer vision algorithms process this data to identify objects, lanes, traffic signals, pedestrians, and other key features. This helps the vehicle make decisions such as when to stop, turn, or accelerate.

Radar: Radar sensors are used to detect objects that might be out of the range of other sensors, especially in adverse weather conditions like fog or rain. Radar is particularly effective for detecting moving objects such as other vehicles or pedestrians.

GPS and Mapping: GPS systems help the car navigate based on real-time satellite positioning, while high-definition maps provide additional contextual information. These maps are regularly updated to ensure the vehicle is aware of any road changes, construction zones, or detours.

Artificial Intelligence and Machine Learning: AI and machine learning algorithms process the data collected by these sensors and allow the vehicle to make complex decisions. Over time, the vehicle's system "learns" from its experiences, improving its ability to handle various driving scenarios and adapt to new situations.

The Benefits of Autonomous Cars

The widespread adoption of autonomous cars promises to bring numerous benefits to society, ranging from safety improvements to environmental advantages. Some of the most significant benefits include:

Improved Safety: Human error is the leading cause of traffic accidents, with factors such as distracted driving, fatigue, and impaired driving contributing to thousands of fatalities each year. Autonomous cars have the potential to significantly reduce accidents by eliminating human error. Sensors and AI systems can react faster than humans, making split-second decisions that can avoid collisions or mitigate the severity of an accident.

Reduced Traffic Congestion: Self-driving cars can communicate with one another and coordinate their movements in real time, which can reduce traffic congestion. By maintaining optimal speeds and adjusting routes based on real-time traffic data, autonomous cars can contribute to smoother traffic flow and fewer bottlenecks.

Fuel Efficiency and Environmental Impact: Autonomous vehicles can optimize their driving patterns, such as accelerating and braking more smoothly, leading to better fuel efficiency. Additionally, the integration of autonomous cars with electric vehicle (EV) technologies could further reduce emissions, making transportation more sustainable.

Accessibility: Autonomous cars can provide a new level of mobility for individuals who are unable to drive due to age, disability, or other factors. By removing the need for a human driver, autonomous vehicles can offer greater independence and access to transportation for these individuals.

Economic Benefits: The widespread adoption of self-driving cars could lead to significant cost savings. From reduced accident-related expenses to increased productivity (since passengers can focus on other tasks instead of driving), autonomous cars have the potential to positively impact economies at both the individual and societal levels.

Challenges in Autonomous Car Development

Despite the many advantages, the development of autonomous cars faces several challenges. Some of the most notable challenges include:

Regulatory Hurdles: Governments around the world are working to establish regulations for the testing and deployment of self-driving cars. These regulations must address safety standards, insurance requirements, liability in case of accidents, and data privacy concerns. The pace of regulatory development has been slow, and different countries have different approaches to autonomous vehicle legislation.

Public Perception and Trust: Many people remain skeptical about the safety of self-driving cars. High-profile accidents involving autonomous vehicles have led to concerns about the technology's reliability. For widespread adoption, consumers must feel confident in the safety and efficacy of autonomous cars, which will require extensive testing, transparency, and education.

Ethical and Legal Issues: Autonomous vehicles face complex ethical decisions, such as how to prioritize lives in the event of an unavoidable accident. These moral dilemmas raise questions about how the AI systems in self-driving cars should be programmed to respond in critical situations. Moreover, questions about liability, insurance, and the accountability of manufacturers also remain unresolved.

Technology Limitations: While autonomous vehicles are making significant progress, they still face challenges in certain environments. For example, self-driving cars may struggle with inclement weather conditions, such as heavy rain, snow, or fog, which can obscure sensor data. Furthermore, they may have difficulty navigating complex road systems or interpreting ambiguous road signs.

Autonomous Logistics Systems

In addition to self-driving cars, autonomous logistics systems are playing a crucial role in the advancement of transportation. These systems involve the use of autonomous trucks, drones, and other vehicles to transport goods and services. The benefits of autonomous logistics are equally transformative, providing significant efficiencies for businesses and consumers.

Autonomous Trucks

Autonomous trucks, also known as self-driving freight vehicles, have the potential to revolutionize the logistics and supply chain industries. These trucks are capable of transporting goods over long distances without the need for human drivers. The key technologies used in autonomous trucks are similar to those in autonomous cars, such as sensors, AI, and machine learning algorithms.

Cost Savings: One of the most significant benefits of autonomous trucks is the potential for cost savings. Trucking companies can eliminate the need for human drivers, reducing labor costs. Additionally, autonomous trucks can operate for longer hours without the need for breaks, increasing efficiency and reducing delivery times.

Improved Safety and Reduced Accidents: Much like self-driving cars, autonomous trucks can reduce accidents caused by human error. These trucks can respond quickly to road conditions, adjust speeds based on traffic, and avoid potential collisions. Furthermore, autonomous trucks can be equipped with advanced monitoring systems to ensure cargo safety during transportation.

Fuel Efficiency: Autonomous trucks can optimize driving patterns, such as maintaining consistent speeds, reducing fuel consumption, and lowering carbon emissions. These trucks can also benefit from platooning, where multiple autonomous trucks travel in a closely spaced formation to reduce air resistance and improve fuel efficiency.

Drone Deliveries

In addition to autonomous trucks, drones are emerging as an alternative method for transporting small packages. Companies like Amazon have already experimented with drone deliveries, and other companies are following suit. Drones can deliver goods quickly and efficiently, especially in urban areas or remote locations where traditional delivery methods may be less practical.

Speed and Efficiency: Drones can bypass traffic and other obstacles, allowing for faster delivery times. This is particularly useful for last-mile deliveries, where traditional vehicles face delays in urban environments. Drones are also more cost-effective for small packages, reducing the need for larger, more expensive vehicles.

Environmental Impact: Drones are typically electric and produce fewer emissions compared to traditional delivery trucks. As such, drone deliveries could reduce the environmental impact of logistics operations, especially in densely populated urban areas.

Regulatory and Safety Concerns: Just like autonomous vehicles, drone deliveries face regulatory challenges. Governments are working to develop rules for the safe and efficient use of drones in airspace, especially in urban areas. Safety concerns, such as preventing collisions and ensuring secure package delivery, must also be addressed.

The Road Ahead: Challenges and Opportunities

The future of autonomous transportation, including self-driving cars and logistics systems, is filled with both opportunities and challenges. As technology advances, new possibilities emerge, but obstacles remain in terms of safety, regulation, and public trust. However, the potential benefits of autonomous transportation systems—such as reduced traffic accidents, lower costs, improved efficiency, and a more sustainable future—are significant.

The next few years will likely see the gradual introduction of autonomous vehicles and logistics systems, with testing, regulation, and consumer acceptance paving the way for broader adoption. As these technologies mature, we can expect a fundamental shift in how people and goods are transported across the globe, opening new avenues for growth and innovation in industries ranging from automotive manufacturing to e-commerce. Autonomous transportation is no longer a futuristic concept—it is quickly becoming a transformative reality.

Chapter 30 Agentic AI in Law and Governance

The rapid advancement of artificial intelligence (AI) technologies has brought about significant transformations in various industries, from healthcare to finance. One area where AI is beginning to show its potential is law and governance. Specifically, agentic AI — AI systems that can perform tasks autonomously, make decisions, and interact with their environment without human intervention — is emerging as a powerful tool in both legal and political contexts. The role of agentic AI in law and governance raises important questions about its capabilities, risks, and the implications for legal frameworks, ethics, and accountability. In this chapter, we explore the potential benefits, challenges, and considerations of incorporating agentic AI into law and governance.

Understanding Agentic AI

Before delving into its role in law and governance, it's important to define what agentic AI is. Agentic AI refers to systems that have the ability to autonomously make decisions and take actions within a specified environment or domain. These AI systems are equipped with reasoning, learning, and decision-making capabilities, often using machine learning algorithms and large datasets to improve their performance over time. Unlike traditional AI, which relies on direct human input for every action, agentic AI can function independently and interact with other systems or entities to achieve specific goals.

In the context of law and governance, agentic AI can be applied in various ways, from assisting in legal research to helping policymakers make data-driven decisions. However, the idea of AI systems that can act independently and make decisions without human oversight presents both opportunities and challenges that must be carefully considered.

The Potential Benefits of Agentic AI in Law and Governance

Efficiency and Automation in Legal Processes

One of the most promising aspects of agentic AI in the legal field is its potential to streamline and automate various legal processes. Legal research, document review, and contract analysis are tasks that require significant time and effort from lawyers and legal professionals. AI systems, especially those powered by natural language processing (NLP) and machine learning, can rapidly analyze vast amounts of legal texts, case precedents, and statutes, providing insights and recommendations for legal practitioners.

For example, AI could automate the process of reviewing and drafting contracts, identifying potential legal issues, and suggesting modifications to ensure compliance with regulations. This would not only save time and resources but also reduce the risk of human error and ensure that legal work is more consistent and accurate.

Enhanced Decision-Making in Governance

In the realm of governance, agentic AI can assist policymakers by analyzing large datasets to identify patterns, trends, and insights that might be overlooked by human analysts. Governments could use AI to evaluate the impact of different policies, predict potential outcomes, and simulate various scenarios to determine the most effective course of action.

For instance, AI could be used to optimize public resource allocation, predict economic trends, or design more efficient healthcare policies. By leveraging data-driven insights, governments can make more informed decisions that are based on evidence rather than political ideology or short-term interests. Moreover, AI could help identify inefficiencies in governance structures, streamline bureaucratic processes, and improve public service delivery.

Access to Justice

Access to justice is a fundamental principle in any legal system. Unfortunately, legal representation and services can often be expensive, leaving many individuals without the resources to defend their rights. AI has the potential to democratize access to legal services by offering low-cost or even free legal advice through chatbots or virtual assistants.

For example, AI-powered platforms could provide legal guidance to individuals facing legal issues, helping them navigate the complexities of the legal system. These platforms could assist with filing complaints, drafting legal documents, or even predicting the outcome of cases based on historical data. This would make legal assistance more accessible to marginalized communities and individuals who may otherwise be excluded from the legal process.

Regulatory Compliance and Monitoring

In the realm of governance, ensuring that organizations comply with laws and regulations is a critical function. AI can be employed to monitor and enforce compliance with various laws, from environmental regulations to financial reporting standards. By continuously analyzing data, AI systems can detect anomalies or violations in real time, alerting authorities to potential breaches of the law.

For example, AI could be used to track financial transactions, ensuring that companies comply with anti-money laundering (AML) regulations or detect fraud in financial reporting. This level of continuous monitoring could lead to more effective enforcement of laws and regulations, reducing the burden on human regulators and increasing the efficiency of enforcement mechanisms.

Challenges and Risks of Agentic AI in Law and Governance

While the potential benefits of agentic AI are vast, there are significant challenges and risks that must be carefully addressed. These concerns primarily revolve around issues of accountability, transparency, bias, and the concentration of power.

Accountability and Responsibility

One of the central challenges in incorporating agentic AI into law and governance is determining who is accountable when an AI system makes a decision or takes an action. If an AI system is capable of making independent decisions, who is responsible if it makes a mistake or causes harm? This issue becomes even more complicated in the context of governance, where AI systems may make decisions that affect the lives of citizens.

For example, if an AI system is used to allocate social welfare benefits and it inadvertently denies benefits to eligible individuals, who should be held accountable for this mistake? The developer of the AI system? The government agency that deployed it? The answer to this question is not clear, and existing legal frameworks may not be sufficient to address the unique challenges posed by AI.

Bias and Fairness

Another significant concern is the potential for bias in AI systems. AI models are trained on data, and if that data contains biases — whether based on race, gender, socioeconomic status, or other factors — the AI system may perpetuate or even amplify these biases in its decisions. This could have serious consequences in the legal and governance domains, where fairness and impartiality are essential.

For example, an AI system used in sentencing decisions could unintentionally favor certain demographic groups over others, leading to unequal treatment in the justice system. Similarly, an AI model used to determine eligibility for government benefits might discriminate against certain groups if it is trained on biased historical data. To mitigate these risks, it is essential to ensure that AI systems are transparent, explainable, and regularly audited for fairness.

Transparency and Explainability

Transparency and explainability are critical for trust in AI systems, especially in law and governance, where decisions can have profound consequences. Many advanced AI systems, particularly those using deep learning, operate as "black boxes," meaning that even their developers may not fully understand how the system arrives at a particular decision. This lack of transparency poses significant challenges when it comes to accountability and public trust.

For example, if an AI system used in the criminal justice system makes a decision to deny parole, the reasons behind that decision may not be clear to the individual or their lawyer. In such cases, the lack of explainability can undermine confidence in the fairness and integrity of the legal process. To address this, it is essential to develop AI systems that are not only accurate but also interpretable and capable of providing clear explanations for their decisions.

Concentration of Power

The deployment of agentic AI in governance could also lead to a concentration of power in the hands of a few tech companies or governments that control these systems. The use of AI to make important decisions about public policy, resource allocation, or criminal justice could give disproportionate influence to those who design and operate these systems, potentially exacerbating existing power imbalances.

For instance, large tech companies with access to vast amounts of data and computational resources could dominate the development of AI systems that influence governance decisions. This could lead to a situation where decisions are made by private entities with little oversight, transparency, or accountability. It is crucial to ensure that AI is deployed in ways that promote democratic values and prevent the undue concentration of power.

The Future of Agentic AI in Law and Governance

As agentic AI continues to evolve, its integration into law and governance will undoubtedly increase. However, this transformation must be approached with caution, ensuring that legal and ethical standards are maintained. Governments, regulators, and technology developers must collaborate to create frameworks that address the unique challenges posed by AI while promoting its potential benefits.

Key steps in this process include developing comprehensive regulations that address AI accountability, transparency, and fairness, as well as establishing independent oversight bodies to monitor the deployment of AI in governance and legal processes. Moreover, efforts should be made to ensure that

AI systems are designed and trained in ways that are inclusive, representative, and free from bias.

In conclusion, agentic AI represents a powerful tool that could revolutionize law and governance, enhancing efficiency, decision-making, and access to justice. However, it also raises significant challenges related to accountability, bias, transparency, and the concentration of power. To fully realize the potential of agentic AI, it is essential to approach its implementation with careful consideration of these issues, ensuring that its use aligns with the values of fairness, justice, and democracy.

Chapter 31 The Next Generation of Agentic AI

The advent of artificial intelligence (AI) has ushered in a transformative era, with AI technologies evolving rapidly to shape various sectors, from healthcare to finance and entertainment. Among the most exciting developments in AI are agentic AI systems—systems designed to autonomously make decisions, take actions, and achieve objectives without continuous human intervention. These AI systems not only process and analyze data but also possess the capability to initiate actions based on reasoning, learning, and adaptability. This chapter explores the next generation of agentic AI, focusing on emerging trends and technologies that are driving advancements in autonomy.

At its core, agentic AI embodies three key characteristics: autonomy, decision-making, and adaptability. Autonomy allows the system to function without constant human input. Decision-making involves evaluating multiple options and selecting the best course of action based on context and objectives. Adaptability ensures that the system can adjust to changing environments or new information, making it robust and versatile.

Trends Shaping the Future of Agentic AI

Autonomous Decision-Making with Reinforcement Learning

One of the most promising advancements in agentic AI is the use of reinforcement learning (RL). RL algorithms allow AI agents to learn through trial and error by interacting with their environment and receiving feedback in the form of rewards or penalties. This iterative learning process enables AI systems to make decisions and refine their strategies over time.

In the context of agentic AI, RL enables systems to autonomously navigate complex decision-making tasks. For instance, autonomous vehicles use RL to optimize driving behavior based on real-time traffic conditions, road networks, and user preferences. Similarly, in robotics, RL allows machines to adapt their movements and strategies based on their environment, improving their efficiency and functionality.

The next generation of agentic AI is likely to see RL-driven systems become more capable of handling increasingly complex tasks. With advancements in deep reinforcement learning (DRL), agentic AI systems can process large volumes of unstructured data to make sophisticated decisions, allowing them to operate in unpredictable and dynamic settings. As RL algorithms become more refined, we can expect AI agents to gain greater levels of autonomy, accuracy, and decision-making capabilities.

Human-AI Collaboration in Complex Tasks

While agentic AI aims to minimize human intervention, the future of autonomous systems will likely involve greater collaboration between humans and AI. In many industries, such as healthcare, manufacturing, and customer service, human expertise remains indispensable for ensuring high-quality outcomes. However, AI can enhance human capabilities by automating repetitive tasks, providing decision support, and offering insights based on data analysis.

Agentic AI systems that excel in human-AI collaboration will have the ability to understand human preferences, provide contextual information, and support human decision-making in real-time. For example, AI-powered diagnostic tools in healthcare can assist doctors in identifying diseases or recommending treatment options, while robots in manufacturing can work alongside human operators to optimize production processes. This symbiotic relationship will allow humans to focus on creative, strategic, and judgment-based tasks while leaving more routine and data-intensive work to AI.

Ethical and Responsible AI in Autonomous Systems

As agentic AI systems become more autonomous, there is an increasing need to address ethical concerns related to their decision-making processes. Autonomous systems that make decisions without human oversight raise questions about accountability, transparency, and fairness. Who is responsible when an autonomous vehicle makes a mistake or when an AI system causes unintended harm? How can we ensure that AI systems make ethical choices in complex, morally ambiguous situations?

The next generation of agentic AI will need to incorporate ethical frameworks and decision-making models that prioritize fairness, accountability, and transparency. Researchers are exploring ways to embed ethical reasoning into AI systems, allowing them to make morally sound decisions based on predefined ethical principles. Additionally, AI governance models that involve human oversight, auditing, and regulatory frameworks will be essential to ensure the responsible deployment of autonomous systems.

To address these challenges, new methods such as explainable AI (XAI) are being developed. XAI seeks to make AI systems' decision-making processes more transparent and understandable to humans. By enabling AI systems to provide explanations for their actions, users can better trust and comprehend how decisions are made, thus fostering accountability and ethical alignment.

Edge Computing for Real-Time Autonomous Decision-Making

Edge computing is a critical enabler of real-time decision-making in agentic AI systems. Edge computing involves processing data locally, near the source of the data generation, rather than relying on distant cloud servers. This approach reduces latency, enables faster response times, and improves efficiency in environments where real-time decisions are crucial.

In the context of agentic AI, edge computing allows autonomous systems such as drones, robots, and self-driving cars to process sensor data and make decisions on the spot, without the need for constant communication with a central server. This is especially important in applications where speed and reliability are paramount, such as autonomous vehicles navigating busy roads or industrial robots performing assembly tasks in fast-paced environments.

As edge computing technologies advance, the next generation of agentic AI systems will become more capable of operating independently in real-time, even in remote or disconnected environments. This will expand the potential use cases for autonomous systems, from disaster response scenarios to remote infrastructure monitoring.

Swarm Intelligence and Collective Autonomy

Swarm intelligence is an emerging concept in AI that draws inspiration from the collective behavior of groups in nature, such as flocks of birds, swarms of insects, or schools of fish. In swarm intelligence, multiple agents collaborate, communicate, and coordinate their actions to solve complex problems that would be difficult for a single agent to address alone.

In agentic AI, swarm intelligence can be applied to create systems of autonomous agents that work together to achieve shared goals. For example, fleets of drones can collaborate to perform tasks such as surveying large areas, mapping terrain, or delivering goods. Each drone in the swarm operates autonomously but communicates and cooperates with others to improve the overall efficiency of the mission.

As technology advances, the next generation of agentic AI will see greater use of swarm intelligence in applications like environmental monitoring, disaster relief, and autonomous manufacturing. These AI systems will be able to coordinate their actions seamlessly, adapting to changing conditions and optimizing resource allocation in real time.

AI-Driven Creativity and Problem Solving

Another exciting trend in agentic AI is its potential for creativity and problem-solving. While AI systems have traditionally been used for tasks like data analysis and automation, newer AI models are beginning to explore creative domains, including music composition, visual arts, and even scientific discovery.

Generative AI models such as GPT (Generative Pretrained Transformer) and DALL-E, which create text and images based on prompts, showcase the potential for AI to assist in creative endeavors. These models can generate novel ideas, suggest solutions, and even create entirely new concepts. As agentic AI systems evolve, we can expect them to take on more complex roles in creative industries, working alongside humans to generate innovative solutions to problems or inspire new artistic expressions.

Moreover, AI's ability to process vast amounts of data and identify patterns that humans might overlook could revolutionize fields like scientific research. Agentic AI systems could autonomously propose new hypotheses, design experiments, or even discover breakthroughs in medicine, materials science, or physics.

Challenges and Considerations for the Future of Agentic AI

While the next generation of agentic AI holds immense promise, several challenges remain to be addressed:

Trust and Transparency: As AI systems become more autonomous, establishing trust between humans and machines will be crucial. Ensuring that AI systems are transparent, explainable, and accountable will be essential for widespread adoption.

Regulation and Governance: With increasing autonomy, there will be a need for regulatory frameworks to ensure that AI systems operate safely and ethically. International cooperation will be necessary to establish global standards for autonomous systems.

Security and Privacy: Autonomous AI systems will generate and process large amounts of sensitive data. Ensuring that these systems are secure and that privacy is protected will be critical to preventing misuse or unauthorized access.

The next generation of agentic AI is poised to revolutionize industries and society, driving advancements in autonomy, decision-making, and collaboration. Emerging trends such as reinforcement learning, human-AI collaboration, ethical AI, edge computing, swarm intelligence, and AI-driven creativity are shaping the future of autonomous systems. As these technologies evolve, the next generation of agentic AI will bring about more intelligent, adaptable, and capable systems that can operate independently and make decisions in dynamic environments. However, addressing the challenges of trust, regulation, and security will be key to ensuring that these systems are deployed responsibly and ethically. The potential of agentic AI is vast, and as we navigate the future, its impact on society will be profound.

Chapter 32 Collaborative Multi-Agent Systems

Collaborative Multi-Agent Systems (CMAS) represent a fascinating and complex area of study in artificial intelligence (AI), where multiple autonomous agents work together to achieve shared goals. These systems are modeled on the behavior of individuals or entities that can make independent decisions but must collaborate with others to fulfill a collective objective. The collaboration of agents, whether in the form of human-robot interaction, smart cities, or industrial applications, has profound implications across various fields such as robotics, economics, game theory, and distributed computing. This chapter explores the concept of Collaborative Multi-Agent Systems, focusing on the nature of agent interactions, their applications, challenges, and future trends.

What is a Collaborative Multi-Agent System?

A Collaborative Multi-Agent System (CMAS) is a system composed of multiple autonomous agents that interact with each other to perform tasks in a coordinated manner. Each agent in the system is an entity capable of perceiving its environment, reasoning about it, and taking actions to achieve specific goals. In CMAS, agents are designed to collaborate with one another, share information, and contribute to a common objective, rather than functioning in isolation or direct competition.

Agents in a CMAS are often viewed as having distinct characteristics:

Autonomy: Each agent can operate independently, making decisions based on local observations without centralized control.

Interdependence: While autonomous, agents in CMAS systems rely on the actions and information provided by other agents to accomplish their goals.

Decentralized Control: The system does not rely on a single central controller. Instead, each agent controls its own actions, often using local knowledge to make decisions.

Interaction: Agents must interact with one another, whether by sharing information, coordinating actions, or negotiating solutions.

Agent Interactions in Collaborative Multi-Agent Systems

The core of Collaborative Multi-Agent Systems lies in the interactions between agents. These interactions can be categorized into several types, each with its own dynamics and strategies for collaboration:

1. Communication-Based Interactions

Communication is a fundamental aspect of CMAS, enabling agents to share information, synchronize actions, and negotiate solutions. The interaction could be explicit, such as an agent sending a message, or implicit, where agents infer information based on actions or environmental cues. Common communication protocols used in CMAS include message passing, shared memory, or broadcast systems.

The communication can be structured or unstructured:

Structured Communication: Agents follow a formalized set of rules or protocols when exchanging messages. Examples include protocols like FIPA-ACL (Foundation for Intelligent Physical Agents - Agent Communication Language), which standardize communication between agents in distributed systems.

Unstructured Communication: Agents exchange messages or cues in an informal manner, often based on learned or adaptive behaviors rather than predefined rules.

2. Coordination-Based Interactions

Coordination between agents is critical for ensuring that they do not work at cross-purposes. In collaborative settings, agents must not only act autonomously but also synchronize their actions to achieve the shared goal. There are several approaches to coordination in CMAS:

Centralized Coordination: One agent or a leader is given the responsibility to coordinate the actions of other agents. While this approach simplifies decision-making, it can also create bottlenecks and reduce scalability.

Decentralized Coordination: Each agent coordinates its own actions, sometimes using local or global strategies, based on its knowledge and the actions of other agents. This approach enhances flexibility but can lead to issues with ensuring optimal collective performance.

Market-based Coordination: Agents can engage in a market-like mechanism, where tasks are allocated according to preferences, bidding, or negotiated agreements.

3. Negotiation and Cooperation

Negotiation is another essential form of interaction within CMAS. Agents may have competing interests, limited resources, or incomplete information, requiring them to negotiate solutions that balance individual needs with collective goals. This is particularly true in scenarios where agents are involved in tasks such as resource allocation, task division, or problem-solving.

The negotiation process in CMAS may involve strategies like:

Bargaining: Agents offer terms and adjust their demands or proposals until a mutual agreement is reached.

Auctions: Agents bid for resources or tasks, allowing them to compete for a limited pool of resources in a structured way.

Coalition Formation: Agents may form coalitions to pool resources, knowledge, or expertise to increase the likelihood of achieving the shared goal.

Cooperation, on the other hand, can be driven by mutual benefit. Agents cooperate to exploit synergies, often through joint action or the sharing of resources. Trust-building mechanisms and reciprocity are vital in fostering long-term cooperation.

Applications of Collaborative Multi-Agent Systems

The applications of CMAS span numerous fields, with a few notable ones including:

1. Robotics and Autonomous Vehicles

In robotics, CMAS is applied to systems where multiple robots work together to achieve common objectives, such as in warehouse automation or disaster response scenarios. These robots can collaborate by sharing information about their environment, coordinating movements to avoid collisions, or distributing tasks based on their capabilities. In autonomous vehicles, CMAS could enable fleets of self-driving cars to coordinate traffic, share road conditions, and optimize route planning.

2. Smart Cities

CMAS plays a crucial role in the development of smart cities, where multiple interconnected devices, sensors, and systems interact autonomously to manage resources, traffic, energy, and services. Traffic lights, waste management systems, public transportation, and energy grids all rely on collaborative interactions among agents to optimize their performance. For example, traffic management systems may adjust traffic signals based on real-time data shared by vehicles and infrastructure agents.

3. Supply Chain Management

In supply chains, CMAS facilitates coordination among various entities, such as suppliers, manufacturers, and distributors, to improve efficiency and reduce costs. Agents within the system may communicate to manage inventories, order supplies, and schedule deliveries. Coordination among these agents is vital for optimizing production schedules, reducing delays, and minimizing resource wastage.

4. Healthcare Systems

Healthcare applications of CMAS involve collaboration between medical devices, healthcare professionals, and administrative systems. For example, in an emergency room, agents representing different systems (e.g., patient monitoring devices, scheduling software, and medical staff) work together to ensure that patients receive timely and appropriate care.

5. Environmental Monitoring

CMAS is used in environmental monitoring systems, where autonomous agents such as drones, satellites, or ground-based sensors work together to gather data about climate conditions, pollution, or wildlife tracking. These agents collaborate by sharing observations, analyzing data, and adjusting their behaviors based on environmental changes.

Challenges in Collaborative Multi-Agent Systems

While the potential benefits of CMAS are immense, there are several challenges that researchers and developers face when implementing these systems:

1. Scalability

As the number of agents in a system increases, the complexity of managing interactions and ensuring effective collaboration grows exponentially. In large-scale systems, ensuring that agents efficiently communicate, coordinate, and make decisions without overwhelming the system or creating bottlenecks is a major challenge.

2. Communication Overhead

In CMAS, continuous communication between agents can lead to significant overhead, especially if messages are complex or require frequent exchanges. This can strain the system's bandwidth, causing delays in decision-making and impacting overall performance. Balancing communication frequency and data volume is key to ensuring efficiency.

3. Trust and Security

Since agents operate autonomously, ensuring that they trust one another and share reliable information is crucial. Security concerns also arise, as malicious agents could infiltrate the system, compromising communication and collaboration. Effective trust-building mechanisms and security protocols are necessary to safeguard the integrity of CMAS.

4. Conflict Resolution

When multiple agents have competing goals or limited resources, conflicts are inevitable. Developing efficient conflict resolution strategies that allow agents to reach mutually beneficial solutions without causing disruption is a challenging task in CMAS. Techniques such as negotiation, game theory, and multi-objective optimization are often employed to mitigate conflict.

Future Trends in Collaborative Multi-Agent Systems

The future of CMAS is exciting, with ongoing research and development promising advancements in several areas:

Deep Learning and AI: Advances in deep learning and reinforcement learning will allow agents to learn from their interactions with the environment and other agents. This will enhance their ability to adapt, collaborate, and make optimal decisions in complex, dynamic environments.

Swarm Intelligence: Inspired by nature, swarm intelligence algorithms enable a group of simple agents to cooperate and solve complex problems collectively. Applications in fields like robotics, environmental monitoring, and traffic management are expected to grow.

Human-Agent Collaboration: The integration of human agents into CMAS (such as in human-robot teams) will further push the boundaries of collaborative systems, leading to more sophisticated, interactive, and efficient teamwork.

Collaborative Multi-Agent Systems represent a rich and evolving field of research with immense practical implications. Through efficient interactions, communication, and coordination, agents can work together autonomously to solve problems and achieve collective goals. Despite challenges such as scalability, communication overhead, and conflict resolution, CMAS holds promise across various domains, from robotics to smart cities and healthcare. With advancements in AI, swarm intelligence, and human-agent collaboration, the potential for CMAS to revolutionize industries and improve everyday life is enormous.

Chapter 33 Quantum Computing and Agentic AI

In the world of artificial intelligence (AI), we are witnessing an unprecedented surge in technological innovation. One of the most transformative fields fueling this evolution is quantum computing, which offers new paradigms for solving complex computational problems that classical computers struggle to address. By merging the powerful capabilities of quantum computing with the growing sophistication of AI, we enter the domain of agentic AI—a term that refers to AI systems that can act autonomously and make decisions in real-time.

This chapter explores how quantum computing is poised to drive smarter AI by augmenting its capabilities, making it more efficient, faster, and more adept at solving a wide range of problems. We will examine the principles behind quantum computing, the concept of agentic AI, and how quantum computing can revolutionize the way we approach intelligent systems.

Quantum Computing: A New Paradigm

Quantum computing represents a radical departure from classical computing. While classical computers store and process data as binary units called "bits" (either 0 or 1), quantum computers utilize quantum bits or "qubits," which can exist in multiple states simultaneously due to a property known as superposition. This allows quantum computers to perform complex calculations in parallel, vastly increasing their computational power.

Additionally, quantum computers exploit entanglement, a phenomenon in which qubits become linked in such a way that the state of one qubit can instantly affect the state of another, no matter how far apart they are. This enables quantum computers to perform highly intricate computations at speeds unthinkable for classical systems.

The potential advantages of quantum computing in various fields—cryptography, optimization, chemistry, and AI—are immense. Quantum computers can tackle problems that require vast amounts of data processing, offering an exponential speed-up in solving complex optimization tasks and simulating molecular structures, which classical computers cannot efficiently handle.

The Intersection of Quantum Computing and AI

Artificial intelligence, particularly machine learning (ML) and deep learning (DL), has already transformed industries like healthcare, finance, transportation, and entertainment. Machine learning algorithms rely heavily on data to train models, and as the size and complexity of datasets increase, so does the computational cost. Classical computers, even with high-performance GPUs, face limits in processing vast amounts of data within a reasonable time frame.

This is where quantum computing can make a significant impact. Quantum computers can process multiple possibilities at once, potentially revolutionizing machine learning algorithms by speeding up the training process and improving their efficiency. By leveraging quantum parallelism, quantum-enhanced machine learning algorithms could uncover patterns and insights within datasets that were previously beyond the reach of classical systems.

Quantum computing could also accelerate optimization tasks. In AI, optimization is central to tasks like reinforcement learning (RL), where agents must find the best sequence of actions to maximize cumulative rewards. Classical optimization methods, such as gradient descent, may become inefficient when dealing with high-dimensional spaces, and quantum computing could offer faster convergence to optimal solutions by processing multiple paths simultaneously.

Agentic AI: Defining Autonomy in Machines

Agentic AI refers to intelligent systems capable of acting autonomously and making decisions based on their observations, reasoning, and goals. These systems are not merely reactive to human inputs but can actively perceive their environment, assess situations, and take actions that further their objectives, much like humans do.

An agentic AI system typically includes the following key components:

Perception: The ability to sense and interpret the environment, which may include both sensory inputs (visual, auditory, etc.) and data from other sources (e.g., social media feeds, sensor networks).

Reasoning and Decision-Making: The ability to process information, weigh options, and choose the best course of action based on available knowledge and context.

Learning: The ability to improve over time by learning from experiences, adapting to new situations, and refining strategies.

Action: The ability to execute actions based on the decisions made, whether in the physical world (e.g., robots) or in the digital domain (e.g., trading algorithms).

In essence, agentic AI systems exhibit a degree of autonomy, allowing them to make decisions without requiring constant human intervention. These systems hold promise in fields such as autonomous vehicles, industrial automation, personal assistants, and decision support systems.

Leveraging Quantum Advancements for Smarter Agentic AI

The fusion of quantum computing with agentic AI presents an exciting opportunity for enhancing the capabilities of autonomous systems. By leveraging quantum advancements, AI systems can become more capable, flexible, and efficient, driving innovation in a variety of sectors. Let's explore how quantum computing can enhance agentic AI across key areas.

1. Improved Optimization for Autonomous Decision-Making

One of the central challenges in agentic AI is optimization—how to make the best decisions in complex, high-dimensional environments. Whether it's a robot determining the most efficient path to navigate through an unknown terrain or an AI trading system selecting the best investment strategy, optimization lies at the heart of autonomous action.

Quantum computing offers significant improvements in optimization tasks through quantum algorithms like Quantum Approximate Optimization Algorithm (QAOA) and Quantum annealing. These algorithms exploit quantum mechanics to explore the solution space more efficiently, potentially solving optimization problems much faster than classical methods.

For agentic AI, this means that systems can make more informed, accurate decisions in less time. For example, an autonomous vehicle could calculate the safest, fastest route in real-time, factoring in dynamic environmental conditions, traffic, and road hazards. Quantum-enhanced decision-making would enable these vehicles to react more quickly and accurately than current systems.

2. Quantum Machine Learning for Smarter AI

Machine learning is a critical component of agentic AI, allowing systems to learn from experience, adapt to new scenarios, and improve their performance over time. Quantum computing can significantly accelerate the process of training machine learning models, especially when dealing with large, complex datasets.

Quantum machine learning (QML) algorithms take advantage of quantum parallelism to process large datasets more efficiently. Techniques like quantum neural networks and quantum support vector machines are being explored to enhance the speed and accuracy of learning algorithms. These quantum-enhanced models can process data at an exponentially faster rate than classical counterparts, enabling faster learning and more precise decision-making.

For agentic AI, faster learning translates into quicker adaptation to new environments. An AI system controlling a drone, for instance, could learn to navigate obstacles more efficiently, improving its performance in real-time. In reinforcement learning, quantum computing could accelerate the training of agents, allowing them to explore complex state spaces more effectively and find optimal strategies in less time.

3. Handling Uncertainty with Quantum Algorithms

A major challenge in agentic AI is dealing with uncertainty. In real-world environments, complete information is rarely available, and AI systems must make decisions based on incomplete or noisy data. Classical AI systems often rely on probabilistic models or heuristics to estimate the likelihood of certain outcomes, but these approaches are limited by computational constraints.

Quantum computing offers a new approach to uncertainty through quantum probability and quantum-enhanced Bayesian inference. Quantum algorithms can simulate more complex probabilistic models, which could improve decision-making under uncertainty. For agentic AI, this means that systems can make more accurate predictions and decisions, even in highly uncertain environments.

For example, an autonomous drone flying in a storm may not have precise data on wind patterns or other environmental factors. Quantum-enhanced probabilistic reasoning could allow the drone to make better-informed decisions about its flight path, improving its ability to navigate safely through the storm.

4. Quantum-Enhanced Simulation for Complex Environments

Quantum computing excels at simulating complex systems, which is valuable for agentic AI systems that need to interact with dynamic, real-world environments. For instance, AI agents in robotics or autonomous systems often need to predict the outcomes of their actions in complex physical spaces.

Quantum computers can simulate physical phenomena at the quantum level, offering a more accurate representation of the real world than classical simulations. For agentic AI, this means that systems can model and predict the consequences of their actions with a higher degree of precision, improving their ability to interact with the environment effectively.

For example, a robot navigating a factory floor could use quantum-enhanced simulations to predict the effects of various movements on its surroundings, allowing it to avoid obstacles or optimize its path in real-time. This capability could be extended to other domains, such as healthcare (predicting patient outcomes) or finance (simulating market behavior).

Quantum computing represents a transformative shift in the way we approach computation, offering unprecedented advantages in speed, efficiency, and complexity. When combined with agentic AI, quantum advancements have the potential to drive smarter, more capable autonomous systems. From optimization and machine learning to probabilistic reasoning and simulation, quantum computing enhances every facet of AI, enabling systems to make better decisions, adapt more rapidly, and solve problems previously beyond the reach of classical computers.

As quantum technologies continue to evolve, the integration of quantum computing with agentic AI will likely revolutionize industries, creating intelligent systems that are faster, more accurate, and more efficient. The fusion of these two groundbreaking technologies promises to unlock new possibilities, bringing us closer to a future where AI can act with true autonomy and intelligence.

Chapter 34 AI Ethics in a Global Context

AI ethics involves the study of how AI systems should be developed and used to benefit humanity, while mitigating potential harm. It is an interdisciplinary field that brings together principles from philosophy, law, engineering, and social sciences to ensure that AI technologies align with human values, promote equity, and are deployed responsibly. However, given the global nature of AI development, establishing ethical guidelines that are consistent across different regions and cultures poses a unique challenge. In this chapter, we will explore the current state of AI ethics, its challenges, and the necessity of harmonizing international guidelines for autonomous systems.

The Global Nature of AI Development

The development of AI technologies is happening on a global scale. Research institutions, tech companies, and governments from all over the world are competing to push the boundaries of AI capabilities. AI is being used in numerous sectors, from self-driving cars to facial recognition and natural language processing, and the pace of innovation is accelerating. With such rapid development, the ethical implications of AI have become a pressing concern.

While the benefits of AI are vast, the potential risks are also significant. For instance, autonomous vehicles can reduce traffic accidents, but they also raise questions about accountability when an accident occurs. Similarly, AI-driven algorithms can improve healthcare by providing accurate diagnoses, but they also risk amplifying biases present in the data, leading to discriminatory outcomes. These risks are not limited to any one country; AI technologies are being developed and deployed in a way that affects people globally. This international interconnectedness makes the need for harmonized guidelines all the more urgent.

Ethical Concerns in Autonomous Systems

Autonomous systems are AI-driven technologies that can operate without human intervention. These systems are designed to make decisions based on algorithms and data inputs, often with little or no human oversight. Autonomous systems raise several ethical concerns, particularly when it comes to accountability, safety, transparency, and fairness.

Accountability and Responsibility: One of the central ethical issues with autonomous systems is determining who is accountable when something goes wrong. For example, if an autonomous vehicle causes an accident, should the manufacturer, the developer, or the owner be held responsible? This question becomes even more complicated in situations involving autonomous weapons or military drones. The issue of accountability is compounded by the fact that AI systems may make decisions based on complex algorithms that are difficult for humans to understand or predict.

Safety and Reliability: Autonomous systems must be designed to ensure the safety and well-being of individuals. In the case of autonomous vehicles, for example, the technology must be able to safely navigate unpredictable environments, such as inclement weather or sudden obstacles. Ensuring that autonomous systems are safe and reliable requires rigorous testing, validation, and ongoing monitoring to minimize risks. However, global standards for these safety measures are still in development, and they vary from country to country.

Transparency and Explainability: AI systems, especially those based on deep learning and neural networks, often function as "black boxes," where the reasoning behind their decisions is not easily understood by humans. This lack of transparency is a significant ethical concern, as it makes it difficult to trust AI systems, especially in high-stakes situations like healthcare or criminal justice. The need for explainability—where AI systems can provide understandable reasons for their decisions—has been recognized as an important ethical principle. However, the technical challenges involved in creating transparent AI systems are still a subject of research.

Bias and Fairness: AI systems are only as good as the data they are trained on. If the data is biased or unrepresentative, the AI system may produce unfair or discriminatory outcomes. For example, facial recognition systems have been found to have higher error rates for people with darker skin tones, leading to concerns about racial bias. Similarly, predictive algorithms used in criminal justice have been shown to disproportionately target minority communities. Ensuring fairness in AI systems requires careful attention to data collection, preprocessing, and model development, and it is essential to address the ethical concerns surrounding bias.

Privacy and Surveillance: As AI technologies become more embedded in society, the collection of personal data has become a major concern. Autonomous systems often rely on vast amounts of data to function effectively, and this data can include sensitive information such as location, health records, and personal behavior. The potential for surveillance—whether by governments, corporations, or other entities—raises significant ethical questions about privacy and individual rights. Striking a balance between the benefits of data-driven AI and the protection of privacy is a critical issue in AI ethics.

The Need for Global AI Ethics Guidelines

Given the global nature of AI development and deployment, it is essential to establish internationally recognized ethical guidelines for autonomous systems. While various countries and organizations have proposed their own AI ethics frameworks, these guidelines often differ in their emphasis and priorities. For instance, the European Union has taken a strong stance on AI ethics, emphasizing human-centric principles such as transparency, accountability, and privacy. The EU has also proposed regulations for AI that aim to ensure that autonomous systems are developed and used in a way that aligns with fundamental rights and values.

In contrast, countries like China and the United States have focused more on the economic and technological aspects of AI development, with less emphasis on regulation. China's AI ethics framework, for example, prioritizes technological advancement and economic competitiveness, while the U.S. has taken a more decentralized approach to AI ethics, relying on industry self-regulation. These differences reflect the diverse cultural, political, and economic contexts in which AI is being developed and deployed, but they also highlight the challenges of establishing global guidelines.

To harmonize AI ethics across borders, it is necessary to find common ground on key principles. International organizations such as the United Nations (UN), the Organization for Economic Co-operation and Development (OECD), and the World Economic Forum (WEF) have recognized the importance of addressing AI ethics in a global context. In 2021, the OECD published guidelines for AI that focus on promoting innovation while ensuring that AI systems are trustworthy, transparent, and aligned with human rights. Similarly, the UN has called for the creation of a global framework for AI governance, with a focus on ensuring that AI benefits all people, not just those in advanced economies.

Challenges to Harmonizing Global AI Ethics

While the need for harmonized AI ethics guidelines is clear, several challenges remain in creating a unified framework for autonomous systems.

Cultural and Political Differences: Different cultures and political systems have varying views on what constitutes ethical behavior. For example, some countries prioritize individual privacy, while others may prioritize national security or economic growth. These differing priorities can make it difficult to create a one-size-fits-all approach to AI ethics. However, it is possible to identify common principles, such as respect for human dignity, fairness, and accountability, that can serve as a foundation for global guidelines.

Economic and Technological Disparities: Countries with advanced AI capabilities, such as the U.S., China, and several European nations, may be more inclined to prioritize the economic and technological benefits of AI, while developing countries may focus more on ensuring that AI technologies do not exacerbate existing inequalities. Striking a balance between promoting innovation and addressing global disparities in access to technology will be crucial in developing ethical guidelines that are inclusive and equitable.

Lack of International Consensus: While there is growing recognition of the need for global AI ethics guidelines, there is no international consensus on how to regulate AI. Different countries have adopted different approaches, and some have been slow to implement AI regulations. Developing a global framework will require extensive dialogue and cooperation between governments, industry leaders, academics, and civil society organizations.

As AI technologies continue to evolve, the need for a harmonized global approach to AI ethics becomes increasingly urgent. Autonomous systems present complex ethical challenges, from accountability and fairness to safety and privacy. Given the global nature of AI development, it is essential to establish international guidelines that promote responsible innovation while addressing the ethical concerns surrounding these technologies.

While challenges such as cultural differences, economic disparities, and the lack of international consensus remain, there is a growing recognition of the need for a unified approach. By building on common ethical principles and fostering international cooperation, it is possible to develop AI ethics guidelines that ensure autonomous systems are developed and deployed in a way that benefits all of humanity.

Ultimately, the goal should be to create an AI landscape that is not only technologically advanced but also ethical, transparent, and aligned with the values that promote social good, fairness, and human dignity on a global scale.

Chapter 35 The Role of Agentic AI in Space Colonization

Space exploration has long captivated humanity's imagination. From the first steps on the Moon to the ongoing missions to Mars, the idea of expanding humanity's presence beyond Earth has driven significant advances in science and technology. As space exploration continues to evolve, the concept of space colonization is becoming increasingly realistic. However, colonizing other planets presents numerous challenges, including the development of self-sustaining systems that can support human life in the harsh environment of space. One of the most promising technological solutions to these challenges is Agentic Artificial Intelligence (Agentic AI).

Agentic AI refers to artificial intelligence systems capable of performing tasks autonomously, making decisions, and executing actions based on those decisions. Unlike traditional AI, which often operates under human supervision or in predefined contexts, Agentic AI has a degree of autonomy and decision-making capacity. This makes it especially valuable for complex and unpredictable environments, such as space. In this chapter, we will explore the role of Agentic AI in space colonization, particularly in the context of building self-sustaining systems for extraterrestrial living.

The Challenges of Space Colonization

Before delving into the role of Agentic AI, it's important to understand the significant challenges that must be overcome for successful space colonization. These challenges include:

Life Support Systems: In space, humans cannot survive without life support systems that provide air, water, food, and temperature regulation. These systems must be robust, self-sustaining, and able to function independently of Earth-based support.

Energy Production and Management: Colonies on other planets will require a reliable energy source to power life support systems, scientific research, and other infrastructure.

Solar power may be one option, but it faces limitations due to the distance from the Sun and the extreme weather conditions that may prevail on some planets.

Resource Utilization and Recycling: Resources like water and oxygen will need to be recycled and replenished on-site. Additionally, raw materials for construction, agriculture, and other purposes must either be sourced from the local environment or transported from Earth.

Environmental Hazards: Planets like Mars or the Moon are inhospitable to humans due to extreme temperatures, radiation, and lack of a breathable atmosphere. Creating habitats that can shield humans from these environmental hazards is crucial.

Psychological and Social Factors: Space colonists will be far from Earth, isolated, and confined to small spaces. Managing mental health and maintaining social cohesion will be a significant challenge.

Given the scale and complexity of these challenges, human intervention alone may not be enough to ensure the survival of a space colony. This is where Agentic AI comes into play.

The Role of Agentic AI in Space Colonization

Agentic AI has the potential to revolutionize space colonization in several key ways:

1. Autonomous Life Support Systems

Agentic AI can play a crucial role in managing life support systems within extraterrestrial habitats. These systems need to be continuously monitored and adjusted to ensure that oxygen, water, food, and waste are properly regulated. While human oversight is essential in the initial stages, Agentic AI could take over many of the repetitive, time-consuming tasks and ensure that the systems are running efficiently.

For example, AI-powered environmental control systems could autonomously adjust temperature, humidity, and air composition within habitats, based on real-time data from sensors embedded throughout the colony. These systems could also handle emergency situations, such as a drop in oxygen levels or water contamination, and take immediate corrective action without needing human intervention.

AI could also assist in optimizing resource usage by monitoring consumption patterns and making adjustments based on available resources. In situations where resources are limited—such as when a colony is on a planet with scarce water—Agentic AI could help conserve and recycle water to ensure sustainability.

2. Energy Production and Management

Energy is one of the most critical resources for space colonization. A reliable, self-sustaining energy supply is necessary for all aspects of colony life, from life support systems to scientific experiments. Agentic AI can enhance energy management by autonomously monitoring energy production, consumption, and storage systems. For instance, on Mars, solar power is a primary energy source due to the lack of a suitable atmosphere for other energy generation methods. However, solar energy is intermittent, and the power supply will need to be managed carefully to ensure a continuous supply.

Agentic AI systems could dynamically adjust energy usage based on the availability of solar power. During the day, when solar power is abundant, AI systems could prioritize high-energy tasks. At night, or during dust storms when solar generation is reduced, the AI could manage power reserves more efficiently, reducing energy consumption in non-essential areas and ensuring that critical systems such as life support are prioritized.

AI could also assist in developing alternative energy solutions, such as harnessing the planet's resources for local energy production. For example, AI could optimize geothermal energy harvesting on Mars or the Moon, using local heat sources to supplement solar energy.

3. Resource Utilization and Recycling

Space colonies will need to be self-sufficient when it comes to resource management. On Earth, resources are abundant, but on distant planets, everything must be carefully recycled and utilized. Agentic AI can help by managing the recycling processes for water, oxygen, and waste. Through the use of AI-powered sensors and automated systems, the colony can ensure that these critical resources are not wasted and are replenished as needed.

Moreover, AI can help manage mining operations for local resources. For instance, if the colony is located on a planet with usable minerals, AI could guide robotic miners to extract these materials efficiently. These resources could be used for construction, manufacturing, or even creating fuel. AI would be able to analyze the quality and quantity of resources in real-time, optimizing extraction processes and ensuring minimal waste.

Agentic AI would also be crucial in managing agriculture, a vital part of a self-sustaining colony. AI could optimize the growing conditions for plants, ensuring that they receive the right amount of water, light, and nutrients. Furthermore, AI could monitor the health of crops and make real-time adjustments to maximize yield. By managing these systems, AI could help maintain a steady food supply without requiring constant human supervision.

4. Hazard Detection and Environmental Protection

Space environments, especially on planets like Mars, pose significant hazards to human life. These include extreme temperatures, radiation, dust storms, and micrometeorite impacts. Agentic AI can be used to detect these hazards in real-time and take action to protect the colony.

AI-powered drones could fly over the colony's surroundings, scanning for potential threats such as incoming meteorites or dust storms. The AI could then analyze the data, predict the potential impact, and take necessary actions. This could include activating protective shields, alerting the inhabitants, or even moving sensitive equipment to safety.

Additionally, radiation levels on planets like Mars are much higher than on Earth due to the absence of a thick atmosphere. Agentic AI could monitor radiation levels in real-time and adjust the colony's shielding or recommend changes in the daily routine to minimize exposure.

5. Autonomous Construction and Maintenance

Building a self-sustaining colony on another planet will require significant infrastructure, including habitats, laboratories, energy generation systems, and communication facilities. Agentic AI could take the lead in autonomous construction and maintenance of these structures. AI-driven robots and drones could build habitats, lay power cables, and set up other essential infrastructure without human intervention.

Additionally, Agentic AI could be responsible for ongoing maintenance. In a space colony, regular maintenance of life support systems, equipment, and structural components will be crucial for survival. AI systems could detect potential issues, diagnose problems, and even carry out repairs autonomously, all without requiring a crew member to perform the task manually.

6. Psychological and Social Wellbeing

The isolation and confinement experienced by space colonists could lead to significant psychological stress. Agentic AI could play a role in managing mental health by detecting signs of depression, anxiety, or social isolation among colonists. AI systems could provide support by suggesting activities, facilitating virtual social interactions, or offering counseling through virtual assistants.

Moreover, AI could assist in maintaining social cohesion within the colony by monitoring interpersonal dynamics. It could identify conflicts between colonists and suggest interventions to prevent escalation. By fostering a healthy social environment, Agentic AI could ensure that the colony remains stable and productive.

Agentic AI has the potential to transform space colonization by providing the autonomous capabilities required to build and maintain self-sustaining systems for extraterrestrial living. From managing life support systems to optimizing energy production, recycling resources, and detecting environmental hazards, AI can perform essential tasks that are vital for the survival of space colonies. As we move closer to the reality of space colonization, the integration of Agentic AI into space exploration and settlement will be indispensable. By leveraging the power of AI, humanity can take its first steps toward establishing thriving, self-sustaining colonies on other planets, ensuring that the dream of space colonization becomes a reality.

Chapter 36 Overcoming Technological Hurdles

In the rapidly advancing landscape of technology, autonomy—whether in the form of self-driving cars, robotic automation, or artificial intelligence (AI)—is one of the most exciting frontiers of innovation. However, despite the great strides made in autonomous systems, there remain significant technological hurdles and unresolved issues that must be addressed for them to function safely, efficiently, and reliably in real-world scenarios. This chapter explores some of the key challenges faced in autonomous technology and outlines potential solutions to overcome these barriers.

1. Safety and Reliability

One of the primary concerns surrounding autonomy, particularly in the realm of self-driving vehicles and robotics, is ensuring safety and reliability. Autonomous systems must be capable of operating under a wide variety of conditions—often far more complex than any controlled laboratory environment can simulate. For example, in autonomous vehicles, environmental variables such as weather, traffic patterns, and unpredictable human behavior present significant challenges.

Challenges:

Sensor Accuracy and Limitations: Autonomous systems rely heavily on sensors (LiDAR, cameras, radar, etc.) to perceive their environment. These sensors, however, are not foolproof. Low-light conditions, heavy rain, fog, and snow can interfere with sensor performance, leading to inaccuracies in detection and decision-making.

Edge Cases and Uncertainty: Autonomous systems must handle edge cases—situations that are rare but critical. For example, what should a self-driving car do if an object unexpectedly crosses its path, or if it encounters a roadblock? The sheer complexity of real-world scenarios makes it impossible to account for every potential edge case.

Solutions:

Sensor Fusion and Redundancy: By combining multiple sensors, the system can cross-check data to compensate for the limitations of individual sensors. This approach, known as sensor fusion, ensures greater accuracy and provides redundancy, meaning that if one sensor fails or becomes unreliable, others can fill in the gap.

Machine Learning and Simulation: To address edge cases, autonomous systems can be trained using vast datasets and sophisticated machine learning algorithms. Simulations can generate millions of different scenarios, allowing autonomous systems to experience rare situations and learn how to react appropriately. Over time, the system becomes better at generalizing from past experiences to handle new situations.

Real-time Decision-Making: AI-powered systems can be designed to make real-time decisions based on constantly updated data from sensors. These decisions must be fast and accurate, relying on powerful processing units that can handle large amounts of data in real-time. The development of faster and more efficient hardware will contribute significantly to this solution.

2. Ethical and Legal Considerations

Autonomous technology raises a host of ethical and legal issues, particularly when it comes to decision-making in life-and-death situations. For example, if a self-driving car must choose between swerving to avoid hitting a pedestrian and hitting a tree, which decision is morally preferable? Who is responsible for the actions of an autonomous system if it causes harm?

Challenges:

Moral Dilemmas: Autonomous systems, especially in applications like self-driving cars or military robots, must sometimes make decisions that could have significant moral implications. The famous "trolley problem" is often cited in discussions of autonomous ethics, where a machine must decide which course of action will result in fewer casualties when it cannot avoid harm altogether.

Accountability and Liability: In the event of an accident involving an autonomous vehicle or robot, who is legally responsible? The manufacturer? The developer of the software? The owner of the system? Current laws are not fully equipped to handle the complexities of autonomous systems, and the legal landscape is still evolving.

Solutions:

Ethical Frameworks and Algorithms: Researchers are working to develop ethical frameworks that can guide autonomous decision-making. One approach is to create algorithms that prioritize minimizing harm based on predefined ethical principles. However, these algorithms are far from perfect, and they may require continuous refinement as new ethical dilemmas arise.

Clear Regulations and Liability Laws: Governments and regulatory bodies must create clear and adaptable legal frameworks to address issues of liability, accountability, and insurance for autonomous systems. This could involve creating new categories of laws specifically for autonomous technologies, ensuring that manufacturers and developers are held accountable for any harm caused by their systems.

Public Dialogue and Transparency: Engaging the public in discussions about the ethical implications of autonomy is crucial. Transparency in how decisions are made by autonomous systems, and who holds responsibility for them, can help to build trust and ensure that these technologies are developed in a way that aligns with societal values.

3. Trust and Acceptance

For autonomous technologies to be widely adopted, they must gain the trust and acceptance of the public. People must feel confident that these systems will perform as expected and that they are safe to use. However, there is often resistance to autonomous systems due to fears about the unknown, the loss of jobs, or the potential for malfunction.

Challenges:

Fear of Technology Failure: Autonomous systems are perceived by many as "black boxes," where the decision-making process is not fully understood or transparent. This lack of clarity can cause anxiety and distrust, particularly in life-critical applications such as healthcare or transportation.

Job Displacement Concerns: As robots and autonomous systems take over tasks traditionally performed by humans, many workers fear that their jobs will become obsolete. The societal impact of automation on employment is a significant concern that must be addressed.

Cultural Resistance: Different cultures and societies may have varying levels of acceptance of autonomy. In some regions, people may feel more comfortable with machines making decisions, while in others, there may be a stronger emphasis on human control and judgment.

Solutions:

Education and Awareness: A key strategy to overcoming distrust is to educate the public about how autonomous systems work and their benefits. Providing clear, accessible information can help demystify these technologies and reduce fear. Public demonstrations and trials of autonomous systems can also help people experience firsthand how they function.

Human-in-the-loop Systems: Many experts advocate for "human-in-the-loop" systems, where humans retain oversight and control over critical decisions made by autonomous systems. This ensures that, even if the machine makes a mistake, a human operator can intervene to prevent harm.

Reskilling and Job Transition Programs: Governments and businesses must invest in retraining programs to help workers transition to new roles created by the rise of autonomous technology. These programs can focus on developing skills in fields like robotics maintenance, AI programming, and data analysis, where the demand for human expertise will likely increase.

4. Data Privacy and Security

As autonomous systems become more integrated into daily life, the vast amounts of data they generate and rely upon raise significant concerns about privacy and security. Self-driving cars, for instance, collect and process a wealth of data about their environment, user preferences, and driving habits. Similarly, AI-powered personal assistants store sensitive information about users' activities and conversations.

Challenges:

Data Security Risks: Autonomous systems, particularly those that rely on the internet and cloud services, are vulnerable to cyberattacks. Hackers could compromise these systems, causing them to malfunction or be used for malicious purposes.

Privacy Concerns: With the continuous collection of data, there is a risk that personal information could be misused, sold, or accessed by unauthorized parties. This is especially concerning for individuals who are concerned about surveillance and the erosion of privacy in a hyper-connected world.

Solutions:

Robust Cybersecurity Measures: To protect autonomous systems from cyber threats, developers must implement advanced encryption, firewalls, and intrusion detection systems. Regular security updates and patches are essential to keeping these systems secure from evolving threats.

Data Anonymization and Control: Implementing strong data anonymization practices can ensure that sensitive information is not linked to individuals without their consent. Additionally, giving users more control over their data, such as allowing them to opt in or out of data collection, can increase trust in autonomous systems.

Transparent Privacy Policies: Companies that develop autonomous systems must be transparent about how they collect, store, and use data. Clear privacy policies and user agreements that outline data usage can help users make informed decisions about their interactions with these technologies.

The journey towards fully autonomous systems is fraught with technological, ethical, legal, and societal challenges. While significant progress has been made, these unresolved issues must be addressed to ensure that autonomy can be safely and responsibly integrated into everyday life. By improving sensor reliability, developing ethical decision-making frameworks, fostering public trust, enhancing data privacy, and ensuring robust cybersecurity, the path to overcoming technological hurdles in autonomy can be cleared. As we move forward, it is essential for stakeholders—including governments, industry leaders, researchers, and the public—to collaborate in shaping a future where autonomous systems enhance human life while minimizing risks and ensuring accountability.

Chapter 37 Ensuring Human Oversight

The rise of autonomous systems is transforming a wide range of industries, from transportation and healthcare to manufacturing and entertainment. These systems, which include self-driving cars, AI-powered medical diagnostic tools, and automated supply chains, promise to revolutionize operations and improve efficiency. However, as autonomous systems grow more sophisticated and capable of making independent decisions, there is a pressing need to address the complex issues of accountability and human oversight.

The Challenge of Autonomous Systems

Autonomous systems are designed to operate independently, often using machine learning, artificial intelligence (AI), and other advanced technologies to make decisions without human intervention. This independence can provide significant advantages, such as reduced human error, cost savings, and enhanced precision. For instance, autonomous vehicles have the potential to reduce traffic accidents caused by human error, while AI in healthcare could enable faster, more accurate diagnoses.

However, this autonomy also raises several concerns, particularly in regard to accountability. When these systems make decisions that lead to unintended or harmful outcomes, questions arise about who is responsible for those actions. Should it be the developers who created the system? The operators who deployed it? Or the AI itself, which may have made an independent decision based on its programming? To ensure that these systems operate ethically and safely, it is essential to maintain a framework of human oversight and accountability.

The Importance of Human Oversight

Human oversight is essential for several reasons. First and foremost, human judgment is necessary to ensure that autonomous systems act in alignment with societal norms, legal frameworks, and ethical principles. While AI systems can process vast amounts of data and recognize patterns far beyond human capabilities, they lack the emotional intelligence, moral reasoning, and contextual understanding that humans bring to decision-making.

For example, autonomous vehicles rely on algorithms that process sensor data to make decisions about acceleration, braking, and steering. While these decisions may be based on real-time data, the vehicle's AI may not be capable of understanding the full context of a situation, such as the ethical implications of prioritizing one life over another in an emergency situation. A human operator or supervisor, however, can exercise judgment in cases where ethical dilemmas or unforeseen circumstances arise.

Moreover, human oversight ensures that autonomous systems remain aligned with human goals and values. As AI systems become more advanced, their decision-making processes become increasingly opaque, often referred to as the "black box" problem. Without human oversight, it can become difficult to understand how an autonomous system arrived at a particular decision. This lack of transparency can undermine trust in the system and hinder the ability to address errors or undesirable outcomes.

Mechanisms for Ensuring Accountability

There are several key mechanisms that can be employed to ensure human oversight and maintain accountability in autonomous systems.

1. Transparent Design and Development

Transparency in the design and development of autonomous systems is one of the first steps in ensuring accountability. This includes clear documentation of the algorithms, data sets, and decision-making processes used by the system. By maintaining transparency, developers make it possible to trace the actions of an autonomous system and identify the factors that influenced its decisions.

Transparency also involves ensuring that autonomous systems can be understood and interpreted by humans, even if those humans are not experts in AI or machine learning. One approach to achieving this is through explainable AI (XAI), a field of research focused on making machine learning models more interpretable and understandable. If an autonomous system can explain the rationale behind its actions, it becomes easier to assess its behavior and hold it accountable when things go wrong.

2. Human-in-the-Loop (HITL) Systems

Another important mechanism for ensuring accountability is the implementation of human-in-the-loop (HITL) systems. HITL refers to systems where humans remain actively involved in the decision-making process, either by monitoring the system or by directly intervening when necessary.

In the context of autonomous vehicles, for instance, HITL might involve a remote operator who can take control of the vehicle in emergency situations. Similarly, in autonomous healthcare systems, a human doctor or medical professional may oversee AI-generated diagnoses and intervene if necessary. These HITL systems help bridge the gap between autonomous decision-making and human judgment, ensuring that the system operates safely and ethically.

HITL systems can also be used to monitor AI performance over time and make adjustments based on real-world data. By keeping a human operator in the loop, these systems can adapt to unexpected circumstances and correct errors that may arise, ultimately ensuring better outcomes.

3. Ethical Frameworks and Regulations

To further ensure human oversight, autonomous systems should be designed and operated within the boundaries of established ethical frameworks and regulations. Governments and regulatory bodies have a critical role to play in ensuring that autonomous systems are subject to appropriate oversight and accountability measures.

For example, autonomous vehicles are already subject to regulatory standards in many countries, requiring them to meet safety protocols and pass rigorous testing before being allowed on the road. Similar regulatory frameworks are needed for other autonomous systems, such as healthcare technologies, robotics, and military applications.

In addition to regulatory oversight, ethical frameworks must be developed to guide the design and deployment of autonomous systems. These frameworks should address issues such as data privacy, bias, fairness, and transparency, ensuring that autonomous systems operate in ways that align with broader societal values. The ethical implications of autonomous decision-making should be considered at every stage of the system's development and deployment, and developers should be held accountable if their systems violate these ethical principles.

4. Liability and Legal Accountability

A key component of ensuring accountability in autonomous systems is determining who is legally responsible when things go wrong. As autonomous systems make more decisions on their own, it becomes increasingly difficult to assign blame when an incident occurs.

In traditional systems, accountability is often clear. If a person makes a mistake while driving a car, they are liable for any resulting damages. However, in the case of an autonomous vehicle, the situation is more complicated. If the vehicle causes an accident, is the manufacturer, the software developer, or the owner of the vehicle responsible?

One potential solution to this issue is to develop new legal frameworks that account for the unique characteristics of autonomous systems. For instance, manufacturers of autonomous systems could be held liable for design flaws or malfunctions, while operators may be responsible for ensuring that the system is functioning correctly and intervening if necessary.

The establishment of clear liability frameworks is essential to ensuring that autonomous systems remain accountable and that individuals and organizations are incentivized to design and operate these systems safely and responsibly.

5. Continuous Monitoring and Auditing

Even with robust human oversight, autonomous systems require continuous monitoring and auditing to ensure they remain accountable. This is especially important as systems evolve over time and learn from new data. Regular audits can help identify potential risks or biases in the system's behavior and address any issues before they lead to harm.

For example, in the case of AI-based hiring systems, continuous monitoring can ensure that the algorithms are not unintentionally discriminating against certain groups of applicants. Similarly, in autonomous vehicles, monitoring systems can ensure that the vehicle continues to operate safely and ethically as it encounters new situations on the road.

Auditing also serves as a mechanism for learning from mistakes and improving the system over time. By identifying where things went wrong, developers can refine the system's algorithms and decision-making processes, reducing the likelihood of future errors and enhancing the system's accountability.

The Role of Public Trust

Ultimately, ensuring human oversight and accountability in autonomous systems is not just a matter of legal and technical measures; it is also about building public trust. People must feel confident that autonomous systems are designed with their safety, privacy, and well-being in mind. This requires transparency, accountability, and a commitment to ethical principles.

To build trust, developers and organizations must engage with the public, policymakers, and other stakeholders to ensure that autonomous systems are aligned with societal values and that there are clear mechanisms for addressing issues when they arise. Public trust is crucial for the widespread adoption of autonomous systems, and it can only be achieved through a transparent, accountable, and ethically guided approach.

As autonomous systems continue to evolve and become more integrated into our daily lives, ensuring human oversight and maintaining accountability will be essential to their success. Transparent design, human-in-the-loop systems, ethical frameworks, legal accountability, and continuous monitoring all play critical roles in ensuring that these systems operate safely and ethically. By prioritizing accountability, we can ensure that autonomous systems serve humanity's best interests and mitigate the risks that come with their increasing autonomy.

Chapter 38 Interfacing Agentic AI with Humans

The evolution of Artificial Intelligence (AI) has witnessed rapid advancements, and one of the most profound developments is the rise of agentic AI—intelligent systems that can autonomously execute tasks and make decisions in dynamic environments. These agents, designed to possess a degree of autonomy and decision-making capabilities, hold enormous potential for transforming industries, healthcare, education, entertainment, and much more. However, as AI continues to integrate into various facets of human life, the key challenge becomes not just creating intelligent machines, but designing intuitive interaction models that bridge the gap between AI agents and human users. The seamless collaboration between agentic AI and humans hinges upon designing interfaces that allow for fluid, effective, and efficient communication.

This chapter explores the principles, challenges, and strategies involved in designing intuitive interaction models for interfacing agentic AI with humans. It focuses on the importance of creating user-friendly experiences that allow non-expert users to harness the power of AI while minimizing friction in interactions. The discussion will cover interaction types, multimodal interfaces, and the role of context in guiding agentic AI decisions. It will also address user trust, ethical considerations, and best practices for creating seamless collaborations between human and AI.

1. Understanding Agentic AI and Human Interaction

Agentic AI refers to AI systems that can make decisions, act autonomously, and exhibit behavior that appears purposeful. These agents might be simple chatbots or sophisticated systems like autonomous vehicles or virtual assistants, which must navigate complex, real-time environments and interact with humans in meaningful ways. Unlike passive AI systems that merely respond to commands, agentic AI has a degree of autonomy that allows it to act without direct human input. This autonomy, however, creates challenges in terms of how humans interact with these systems and how they can be effectively guided in decision-making processes.

Human-AI Interaction Models: Humans and AI need to collaborate in ways that allow humans to trust the AI's decisions and feel confident in its actions. For instance, an autonomous vehicle must communicate its intentions to passengers so they can understand and react accordingly. Similarly, a virtual assistant should be able to handle tasks with efficiency while also explaining its reasoning to users when necessary.

Interaction models between agentic AI and humans generally fall into three broad categories:

Command-based interaction: The user provides specific instructions, and the AI responds accordingly, often without further explanation or feedback.

Dialogue-based interaction: The AI communicates with the user through text, voice, or other means to perform tasks or provide information. This mode is often used in virtual assistants and customer service bots.

Collaborative interaction: Here, the AI works alongside the human, offering suggestions or taking actions autonomously, but within a framework where the human and AI share decision-making responsibility.

In all cases, the goal is to design a model that allows humans to interface with AI easily, efficiently, and intuitively.

2. The Importance of Intuitive Interfaces

An intuitive interface is one that is easy for users to understand and use without needing specialized knowledge or training. When it comes to agentic AI, intuitive interfaces are crucial for several reasons:

User Adoption: If AI systems are difficult to use or understand, people will resist incorporating them into their daily lives or workplaces. By designing intuitive interfaces, developers ensure that the AI is accessible to a broader audience.

Minimizing Cognitive Load: Human users often come with varying levels of technical expertise. A good interface reduces the cognitive load by offering easy-to-understand feedback, clear instructions, and predictable actions.

Reducing Errors: Clear and intuitive interactions can help users avoid errors and miscommunications with the AI. This is particularly important in high-stakes environments such as healthcare or transportation, where mistakes can have serious consequences.

3. Designing Interaction Models for Agentic AI

When designing interaction models for agentic AI, several key principles must be considered to ensure that the interface is intuitive and effective:

a) Context Awareness and Adaptability

One of the defining features of agentic AI is its ability to adapt to changing contexts. Context-awareness allows the AI to understand the situation in which it operates, making decisions based on relevant factors such as time, location, user preferences, and more. For instance, a smart home assistant could adjust its recommendations based on whether the user is at home or away, or a personal assistant could modify its actions based on calendar events and past behavior.

Designing context-aware interactions involves:

Understanding the environment in which the user is operating, including any external factors that might influence the interaction.

Customizing behavior based on previous interactions, preferences, and the user's needs at any given time.

When AI systems can "read" and respond to context, it enhances user experience, making interactions feel more personalized and natural.

b) Multimodal Interaction

Humans interact with the world in multiple ways, such as through sight, sound, touch, and gesture. AI systems that can accommodate these multiple modalities create more natural and intuitive experiences. For example, a voice-activated AI assistant can understand spoken commands, but if the assistant also has a visual interface that shows relevant information (such as a map or a list), users are more likely to feel comfortable engaging with it.

Multimodal interaction models involve:

Voice recognition and synthesis: Enables users to speak naturally with AI, allowing for hands-free and highly intuitive interactions.

Touch interfaces: For smartphones, tablets, and other devices, touch-based interfaces allow users to interact through gestures.

Visual and gesture recognition: Advanced AI can recognize hand movements, facial expressions, or even eye movements to understand user intent.

Text-based communication: Many AI systems still rely on text input and output, particularly in applications like chatbots.

By integrating these modalities, AI systems can offer a more holistic and adaptable user experience.

c) Transparency and Explainability

A common challenge with agentic AI is the opacity of decision-making. Many AI systems, especially deep learning-based models, can make decisions that are not easily understood by humans. For effective collaboration between humans and AI, it is crucial that users can trust the system. Therefore, the design of interaction models must incorporate explainability features, which provide insights into how and why the AI arrived at certain decisions.

Explanation can take many forms:

Justifications for decisions: When the AI makes a decision, it can explain its reasoning in simple terms. For example, an AI medical assistant might explain why it recommends a specific treatment based on a patient's medical history.

Visual explanations: Showing users how the AI arrived at a decision through a series of visual steps or graphs helps users understand the logic behind the AI's actions.

d) Trust Building

User trust is a critical element in designing successful human-AI interactions. If users do not trust the AI, they will be less likely to follow its recommendations or rely on its decisions. Building trust involves:

Consistency and reliability: The AI must perform as expected and consistently provide accurate results.

User control: Allowing users to make adjustments and modifications to the AI's behavior fosters a sense of control, which is crucial for trust.

Transparency: As mentioned above, providing insight into the AI's decision-making process helps users understand and trust its actions.

e) Emotion and Empathy

To enhance the interaction between humans and agentic AI, designers should consider the emotional aspects of the relationship. AI systems that can detect emotions (via voice tone, facial expression, etc.) and respond empathetically can create more meaningful connections. For example, an AI assistant that recognizes frustration in a user's voice and adjusts its tone or responses accordingly can lead to a more positive user experience.

4. Challenges in Designing Intuitive AI Interaction Models

Despite the potential for highly intuitive interaction models, there are several challenges that developers and designers face:

a) Understanding and Predicting User Behavior

Users are not always predictable. Their preferences, emotions, and interactions can vary widely. Designing a model that can adapt to these variations while maintaining usability is a significant challenge.

b) Balancing Autonomy and Control

Agentic AI systems are designed to act autonomously, but they must still offer users a sense of control. Striking the right balance between AI autonomy and user intervention is key to building trust and ensuring that the AI behaves in a way that aligns with user goals.

c) Ethical Considerations

The design of AI interactions must take into account the ethical implications of decision-making. For example, in a healthcare setting, AI systems must ensure that their decisions are aligned with ethical standards and respect for patient autonomy.

Interfacing agentic AI with humans in an intuitive and effective manner is a complex but crucial task for the continued development of AI systems that will work in concert with people. Designing interaction models that are context-aware, multimodal, transparent, and empathetic can greatly enhance the user experience and foster trust between humans and AI. As technology advances, the future of AI-human interaction will depend not only on the sophistication of the AI but also on how well it can communicate, understand, and adapt to human needs and behaviors. Through thoughtful design, AI has the potential to become a seamless and beneficial partner for users across a wide range of applications.

Chapter 39 Mitigating Environmental Impact

In the modern world, artificial intelligence (AI) has evolved to become one of the most transformative technologies, with applications spanning healthcare, finance, education, entertainment, and beyond. However, as AI systems continue to grow in complexity and power, their environmental footprint is becoming a growing concern. The energy demands of training and running AI models, particularly large deep learning systems, require substantial computational resources, which in turn have significant environmental consequences. With global efforts to reduce carbon emissions and mitigate climate change, the development of eco-friendly AI systems is more crucial than ever.

This chapter explores the environmental impact of AI, the importance of building eco-friendly AI systems, and strategies to mitigate the carbon footprint of AI technologies. It discusses the challenges and opportunities in making AI more sustainable, focusing on energy-efficient models, green data centers, renewable energy sources, and a more circular approach to AI hardware.

1. The Environmental Footprint of AI

AI's environmental impact primarily stems from the energy consumption required to train and deploy large-scale models. Deep learning, a subset of AI, has been particularly criticized for its immense energy requirements. Training a state-of-the-art deep learning model can consume hundreds or even thousands of kilowatt-hours of electricity, which translates into high carbon emissions, especially if the energy comes from non-renewable sources.

A 2019 study by researchers at the University of Massachusetts Amherst found that training a large natural language processing model (such as GPT-3) could emit as much carbon dioxide as five cars over their entire lifetimes. The carbon footprint of AI is not limited to model training; once deployed, AI models require continuous energy for inference, data storage, and maintenance. This means the environmental burden of AI is not a one-time concern but a long-term issue that requires ongoing efforts to address.

2. Energy Efficiency in AI Models

One of the key strategies to reduce the environmental impact of AI is to improve the energy efficiency of the models themselves. This can be achieved through various approaches, such as reducing the size and complexity of models, optimizing training algorithms, and improving the use of hardware.

2.1. Model Compression and Knowledge Distillation

Model compression is the process of reducing the size of an AI model without sacrificing its performance. This can be done by pruning unnecessary parameters, quantizing weights, or using techniques like knowledge distillation. Knowledge distillation involves training a smaller model (the student) to mimic the behavior of a larger, more complex model (the teacher). This allows the smaller model to achieve comparable performance with much less computational cost, leading to lower energy consumption during both training and inference.

2.2. Algorithmic Optimizations

Another way to enhance the energy efficiency of AI systems is to optimize the underlying algorithms. Researchers have been developing more efficient training algorithms that require fewer iterations or less data to achieve high accuracy. For example, adaptive optimization techniques like Adam and LAMB have been shown to improve the convergence speed of neural networks, thus reducing the computational resources required for training.

2.3. Transfer Learning and Pre-trained Models

Transfer learning, where a pre-trained model is fine-tuned on a specific task, has gained popularity as an energy-efficient alternative to training models from scratch. By leveraging pre-existing models, AI developers can significantly reduce the amount of data and computational power needed to develop effective solutions for new tasks, ultimately lowering the environmental cost.

3. Eco-Friendly Hardware and Data Centers

Even with energy-efficient algorithms and models, the physical infrastructure used to train and run AI systems can still contribute significantly to their environmental impact. The power consumption of data centers, which house the servers that perform AI computations, is a key factor in this.

3.1. Green Data Centers

A green data center is one that is designed to minimize its environmental impact through energy-efficient technologies, renewable energy sources, and innovative cooling techniques. Traditional data centers often rely on air conditioning systems to maintain optimal temperatures for servers, consuming significant amounts of energy. However, more eco-friendly alternatives, such as liquid cooling and free-air cooling, can drastically reduce energy consumption by harnessing natural environmental factors.

Furthermore, green data centers prioritize the use of renewable energy sources, such as solar, wind, and hydropower, to power their operations. Major tech companies like Google, Microsoft, and Amazon have committed to running their data centers entirely on renewable energy. Google, for example, has been carbon-neutral since 2007 and is on track to run all of its data centers on renewable energy.

3.2. Energy-Efficient Hardware

The energy efficiency of the hardware used in AI systems plays a critical role in reducing their environmental impact. Specialized hardware, such as Graphics Processing Units

(GPUs) and Tensor Processing Units (TPUs), are designed to accelerate machine learning computations and are often more energy-efficient than traditional CPUs. Moreover, custom-built AI chips optimized for specific tasks can provide significant performance improvements while consuming less energy.

In addition to using energy-efficient hardware, it is also essential to implement better hardware lifecycle management. Rather than discarding outdated equipment, tech companies can recycle or repurpose hardware to reduce e-waste and extend the life cycle of their components.

4. Sustainable AI in Practice: Case Studies and Innovations

Several companies and research initiatives are leading the way in building eco-friendly AI systems. These efforts highlight the potential for AI to be both powerful and sustainable.

4.1. Google's Sustainability Initiatives

As one of the leading tech companies, Google has committed to minimizing the environmental impact of its AI systems. In addition to powering its data centers with renewable energy, Google has invested in developing more energy-efficient AI algorithms. The company has also open-sourced some of its energy-efficient machine learning models, enabling other developers to benefit from these innovations.

Google has also created AI tools that help other industries become more sustainable. For example, its DeepMind division has worked on optimizing energy usage in data centers by using AI to predict and manage power consumption. This initiative has reportedly led to a 40% reduction in the amount of energy required to cool Google's data centers.

4.2. Microsoft's AI for Good

Microsoft has developed a program called "AI for Good" which leverages AI to address global sustainability challenges. One of its most notable initiatives is using AI to improve energy efficiency in buildings. Through the analysis of data from sensors embedded in smart buildings, Microsoft's AI models can predict when heating, cooling, and lighting systems should be adjusted to minimize energy consumption without sacrificing comfort.

In addition to these applications, Microsoft is also committed to achieving carbon neutrality by 2030. This includes reducing the energy consumption of its AI systems and offsetting the emissions from its operations.

5. Building a Circular Economy for AI

The concept of a circular economy, which focuses on reducing waste and reusing resources, is increasingly being applied to AI. In the context of AI, a circular approach could involve the recycling of hardware components, repurposing of data, and extending the life cycle of AI models and infrastructure.

5.1. Hardware Recycling and Repurposing

AI hardware, particularly GPUs and TPUs, can be expensive and energy-intensive to manufacture. To reduce the environmental impact, companies can prioritize the recycling and repurposing of hardware components. This not only reduces e-waste but also minimizes the need for new materials. Additionally, AI hardware that is no longer suitable for cutting-edge tasks can be repurposed for less resource-intensive applications, extending its lifespan and reducing waste.

5.2. Data Reuse and Model Sharing

Data is a critical resource in the development of AI models, and it is often collected from various sources to create large training datasets. However, creating new datasets can be energy-intensive, both in terms of data collection and processing. One solution is to reuse existing datasets across different projects and industries, reducing the need for redundant data collection. Similarly, sharing pre-trained models across organizations can help mitigate the need for retraining large models from scratch, saving energy and computational resources.

6. The Future of Eco-Friendly AI

As the AI industry continues to grow, it will be increasingly important to prioritize sustainability. The environmental challenges posed by AI are not insurmountable, but they require collaboration and innovation across the industry. By focusing on energy-efficient algorithms, green data centers, eco-friendly hardware, and circular economy practices, we can significantly reduce the environmental impact of AI systems.

In the coming years, it is likely that governments, regulators, and industry leaders will implement stricter environmental standards for AI development, incentivizing the use of sustainable technologies. Additionally, consumer demand for eco-friendly products and services will drive the adoption of more sustainable AI practices. Ultimately, the goal is to create AI systems that are not only powerful and effective but also responsible stewards of the planet's resources.

AI has the potential to shape a sustainable future, but it must first address its own environmental impact. Building eco-friendly AI systems requires a holistic approach that includes energy-efficient algorithms, green data centers, and a circular economy mindset for hardware and data. Through collaboration, innovation, and the adoption of best practices, the AI industry can help reduce its carbon footprint while continuing to drive technological advancements that benefit society.

Chapter 40 Preparing Society for Agentic AI

As artificial intelligence (AI) rapidly evolves, society is on the cusp of an era marked by the rise of agentic AI — autonomous systems capable of making decisions, learning from experiences, and performing tasks without human intervention. These intelligent systems are designed to be proactive, self-directed, and adaptive, rather than simply reacting to inputs from humans. While the potential benefits of agentic AI are immense, ranging from automation of complex tasks to the acceleration of innovation, there are significant challenges to overcome. One of the most pressing challenges is preparing both the public and the workforce for the shifts that agentic AI will bring.

This process requires thoughtful, proactive efforts to ensure that people not only understand the implications of these technologies but also acquire the necessary skills to thrive in an autonomous, AI-driven world. As the technology becomes more embedded in daily life, it is essential to consider how education and workforce training can support a smooth transition, while also addressing concerns around ethical, economic, and social impacts.

1. Understanding Agentic AI and Its Implications

Agentic AI refers to systems that operate with a level of autonomy, allowing them to make decisions and take actions without continuous human oversight. These systems are often powered by machine learning algorithms that allow them to adapt to new situations based on data, experience, and feedback. As AI systems become more capable, they will be entrusted with increasingly complex tasks across a wide range of industries, from healthcare and finance to transportation and manufacturing.

The impact of agentic AI on society will be profound. For instance, self-driving cars, which rely on autonomous decision-making, could radically transform the transportation sector, leading to improved efficiency and safety. In healthcare, AI-powered diagnostic tools could enhance medical decision-making, potentially saving lives and reducing errors. However, these advancements also come with concerns. As AI systems gain more autonomy, questions about accountability, transparency, privacy, and security will inevitably arise. Who is responsible when an autonomous system makes a wrong decision? How do we ensure that these systems are free from biases and designed in a way that aligns with human values?

Before addressing these concerns, it is important to lay a strong foundation for educating the public and the workforce about the implications of agentic AI. The primary goal is to foster awareness and understanding of the technology so that society can make informed decisions and effectively navigate the changing landscape.

2. Educating the Public on Agentic AI

Public education plays a critical role in preparing society for the age of agentic AI. While there is an increasing awareness of AI technologies, the general public's understanding of their complexities and potential societal implications remains limited. To ensure that individuals are equipped to engage with AI-driven changes, education efforts must focus on demystifying AI and fostering critical thinking.

2.1. Incorporating AI Education into School Curricula

One of the most effective ways to build public understanding is by integrating AI education into primary and secondary school curricula. Just as math, science, and language arts are considered foundational subjects, AI literacy should be treated as essential knowledge for the future. Children and young adults should be taught not only how AI works but also its ethical implications, potential risks, and benefits.

Curricula could include basic programming and computational thinking, alongside lessons on how AI systems are developed and deployed in the real world. Students could also explore the philosophical, ethical, and societal questions raised by AI, such as privacy, fairness, and the role of human agency in decision-making. By incorporating AI education from an early age, future generations will be better prepared to navigate a world where autonomous systems play an increasing role.

2.2. Public Awareness Campaigns

In addition to school-based education, public awareness campaigns can help bridge the knowledge gap for adults. These campaigns should focus on dispelling common misconceptions about AI and highlighting its benefits and challenges. Effective communication strategies will be crucial in making AI accessible and engaging to people from diverse backgrounds.

Media outlets, community centers, and public libraries can be valuable partners in delivering AI education. These platforms can host informational sessions, workshops, and discussions that provide accessible explanations of AI concepts. Moreover, collaboration with industry leaders, policymakers, and academic institutions can ensure that the information provided is accurate, timely, and relevant.

3. Preparing the Workforce for the Autonomous Era

While educating the public is vital, preparing the workforce for the autonomous era is equally important. As AI systems take over more routine and manual tasks, the nature of work will change, and many existing jobs may become obsolete. However, new roles will also emerge that require advanced skills in working with, managing, and developing AI systems. The key challenge is ensuring that workers are equipped with the skills needed to thrive in this evolving environment.

3.1. Lifelong Learning and Reskilling

The rapid pace of technological advancement necessitates a shift toward lifelong learning. As AI becomes more pervasive, workers must continuously update their skills to remain relevant in the job market. Governments, businesses, and educational institutions should collaborate to create accessible reskilling programs that provide workers with the opportunity to learn new skills and adapt to AI-driven changes.

Reskilling efforts could focus on both technical and non-technical skills. On the technical side, workers may need to learn how to interact with AI systems, use AI-powered tools, and even program and develop their own algorithms. Non-technical skills, such as emotional intelligence, creative problem-solving, and leadership, will also remain essential, as these are areas where AI is less likely to replace human workers in the near future.

Reskilling programs should be designed with flexibility in mind, offering courses that workers can take at their own pace, through online platforms or community-based learning hubs. By making learning opportunities more accessible, society can ensure that workers are empowered to embrace new roles and opportunities in the age of AI.

3.2. Industry-Specific Training Programs

While broad-based reskilling is essential, there will also be a need for industry-specific training programs that cater to the unique needs of different sectors. For example, healthcare professionals may need specialized training in how to use AI-driven diagnostic tools, while workers in logistics and transportation will require knowledge of autonomous vehicles and AI-powered supply chain management systems.

By focusing on industry-specific needs, training programs can ensure that workers have the practical knowledge and hands-on experience required to excel in their fields. Collaboration between businesses, academic institutions, and government agencies will be crucial in developing these targeted programs and ensuring that they align with the needs of the workforce and the job market.

3.3. Fostering an Ethical Mindset in the Workforce

As AI systems become more autonomous, workers will need to make ethical decisions regarding their use and deployment. It will be essential to foster an ethical mindset among those who develop, manage, and interact with AI systems. Ethical AI practices should be integrated into both technical and managerial training programs.

This includes teaching workers about the potential risks of AI, such as algorithmic biases, privacy violations, and the consequences of flawed decision-making. By instilling a sense of responsibility and ethics in AI-related roles, society can help ensure that AI systems are developed and used in ways that benefit all people and avoid unintended harm.

4. Addressing Societal Concerns and Ethical Considerations

As we prepare for the widespread adoption of agentic AI, it is essential to address societal concerns and ethical considerations. Public and workforce education must be complemented by strong regulatory frameworks and policies that ensure the responsible development and use of AI technologies.

4.1. Establishing Clear Regulations

Governments must play a key role in establishing clear regulations that govern the development, deployment, and oversight of agentic AI systems. These regulations should address issues such as data privacy, accountability, and transparency, ensuring that AI systems operate in ways that align with societal values.

Moreover, international cooperation will be necessary to ensure that AI standards are consistent across borders. AI systems do not recognize national boundaries, so global frameworks and agreements will be essential in addressing the ethical challenges posed by autonomous systems.

4.2. Involving Diverse Stakeholders

Preparing society for agentic AI requires input from a broad range of stakeholders, including ethicists, technologists, policymakers, business leaders, and the general public. Engaging diverse voices in the conversation will help ensure that AI development is guided by a variety of perspectives and that its impact on society is thoroughly considered.

Public consultation, open forums, and collaborative platforms can facilitate dialogue between stakeholders and help shape AI policy in ways that reflect the values and needs of society as a whole.

The advent of agentic AI promises to bring about transformative changes across all sectors of society. While these advancements present significant opportunities, they also raise important challenges that must be addressed. By prioritizing education and workforce preparation, we can ensure that individuals are equipped to thrive in the autonomous era. Through comprehensive AI education, reskilling initiatives, and ethical training, society can embrace the potential of agentic AI while mitigating its risks. By fostering a proactive and informed approach to AI, we can build a future where both humans and intelligent systems coexist and collaborate for the greater good.

Chapter 41 Philosophical Reflections on Agency

The concept of agency has long been a central topic in philosophy, often associated with human action, free will, and moral responsibility. Traditionally, agency refers to the capacity of an individual to act intentionally, to make decisions, and to initiate actions based on internal desires, intentions, and goals. It has been a focal point of discussions in ethics, metaphysics, and epistemology. However, with the advent of artificial intelligence (AI) and advanced machine systems, the concept of agency is undergoing significant reconsideration. Machines, which were once regarded as mere tools or extensions of human will, are now increasingly capable of performing tasks autonomously, making decisions based on data and algorithms, and even adapting to unforeseen circumstances. This raises important philosophical questions about the nature of machine agency, its implications for human agency, and the ethical considerations surrounding machines that act without direct human intervention.

1. The Nature of Agency

At its core, agency is typically understood as the capacity to act with intention and purpose. Philosophers have long debated the nature of this capacity, questioning whether it is exclusive to humans, or whether other entities, such as animals, artificial intelligences, or even non-human entities like corporations or nations, can also be agents. The traditional view of agency is closely linked to human consciousness and free will. For instance, Immanuel Kant argued that true agency is grounded in the autonomy of the will, the ability to act in accordance with rational principles rather than mere desires or external forces. For Kant, human agency is distinct because it is tied to moral responsibility—the capacity to act according to moral law and to be held accountable for one's actions.

However, as AI systems and machines become more sophisticated, these traditional notions of agency are increasingly being challenged. Can a machine have agency in the same way humans do? If so, what would that imply about our understanding of action, decision-making, and responsibility?

2. Machine Agency: A New Paradigm

The rise of AI and machine learning (ML) has introduced a new dimension to the concept of agency. Unlike traditional machines, which were designed to perform specific tasks under human control, modern AI systems can operate autonomously, making decisions based on complex algorithms and vast datasets. These systems can learn from experience, adapt to changing conditions, and optimize their behavior over time. In many ways, they exhibit behaviors that resemble those of human agents, such as problem-solving, decision-making, and even creativity.

Consider the example of a self-driving car. These vehicles are equipped with sensors, cameras, and algorithms that allow them to navigate roads, avoid obstacles, and make decisions in real time. While human operators may program and monitor these cars, they are capable of making decisions about how to respond to various driving scenarios without direct human intervention. This raises the question: can a self-driving car be considered an agent in the same way that a human driver is? The car is capable of autonomous action, but its actions are determined by pre-programmed algorithms and data inputs, rather than conscious intentions or moral reasoning. Is this enough to qualify the car as an agent?

Philosophical discussions about machine agency often draw distinctions between different types of agency. One important distinction is between "weak agency" and "strong agency." Weak agency refers to the ability of machines or systems to perform actions based on predefined rules, heuristics, or learning algorithms, without any true understanding of the consequences or ethical implications of those actions. Strong agency, on the other hand, would involve the capacity for autonomous decision-making based on subjective experience, moral reasoning, and the ability to make choices that reflect values or purposes beyond mere task completion.

At present, most machines possess weak agency—they can act autonomously, but their actions are still determined by human designers or external factors. However, as AI technology advances, it is possible that machines may begin to exhibit more complex forms of agency, blurring the lines between weak and strong agency.

3. Autonomy and Decision-Making

One key feature of agency is autonomy—the ability to make decisions independently of external control. Autonomy is a central component of human agency, as it is often associated with the freedom to choose one's actions and to pursue goals based on internal motivations and desires. But what does autonomy mean in the context of machines?

In the case of AI systems, autonomy can be understood as the ability of a machine to make decisions based on its internal programming and learning processes, without direct human oversight. This is particularly evident in systems that utilize machine learning, where an algorithm "learns" from data and adjusts its behavior accordingly. For example, an AI-powered recommendation system on a streaming platform can autonomously suggest content based on a user's past behavior, preferences, and patterns. While the algorithm's behavior is influenced by the data it receives, it operates without explicit human instructions at each step.

However, this type of autonomy is distinct from human autonomy in significant ways. Human autonomy is often linked to moral and ethical decision-making—choices that reflect our values, principles, and considerations of right and wrong. A machine, on the other hand, lacks intrinsic values or moral reasoning. Its "decisions" are the result of mathematical optimization and data processing, rather than conscious deliberation.

The ethical implications of autonomous machines are profound. If machines can make decisions independently, who is responsible for those decisions? If a self-driving car causes an accident, should the responsibility fall on the car's designers, the manufacturers, the passengers, or the machine itself? In this context, the concept of responsibility becomes increasingly complex, as it may not be clear whether the machine is merely carrying out its programmed instructions or whether it is truly acting as an autonomous agent.

4. Moral Agency and Ethical Considerations

The issue of moral agency is another critical consideration in the philosophy of machine agency. Moral agency refers to the capacity to act in accordance with moral principles and to be held accountable for one's actions. This capacity is central to human agency, as it underpins our ability to make ethical choices and to take responsibility for our actions. But can machines be morally accountable?

At present, machines are not considered moral agents in the same sense as humans. They do not possess the ability to reflect on their actions, to experience emotions such as guilt or remorse, or to understand the ethical implications of their decisions. A machine's "choices" are based on predetermined algorithms or learned patterns, not on an understanding of right or wrong.

Nevertheless, as AI systems become more sophisticated, the question of moral agency becomes more pressing. If a machine were to make decisions that have ethical consequences—such as allocating resources in a healthcare system or making judgments about criminal sentencing—how should we assign responsibility for those decisions? Should the designers of the machine be held accountable for the outcomes of the machine's actions, or should the machine itself be treated as a moral agent? These questions challenge traditional conceptions of moral responsibility and agency, as they force us to reconsider the nature of accountability in a world where machines are increasingly involved in decision-making processes.

5. The Future of Machine Agency

As AI technology continues to evolve, the concept of machine agency will likely undergo further transformation. While current machines are limited in their ability to act autonomously and make decisions, future developments may lead to machines that exhibit more advanced forms of agency, including the potential for moral reasoning and self-awareness. The advent of artificial general intelligence (AGI), which aims to create machines with human-like cognitive abilities, may push the boundaries of machine agency even further.

At that point, the philosophical questions surrounding machine agency will become even more urgent. If machines are capable of autonomous decision-making, moral reasoning, and self-reflection, how should we treat them? What rights, responsibilities, or obligations might humans have toward these machines? And how will the rise of machine agency reshape our understanding of human agency, free will, and moral responsibility?

Ultimately, the question of machine agency challenges us to rethink fundamental assumptions about what it means to be an agent. It forces us to confront the possibility that agency is not an exclusive domain of humans, but rather a broader phenomenon that may extend to machines, algorithms, and other forms of artificial intelligence. The implications of this shift are far-reaching, touching on issues of ethics, technology, and the future of human society.

In conclusion, the philosophical reflections on machine agency invite us to reconsider the nature of action, responsibility, and autonomy in a world increasingly shaped by artificial intelligence. As machines become more capable of autonomous decision-making, the traditional boundaries between human and machine agency will continue to blur, forcing us to rethink what it means to be an agent in the modern world.

Chapter 42 The Future of Work with Agentic AI

As the digital age continues to evolve, one of the most transformative forces impacting industries and the workforce is the rise of Agentic AI—autonomous technologies capable of making decisions, learning from their environment, and acting independently to achieve specific goals. This advancement is not just about the automation of tasks but the broader potential for machines to take on roles that were traditionally the domain of human workers. The future of work is being shaped by these technologies, presenting both opportunities and challenges as industries adapt to new realities.

Agentic AI refers to autonomous systems equipped with the ability to act as agents in a given environment, much like a

414

human would in a similar context. These systems use advanced machine learning algorithms, deep learning, and reinforcement learning to make decisions based on data inputs without direct human intervention. These AI agents can sense their environment, reason through complex scenarios, and execute actions aimed at achieving pre-defined goals. Unlike traditional AI, which requires human programming for every task, agentic AI has the capability to learn and improve from experience, making it highly adaptable to changing conditions.

For instance, in industries such as manufacturing, autonomous robots powered by agentic AI can detect inefficiencies in the production line, reconfigure processes, and optimize workflows without requiring constant human oversight. Similarly, in customer service, AI-driven chatbots are already taking over basic inquiries and even more complex interactions, learning from each exchange to better serve customers over time.

The Impact of Agentic AI on the Workforce

Displacement of Jobs

One of the most immediate and discussed consequences of the rise of agentic AI is the potential for job displacement. As machines become more capable of performing tasks that once required human intervention, industries ranging from transportation to healthcare, finance, and customer service may see a significant shift in labor demand. According to estimates from McKinsey Global Institute, automation could replace up to 30% of global jobs by 2030.

For example, in the automotive industry, autonomous vehicles powered by AI could eliminate the need for human drivers, potentially displacing millions of workers who rely on transportation and delivery jobs. In healthcare, AI-driven diagnostic tools could replace certain tasks performed by medical professionals, such as analyzing medical images or making treatment recommendations based on patient data.

While these shifts in the workforce will result in the loss of some jobs, they will also create opportunities for workers to engage in more complex and creative roles that cannot be easily automated. The key challenge will be to manage this transition, ensuring that displaced workers have access to the skills and resources necessary to thrive in a rapidly changing job market.

The Creation of New Roles

On the flip side, the rise of agentic AI will also lead to the creation of entirely new roles. While autonomous systems can take over routine tasks, they will still require human oversight and interaction. New jobs will emerge in areas such as AI programming, ethics, supervision, and system maintenance. Additionally, as more industries incorporate AI into their operations, professionals who can bridge the gap between AI technologies and business strategies will be in high demand.

For instance, data scientists and AI specialists will continue to be vital in developing and refining the systems that power agentic AI. Furthermore, human-AI collaboration will become a central feature of many industries. Rather than replacing workers entirely, AI could augment human capabilities, enabling individuals to focus on higher-level decision-making and creativity while the AI handles repetitive tasks.

Transformation of Workplaces

The very nature of workplaces will also undergo significant change as agentic AI is incorporated into daily operations. Many businesses will shift toward hybrid models, where human workers collaborate with AI to perform tasks. This collaboration will be most pronounced in industries where cognitive tasks—such as problem-solving, strategy development, and customer interaction—are central. In fields like law, finance, and marketing, agentic AI could be used to analyze large amounts of data and generate insights, which human workers can then use to make informed decisions.

The workplace itself may become increasingly decentralized as AI-enabled technologies allow remote work to be more efficient and widespread. Tools powered by AI will facilitate communication, project management, and collaboration across teams, even in virtual environments. Companies will likely embrace flexible working arrangements, allowing workers to interact with AI systems from various locations, further blurring the line between the office and home.

AI in Industry Transformation

Manufacturing and Supply Chains

In manufacturing, agentic AI is already beginning to revolutionize how products are designed, produced, and distributed. Autonomous robots, equipped with sophisticated sensors and AI algorithms, are capable of performing a range of tasks traditionally handled by human workers, such as assembly, inspection, and packaging. These robots can also detect and resolve issues in real-time, improving efficiency and reducing the potential for human error.

AI systems are also transforming supply chain management. By using predictive analytics and machine learning, AI can help businesses anticipate demand, optimize inventory levels, and make real-time adjustments to supply chain operations. This increases the speed of production, reduces costs, and allows businesses to be more responsive to market changes.

Healthcare and Medicine

In healthcare, agentic AI is poised to play an instrumental role in diagnostics, treatment planning, and patient care. AI-powered diagnostic tools are already being used to analyze medical images, detect early signs of diseases such as cancer, and predict patient outcomes. In the future, AI may even be capable of designing personalized treatment plans based on an individual's genetic profile, lifestyle, and medical history.

In addition, autonomous systems could assist in surgical procedures, reducing the risk of human error and improving the precision of operations. Robots already assist in minimally invasive surgeries, and advancements in AI could further enhance their capabilities, allowing them to perform complex surgeries autonomously under the guidance of human medical professionals.

Financial Services and Insurance

In the financial services industry, agentic AI is transforming everything from banking and investment to risk management and insurance underwriting. AI-driven algorithms can analyze vast amounts of financial data to identify investment opportunities, predict market trends, and even offer personalized financial advice to clients. These tools can automate routine tasks, such as processing loans or managing portfolios, freeing up human workers to focus on more strategic, high-value work.

In the insurance industry, AI is helping to streamline the claims process, assess risk more accurately, and detect fraudulent claims. Autonomous systems can process and evaluate insurance applications in real-time, reducing the time and cost associated with underwriting. Similarly, predictive analytics can help insurers anticipate future claims and develop more accurate pricing models.

As agentic AI becomes more integrated into the workforce, a host of ethical issues and challenges will arise. One of the most pressing concerns is ensuring that the deployment of AI systems is done responsibly and equitably. AI technologies, if not carefully managed, could exacerbate inequalities in the workforce, especially if certain groups are disproportionately displaced by automation.

Moreover, as AI takes on more decision-making roles, questions of accountability and transparency become critical. In industries like healthcare or criminal justice, where AI systems are making decisions that impact people's lives, it will be crucial to ensure that these systems are transparent, fair, and free from bias. There will be a need for strict regulations to govern how AI technologies are used, ensuring that they operate ethically and in the best interest of society.

Another challenge is the potential for job displacement. Governments, businesses, and educational institutions will need to work together to create upskilling and reskilling programs that help workers transition to new roles. This will require significant investment in education and training to ensure that the workforce is prepared for the changes ahead.

The future of work with agentic AI is both exciting and challenging. Autonomous technologies have the potential to reshape industries, streamline operations, and create new opportunities for innovation and creativity. However, the impact on the workforce cannot be overlooked. As AI takes on more complex and decision-making roles, industries must carefully manage the transition to ensure that workers are supported and equipped to thrive in a new economy.

The future of work will likely be one of collaboration between humans and machines, where AI handles repetitive tasks and augments human decision-making, allowing workers to focus on higher-order cognitive skills. By embracing these changes and preparing for the challenges ahead, industries can create a future where agentic AI enhances human potential, rather than replacing it.

Chapter 43 Ethical Dilemmas and Moral Questions

Ethical dilemmas and moral questions have been at the center of human existence for millennia. They challenge our understanding of right and wrong, good and bad, and often compel us to make difficult choices that reflect not only our values but also our broader societal norms. These unresolved challenges are pervasive, impacting personal decisions, professional conduct, scientific advancements, and public policies. They force us to examine the complexity of human behavior, the moral implications of our actions, and the sometimes contradictory nature of ethical principles.

Understanding Ethical Dilemmas

An ethical dilemma arises when a person faces a situation in which they must choose between two or more actions, each of which is morally acceptable, but each choice may lead to a different, sometimes conflicting, outcome. The crux of the dilemma is the inability to satisfy all moral values simultaneously. Ethical dilemmas often involve a conflict between duties, rights, and consequences, and there is often no clear right or wrong answer.

For example, the classic "trolley problem" presents a scenario where a person must choose between pulling a lever to divert a runaway trolley, killing one person to save five, or doing nothing, letting the trolley continue on its path and kill the five people. In this case, the ethical question revolves around utilitarianism—the greatest good for the greatest number—versus deontological ethics, which stresses the importance of individual rights and duties. Resolving such dilemmas requires not only rational reasoning but also deep moral reflection, often leading to more questions than answers.

The Role of Ethics in Decision Making

Ethical decision-making plays a crucial role in both individual and societal functioning. The decisions we make daily, from choosing whether to help a stranger to navigating professional conflicts, are all shaped by underlying ethical principles. In personal contexts, ethical considerations affect our relationships, how we treat others, and how we perceive justice. In professional settings, especially those involving health care, law, business, or technology, ethical standards ensure that actions are aligned with societal expectations of fairness, justice, and responsibility.

Despite its importance, ethical decision-making is often complicated by various factors, including cultural differences, personal biases, the pressure to conform to norms, and the inherent uncertainty of predicting outcomes. For instance, in a workplace setting, an individual may be forced to choose between following company policies that might negatively affect employees or acting against the policy to do what seems ethically right, such as advocating for a more humane treatment of workers.

Unresolved Ethical Challenges in Modern Society

In modern society, there are numerous unresolved ethical challenges that continue to spark debate and cause concern. As technology advances and global interconnectivity increases, these dilemmas often take on new dimensions, requiring fresh perspectives and innovative solutions. Below are some of the most pressing unresolved ethical questions of our time:

1. Artificial Intelligence and Automation

With the rapid development of artificial intelligence (AI) and automation, ethical concerns regarding the potential impact on jobs, privacy, and autonomy have become a significant topic of discussion. On one hand, AI promises to revolutionize industries, increase efficiency, and even solve complex problems such as climate change or disease prevention. However, the ethical dilemma arises when we consider the potential consequences of AI on human employment, as automation could render many jobs obsolete, leading to unemployment and economic inequality.

Another challenge is the issue of privacy. AI technologies such as facial recognition, predictive algorithms, and data mining can collect and analyze vast amounts of personal data, raising concerns about surveillance and the erosion of individual rights. There is also the risk of bias in AI systems, as they may inadvertently reflect and perpetuate societal inequalities.

2. Genetic Engineering and Designer Babies

The ethical implications of genetic engineering, particularly in the context of gene editing technologies like CRISPR, have raised significant moral questions. While the potential to eradicate genetic diseases and enhance human capabilities is promising, it also presents profound ethical challenges.

Should humans have the right to "design" their children, choosing traits such as intelligence, physical appearance, or even personality?

The concern lies in the potential for creating a class divide where only the wealthy can afford genetic enhancements, exacerbating existing social inequalities. Furthermore, the concept of "designer babies" raises questions about the natural course of human evolution and the potential unforeseen consequences of altering the human genome.

3. Climate Change and Environmental Responsibility

The ethical implications of climate change are both urgent and complex. Climate change poses a moral dilemma in terms of responsibility, particularly when it comes to the question of who should bear the brunt of the responsibility for addressing environmental degradation. Industrialized nations, which have historically contributed the most to global emissions, face the ethical challenge of compensating developing nations that are now most vulnerable to the impacts of climate change.

Furthermore, individuals are often faced with the ethical question of how to balance their consumption habits, such as choosing environmentally friendly products, while also considering economic constraints and personal convenience. These dilemmas highlight the tension between personal freedom and collective responsibility in addressing the global environmental crisis.

4. Medical Ethics and End-of-Life Decisions

Medical ethics has long been a domain where ethical dilemmas are prevalent. Issues such as euthanasia, assisted suicide, and the right to die continue to provoke intense debate. At the core of these dilemmas is the conflict between respecting individual autonomy—the right to make decisions about one's own life—and the moral obligation to preserve life.

In many countries, euthanasia and assisted suicide remain illegal, largely due to the belief that life is sacred and should be protected at all costs. However, advocates argue that individuals should have the right to die with dignity, especially in cases where they are suffering from terminal illness or extreme pain. This debate raises fundamental questions about the value of life, the rights of individuals, and the role of healthcare providers in end-of-life decisions.

5. Social Justice and Inequality

Social justice concerns, particularly related to race, gender, and economic inequality, remain at the forefront of ethical discussions. The unresolved ethical challenges here often involve questions of fairness, equality, and the redistribution of wealth and resources. Systemic inequality, whether based on race, gender, or class, perpetuates social divisions and denies certain groups access to opportunities, healthcare, education, and justice.

Efforts to address these issues, such as affirmative action or wealth redistribution policies, often raise ethical dilemmas regarding fairness and merit. For instance, should preferential treatment be given to historically marginalized groups, or should individuals be evaluated solely on their merit, irrespective of their background? The tension between equality of opportunity and equality of outcome is a complex issue that continues to challenge policymakers and ethicists alike.

6. The Ethics of Surveillance and Privacy

With the increasing implementation of surveillance technologies, from CCTV cameras to online data tracking, the ethics of privacy and individual freedom have come into sharp focus. Governments and corporations argue that surveillance is necessary for national security, public safety, and business interests. However, this raises ethical concerns about the balance between safety and personal privacy.

Surveillance may prevent crimes, but it can also lead to the infringement of civil liberties, creating a society where individuals are constantly monitored. The challenge lies in determining the appropriate level of surveillance, ensuring that it does not overreach and violate personal freedoms or disproportionately target certain groups.

Addressing Ethical Challenges

Addressing unresolved ethical challenges requires a multidisciplinary approach that incorporates insights from philosophy, sociology, law, psychology, and other fields. One key aspect of navigating ethical dilemmas is recognizing that there is rarely a one-size-fits-all solution. Ethical frameworks, such as utilitarianism, deontological ethics, virtue ethics, and care ethics, provide different perspectives on how to evaluate and approach these challenges.

Utilitarianism, for example, focuses on maximizing overall happiness and minimizing harm. This perspective may justify actions that benefit the majority, even if they cause harm to a minority. In contrast, deontological ethics emphasizes moral duties and rules, often prioritizing individual rights over outcomes. Virtue ethics focuses on character and the cultivation of moral virtues, while care ethics emphasizes empathy and the relationships that bind people together.

Ultimately, ethical dilemmas demand that individuals and societies make difficult decisions, often with incomplete information and competing interests. It is essential to engage in thoughtful reflection, open dialogue, and a commitment to justice when grappling with these challenges. As society continues to evolve, new ethical questions will emerge, and addressing them will require adaptability, compassion, and a strong moral compass.

Ethical dilemmas and moral questions are an integral part of human existence. They force us to confront difficult choices, weigh competing values, and reflect on our personal and collective responsibilities. From AI and genetic engineering to climate change and social justice, unresolved ethical challenges are central to the ongoing evolution of society. As we navigate these complex issues, it is essential to engage in critical thinking, empathy, and a commitment to ethical principles that uphold the dignity, rights, and well-being of all individuals. Addressing these dilemmas will require not only philosophical inquiry but also practical solutions that can balance competing moral demands and contribute to the greater good.

Chapter 44 Collaboration Between AI and Humanity

As artificial intelligence (AI) continues to advance at an exponential rate, the potential for collaboration between AI and humanity grows significantly. AI, with its incredible processing power, ability to analyze vast amounts of data, and potential to solve complex problems, can play an integral role in shaping a better future. However, the key to achieving this lies not in seeing AI as a threat but in leveraging its capabilities in partnership with human creativity, empathy, and judgment.

In this chapter, we will explore how AI and humanity can collaborate effectively, the benefits of such partnerships, the challenges they present, and the steps needed to build a harmonious relationship between these two forces.

The Role of AI in Shaping the Future

Artificial intelligence has already shown its immense potential across various industries. From healthcare and education to finance and entertainment, AI is streamlining processes, increasing efficiency, and unlocking new opportunities. For instance, in healthcare, AI-driven tools can analyze medical images more accurately than humans, enabling early detection of diseases like cancer. In education, AI can provide personalized learning experiences for students, adapting to their individual learning speeds and styles.

Additionally, AI is transforming industries such as agriculture, transportation, and manufacturing by optimizing supply chains, improving energy efficiency, and even reducing environmental impacts. Self-driving vehicles, for example, are expected to reduce traffic accidents and pollution, while AI-powered agricultural technologies help farmers increase crop yields with fewer resources.

Despite these promising advancements, AI is still in its infancy. While we have only scratched the surface of what is possible, the full potential of AI lies in its integration with human creativity and decision-making. This partnership can lead to breakthroughs that neither could achieve alone.

The Power of Human Creativity and Judgment

While AI can process vast amounts of data and identify patterns that might elude even the sharpest human minds, it lacks the ability to think creatively, feel emotions, or make ethical decisions. Human beings are uniquely equipped to combine logic with emotion, imagination with reason. We can intuitively understand social dynamics, interpret complex situations, and make judgments based on our values, something AI is far from capable of doing.

One of the greatest strengths of humanity is the ability to approach problems from a multidimensional perspective, incorporating values such as compassion, fairness, and justice into decision-making. For example, in the context of healthcare, while AI can suggest the most effective treatment based on a patient's medical history, it is human doctors who bring empathy, understanding, and ethical considerations to the table, ensuring that each patient receives personalized care.

Moreover, human creativity is boundless. It's humans who have created art, music, literature, and innovations that have changed the course of history. While AI can assist in the creative process, offering suggestions or generating new ideas, it cannot replace the deeply personal and cultural dimensions that human creativity embodies. The partnership between AI and humanity thus becomes a synthesis—AI provides the tools and data-driven insights, while humans provide the vision and direction.

Collaborative Benefits: Synergy Between AI and Humanity

The collaboration between AI and humanity has the potential to bring about numerous benefits across diverse fields. Below are a few key areas where this partnership can be particularly transformative:

1. Solving Global Challenges

AI holds the promise of solving some of the most pressing global challenges, from climate change to poverty and disease. For example, AI systems can model climate change patterns, predict natural disasters, and propose solutions for mitigating environmental damage. With human ingenuity, these AI models can then be used to inform policy decisions and guide global initiatives to combat climate change.

In addressing poverty, AI can help by analyzing economic data and identifying effective intervention strategies. AI can also aid in developing solutions for global food shortages by optimizing agricultural practices, reducing waste, and predicting supply chain disruptions.

Furthermore, in the fight against infectious diseases, AI has proven to be a valuable ally. The rapid development of vaccines for COVID-19, for instance, was accelerated by AI models that predicted the protein structure of the virus, enabling researchers to design effective vaccines more quickly. In partnership with scientists, AI can help uncover cures for other diseases that have long eluded treatment.

2. Enhancing Education and Learning

Education is one of the most powerful tools for shaping the future, and AI can be a valuable partner in enhancing the learning experience. Personalized learning platforms powered by AI can adapt to each student's pace, identify areas where they may be struggling, and provide tailored resources to help them succeed.

AI also opens up new opportunities for education in underserved areas. For instance, AI-powered tutoring systems can provide students with one-on-one assistance in regions with limited access to qualified teachers. In addition, AI can assist teachers in managing classrooms, identifying at-risk students, and tailoring lesson plans to suit the needs of diverse learners.

In this collaborative model, AI acts as a support system, enhancing the teacher's ability to reach and teach students effectively. Teachers, in turn, bring the human touch—guiding, mentoring, and fostering a love of learning.

3. Advancing Healthcare

The potential of AI to revolutionize healthcare is immense. By processing large datasets of medical records, AI can identify correlations and trends that humans might overlook, leading to more accurate diagnoses and better treatment plans. AI is also helping researchers develop new drugs and therapies by simulating molecular interactions and predicting the outcomes of clinical trials.

However, the true power of AI in healthcare comes when it works alongside human expertise. Doctors and medical professionals remain the decision-makers, bringing their clinical experience and ethical judgment to the process. AI can assist by offering insights and recommendations, but the final decisions about patient care are made by humans.

Additionally, AI can alleviate the administrative burden on healthcare providers, allowing them to focus more on patient care. AI-driven systems can manage scheduling, medical records, and billing, freeing up time for doctors and nurses to spend more time with patients.

4. Enhancing Creativity and Innovation

AI is already transforming creative fields like music, film, and design. By analyzing vast databases of creative works, AI can generate new ideas, recommend improvements, and help creatives overcome creative blocks. For example, AI algorithms can help musicians compose melodies, suggest lyrics, or even generate entire symphonies.

However, while AI can assist in the creative process, the human touch remains essential. Creativity is not just about producing new ideas—it is about connecting with people on an emotional level. The best works of art, music, literature, and design come from a place of deep human experience. AI can help unlock new possibilities, but it cannot replace the soul of human creativity.

In the collaboration between AI and humanity, the artist or innovator can use AI tools to experiment with new techniques, explore uncharted territory, and refine their work. Together, they can push the boundaries of creativity and innovation in ways that were once unimaginable.

Overcoming Challenges in AI-Human Collaboration

While the potential for AI-human collaboration is enormous, there are challenges that must be addressed to ensure a positive future. These include:

1. Ethical Considerations

AI has the potential to exacerbate existing inequalities if not properly managed. For example, if AI systems are trained on biased data, they may perpetuate discrimination in hiring, law enforcement, and lending practices. It is crucial that AI development incorporates ethical considerations from the outset, ensuring that AI systems are transparent, fair, and accountable.

Human oversight is vital in ensuring that AI is used ethically and responsibly. Establishing global guidelines for AI development and deployment, with input from diverse stakeholders, is crucial in creating a future where AI serves the common good.

2. Job Displacement and Economic Impact

The rise of AI has led to concerns about job displacement, as automation replaces certain tasks traditionally performed by humans. However, rather than fearing job loss, we should view AI as an opportunity to redefine work and create new roles that leverage human skills in conjunction with AI.

Upskilling and reskilling programs can help workers transition to new roles in industries where AI is used to augment human capabilities rather than replace them.

3. Security and Privacy

As AI becomes more integrated into our lives, issues of security and privacy will become increasingly important. AI systems can process vast amounts of personal data, raising concerns about how this data is used, protected, and shared. Strong cybersecurity measures and data privacy regulations will be necessary to protect individuals from potential misuse of AI technologies.

Building Partnerships for a Better Future

The collaboration between AI and humanity offers immense potential to create a better, more equitable, and sustainable future. By harnessing AI's capabilities in combination with human creativity, empathy, and ethical judgment, we can solve some of the world's most pressing challenges, improve our quality of life, and foster innovation in ways never before possible.

To ensure that AI benefits humanity, we must build this partnership with care, establishing ethical guidelines, promoting transparency, and ensuring that AI is used to complement rather than replace human workers. In doing so, we can create a world where both AI and humanity thrive together, unlocking a future that is brighter for all.

Chapter 45 Beyond Agency: The Next Frontier in AI

As artificial intelligence (AI) continues to advance at an exponential rate, the potential for collaboration between AI and humanity grows significantly. AI, with its incredible processing power, ability to analyze vast amounts of data, and potential to solve complex problems, can play an integral role in shaping a better future. However, the key to achieving this lies not in seeing AI as a threat but in leveraging its capabilities in partnership with human creativity, empathy, and judgment.

In this article, we will explore how AI and humanity can collaborate effectively, the benefits of such partnerships, the challenges they present, and the steps needed to build a harmonious relationship between these two forces.

The Role of AI in Shaping the Future

Artificial intelligence has already shown its immense potential across various industries. From healthcare and education to finance and entertainment, AI is streamlining processes, increasing efficiency, and unlocking new opportunities. For instance, in healthcare, AI-driven tools can analyze medical images more accurately than humans, enabling early detection of diseases like cancer. In education, AI can provide personalized learning experiences for students, adapting to their individual learning speeds and styles.

Additionally, AI is transforming industries such as agriculture, transportation, and manufacturing by optimizing supply chains, improving energy efficiency, and even reducing environmental impacts. Self-driving vehicles, for example, are expected to reduce traffic accidents and pollution, while AI-powered agricultural technologies help farmers increase crop yields with fewer resources.

Despite these promising advancements, AI is still in its infancy. While we have only scratched the surface of what is possible, the full potential of AI lies in its integration with human creativity and decision-making. This partnership can lead to breakthroughs that neither could achieve alone.

The Power of Human Creativity and Judgment

While AI can process vast amounts of data and identify patterns that might elude even the sharpest human minds, it lacks the ability to think creatively, feel emotions, or make ethical decisions. Human beings are uniquely equipped to combine logic with emotion, imagination with reason. We can intuitively understand social dynamics, interpret complex situations, and make judgments based on our values, something AI is far from capable of doing.

One of the greatest strengths of humanity is the ability to approach problems from a multidimensional perspective, incorporating values such as compassion, fairness, and justice into decision-making. For example, in the context of healthcare, while AI can suggest the most effective treatment based on a patient's medical history, it is human doctors who bring empathy, understanding, and ethical considerations to the table, ensuring that each patient receives personalized care.

Moreover, human creativity is boundless. It's humans who have created art, music, literature, and innovations that have changed the course of history. While AI can assist in the creative process, offering suggestions or generating new ideas, it cannot replace the deeply personal and cultural dimensions that human creativity embodies. The partnership between AI and humanity thus becomes a synthesis—AI provides the tools and data-driven insights, while humans provide the vision and direction.

Collaborative Benefits: Synergy Between AI and Humanity

The collaboration between AI and humanity has the potential to bring about numerous benefits across diverse fields. Below are a few key areas where this partnership can be particularly transformative:

1. Solving Global Challenges

AI holds the promise of solving some of the most pressing global challenges, from climate change to poverty and disease. For example, AI systems can model climate change patterns, predict natural disasters, and propose solutions for mitigating environmental damage. With human ingenuity, these AI models can then be used to inform policy decisions and guide global initiatives to combat climate change.

In addressing poverty, AI can help by analyzing economic data and identifying effective intervention strategies. AI can also aid in developing solutions for global food shortages by optimizing agricultural practices, reducing waste, and predicting supply chain disruptions.

Furthermore, in the fight against infectious diseases, AI has proven to be a valuable ally. The rapid development of vaccines for COVID-19, for instance, was accelerated by AI models that predicted the protein structure of the virus, enabling researchers to design effective vaccines more quickly. In partnership with scientists, AI can help uncover cures for other diseases that have long eluded treatment.

2. Enhancing Education and Learning

Education is one of the most powerful tools for shaping the future, and AI can be a valuable partner in enhancing the learning experience. Personalized learning platforms powered by AI can adapt to each student's pace, identify areas where they may be struggling, and provide tailored resources to help them succeed.

AI also opens up new opportunities for education in underserved areas. For instance, AI-powered tutoring systems can provide students with one-on-one assistance in regions with limited access to qualified teachers. In addition, AI can assist teachers in managing classrooms, identifying at-risk students, and tailoring lesson plans to suit the needs of diverse learners.

In this collaborative model, AI acts as a support system, enhancing the teacher's ability to reach and teach students effectively. Teachers, in turn, bring the human touch—guiding, mentoring, and fostering a love of learning.

3. Advancing Healthcare

The potential of AI to revolutionize healthcare is immense. By processing large datasets of medical records, AI can identify correlations and trends that humans might overlook, leading to more accurate diagnoses and better treatment plans. AI is also helping researchers develop new drugs and therapies by simulating molecular interactions and predicting the outcomes of clinical trials.

However, the true power of AI in healthcare comes when it works alongside human expertise. Doctors and medical professionals remain the decision-makers, bringing their clinical experience and ethical judgment to the process. AI can assist by offering insights and recommendations, but the final decisions about patient care are made by humans.

Additionally, AI can alleviate the administrative burden on healthcare providers, allowing them to focus more on patient care. AI-driven systems can manage scheduling, medical records, and billing, freeing up time for doctors and nurses to spend more time with patients.

4. Enhancing Creativity and Innovation

AI is already transforming creative fields like music, film, and design. By analyzing vast databases of creative works, AI can generate new ideas, recommend improvements, and help creatives overcome creative blocks. For example, AI algorithms can help musicians compose melodies, suggest lyrics, or even generate entire symphonies.

However, while AI can assist in the creative process, the human touch remains essential. Creativity is not just about producing new ideas—it is about connecting with people on an emotional level. The best works of art, music, literature, and design come from a place of deep human experience. AI can help unlock new possibilities, but it cannot replace the soul of human creativity.

In the collaboration between AI and humanity, the artist or innovator can use AI tools to experiment with new techniques, explore uncharted territory, and refine their work. Together, they can push the boundaries of creativity and innovation in ways that were once unimaginable.

Overcoming Challenges in AI-Human Collaboration

While the potential for AI-human collaboration is enormous, there are challenges that must be addressed to ensure a positive future. These include:

1. Ethical Considerations

AI has the potential to exacerbate existing inequalities if not properly managed. For example, if AI systems are trained on biased data, they may perpetuate discrimination in hiring, law enforcement, and lending practices. It is crucial that AI development incorporates ethical considerations from the outset, ensuring that AI systems are transparent, fair, and accountable.

Human oversight is vital in ensuring that AI is used ethically and responsibly. Establishing global guidelines for AI development and deployment, with input from diverse stakeholders, is crucial in creating a future where AI serves the common good.

2. Job Displacement and Economic Impact

The rise of AI has led to concerns about job displacement, as automation replaces certain tasks traditionally performed by humans. However, rather than fearing job loss, we should view AI as an opportunity to redefine work and create new roles that leverage human skills in conjunction with AI. Upskilling and reskilling programs can help workers transition to new roles in industries where AI is used to augment human capabilities rather than replace them.

3. Security and Privacy

As AI becomes more integrated into our lives, issues of security and privacy will become increasingly important. AI systems can process vast amounts of personal data, raising concerns about how this data is used, protected, and shared. Strong cybersecurity measures and data privacy regulations will be necessary to protect individuals from potential misuse of AI technologies.

Conclusion: Building Partnerships for a Better Future

The collaboration between AI and humanity offers immense potential to create a better, more equitable, and sustainable future. By harnessing AI's capabilities in combination with human creativity, empathy, and ethical judgment, we can solve some of the world's most pressing challenges, improve our quality of life, and foster innovation in ways never before possible.

To ensure that AI benefits humanity, we must build this partnership with care, establishing ethical guidelines, promoting transparency, and ensuring that AI is used to complement rather than replace human workers. In doing so, we can create a world where both AI and humanity thrive together, unlocking a future that is brighter for all.

Chapter 46 Beyond Agency: The Next Frontier in AI

From recommendation algorithms to autonomous vehicles, AI has redefined what machines can do. However, as we stand on the cusp of new advancements, the conversation is shifting from "What can AI do?" to "What should AI do?" This question underscores the need to explore the next frontier of AI: moving beyond agency to create systems that harmonize with human creativity and judgment while overcoming inherent challenges in AI-human collaboration.

The Role of AI in Shaping the Future

AI's role in shaping the future cannot be overstated. Its capabilities extend far beyond automation; it enables solutions to problems that were previously insurmountable. In healthcare, AI-driven diagnostic tools are improving patient outcomes by detecting diseases earlier and with greater accuracy. In education, adaptive learning platforms provide personalized experiences tailored to individual needs, democratizing access to quality instruction. Furthermore, AI is pivotal in tackling global challenges such as climate change, through predictive models for weather patterns and optimization of energy consumption.

The potential of AI lies in its ability to analyze vast amounts of data, identify patterns, and make predictions at speeds and scales far beyond human capability. This prowess positions AI as a critical partner in decision-making processes across industries. For example, financial institutions use AI to detect fraudulent transactions in real time, while urban planners rely on AI to design smarter, more sustainable cities.

However, the transformative potential of AI also raises ethical and practical questions. As AI systems become more autonomous, how do we ensure they align with human values? What safeguards can be implemented to prevent misuse? These questions highlight the dual role of AI as both a tool and a decision-maker, making its integration into society a matter of profound importance.

The Power of Human Creativity and Judgment

Despite the extraordinary capabilities of AI, it is essential to recognize the unique power of human creativity and judgment. Machines excel at processing information and identifying correlations, but they lack the contextual understanding, emotional intelligence, and moral reasoning that underpin human decision-making. Creativity—the ability to generate novel ideas, art, and solutions—remains a distinctly human trait. Similarly, judgment, which involves weighing complex factors and making nuanced decisions, is an area where humans surpass even the most advanced AI systems.

Human creativity drives innovation. It was human ingenuity that envisioned AI in the first place, crafting algorithms that mimic cognitive functions. It is also human creativity that continues to push the boundaries of what AI can achieve, exploring its applications in fields as diverse as neuroscience and entertainment. From composing symphonies to designing cutting-edge technologies, humans infuse their creations with cultural, historical, and ethical dimensions that machines cannot replicate.

Judgment is equally crucial, particularly in scenarios where decisions carry significant moral or ethical implications. Consider autonomous vehicles: while AI can process data to make split-second driving decisions, it cannot yet navigate the moral dilemmas involved in unavoidable accidents. Should the vehicle prioritize the safety of its passengers over pedestrians? Such questions require human input to define the ethical frameworks within which AI operates.

The interplay between AI and human judgment is not about competition but collaboration. By leveraging the computational power of AI and the creative and moral faculties of humans, we can address complex challenges more effectively. For example, in medicine, AI can assist doctors by analyzing imaging data to identify anomalies, while the final diagnosis and treatment plan remain under the purview of the physician, ensuring a holistic approach to patient care.

Overcoming Challenges in AI-Human Collaboration

While the synergy between AI and human intelligence holds immense promise, realizing this potential requires overcoming significant challenges. These challenges can be broadly categorized into technical, ethical, and societal dimensions.

1. Technical Challenges

The development of AI systems that can seamlessly integrate with human workflows is a daunting task. One major challenge is creating algorithms that are not only accurate but also interpretable. Many AI models, particularly deep learning systems, operate as "black boxes," making it difficult to understand how they arrive at specific decisions. This lack of transparency can erode trust and limit adoption.

Another technical hurdle is the bias inherent in AI systems. Since AI learns from historical data, it often inherits and amplifies the biases present in those datasets. For example, facial recognition systems have been shown to perform poorly on individuals with darker skin tones due to biased training data. Addressing these biases requires diverse datasets and rigorous testing to ensure fairness and inclusivity.

2. Ethical Challenges

AI's ability to make decisions raises profound ethical questions. How do we define the values that guide AI systems? Who is accountable when an AI system makes a mistake? These questions are particularly pressing in areas like criminal justice, where AI tools are used for predictive policing and sentencing recommendations. Without careful oversight, such applications risk perpetuating systemic inequalities.

Privacy is another critical concern. AI systems often rely on vast amounts of personal data to function effectively, raising questions about how this data is collected, stored, and used. Striking a balance between innovation and individual privacy rights is essential to maintain public trust.

3. Societal Challenges

The integration of AI into society has far-reaching implications for employment and education. While AI creates new opportunities, it also disrupts traditional job markets, particularly in roles involving routine tasks. Preparing the workforce for this transition requires a focus on reskilling and upskilling, emphasizing skills that complement AI, such as critical thinking, creativity, and emotional intelligence.

Moreover, the digital divide—the gap between those with access to AI technologies and those without—risks exacerbating existing inequalities. Ensuring equitable access to AI tools and education is essential to prevent a widening disparity between developed and developing regions.

4. Building Trust and Collaboration

Fostering trust in AI systems is crucial for effective collaboration. Transparency, accountability, and ethical governance are key components in building this trust. One approach is to involve diverse stakeholders in the design and deployment of AI systems, including ethicists, sociologists, and end-users. This collaborative approach ensures that AI systems reflect a broad spectrum of perspectives and values.

Additionally, creating user-friendly interfaces that facilitate interaction between humans and AI is vital. AI systems should be designed to augment human capabilities rather than replace them, emphasizing collaboration over automation. For instance, in customer service, AI chatbots can handle routine inquiries, allowing human agents to focus on complex or emotionally sensitive interactions.

The next frontier in AI is not merely about advancing technology but about redefining the relationship between humans and machines. By leveraging the strengths of both, we can create systems that enhance human creativity and judgment while addressing the challenges inherent in AI-human collaboration. This requires a holistic approach that prioritizes ethical considerations, fosters trust, and emphasizes inclusivity.

As we move beyond agency, the future of AI lies in its ability to serve as a true partner to humanity. By embracing this partnership, we can unlock unprecedented opportunities to solve global challenges, enrich human experiences, and build a more equitable and sustainable world. The journey ahead is not without obstacles, but with a shared vision and collaborative effort, we can navigate this uncharted territory and realize the full potential of AI in shaping our collective future.

Chapter 47 The Evolution of Autonomous Systems

The journey of autonomous systems began with humanity's quest to create machines capable of performing tasks without direct human intervention. The term "autonomous system" encompasses a broad spectrum of technologies, from automated machinery to sophisticated artificial intelligence (AI)-driven robots. Understanding the historical trajectory of autonomous systems reveals the foundation upon which modern innovations are built.

Early Concepts and Foundations

The idea of creating self-operating machines dates back to antiquity. Ancient civilizations like the Greeks and Egyptians envisioned mechanical devices that could mimic human actions. The Greek engineer Hero of Alexandria designed primitive automata powered by steam and water pressure. These devices, while rudimentary, showcased early efforts to create machines that could function independently within a specific scope.

The Industrial Revolution marked a significant leap forward. The invention of automated looms and steam engines introduced the concept of mechanization—machines performing repetitive tasks more efficiently than humans. While these were not truly autonomous, they laid the groundwork for the automation of labor-intensive processes.

The Rise of Computing and Robotics

The 20th century saw the advent of computing, which transformed the capabilities of machines. Alan Turing's theoretical work on computation in the 1930s and the development of early computers in the 1940s enabled the creation of programmable machines. These machines could follow pre-set instructions, marking a shift from mechanical automation to digital autonomy.

In the 1950s and 1960s, robotics emerged as a distinct field. General Motors deployed the first industrial robot, Unimate, on its assembly line in 1961. This marked the beginning of autonomous systems in manufacturing, where robots could perform tasks like welding and material handling without human supervision.

From Automation to Autonomy

The development of artificial intelligence (AI) in the mid-20th century propelled the evolution from automation to autonomy. Early AI systems, like the Logic Theorist (1956) and ELIZA (1964), demonstrated that machines could mimic certain aspects of human reasoning and communication. As AI algorithms became more sophisticated, autonomous systems gained the ability to adapt to dynamic environments and make decisions based on real-time data.

The late 20th century saw the integration of sensors, actuators, and control systems, enabling machines to interact with their surroundings. Technologies like GPS and early forms of machine learning further enhanced the autonomy of systems, setting the stage for the advanced applications we see today.

Current Trends and Future Directions

Autonomous systems have reached a level of complexity and capability unimaginable just a few decades ago. Today, they are embedded in various aspects of daily life and are at the forefront of technological innovation. Examining current trends and projecting future directions offers insight into the potential of these systems.

Current Trends

Artificial Intelligence and Machine Learning Modern autonomous systems rely heavily on AI and machine learning. Techniques like deep learning enable systems to process vast amounts of data, recognize patterns, and make informed decisions. Autonomous vehicles, for instance, use neural networks to interpret sensor data and navigate complex environments.

Edge Computing and IoT Integration Edge computing allows autonomous systems to process data locally, reducing latency and dependence on centralized servers. When combined with the Internet of Things (IoT), autonomous systems can communicate and collaborate in real-time. For example, smart factories utilize interconnected robots and sensors to optimize production processes.

Human-Machine Collaboration The trend toward collaborative robots, or cobots, highlights the growing emphasis on human-machine interaction. These systems are designed to work alongside humans, enhancing productivity and safety in industries such as healthcare and manufacturing.

Ethical and Regulatory Considerations As autonomous systems become more prevalent, questions about ethics, accountability, and regulation have emerged. Governments and organizations are working to establish frameworks that ensure the safe and responsible deployment of these technologies.

Future Directions

Autonomous Vehicles The development of fully autonomous vehicles is a key focus area. Advances in sensor technology, AI, and connectivity are bringing us closer to achieving Level 5 autonomy, where vehicles can operate without any human intervention.

Personalized Autonomous Systems Future autonomous systems will be tailored to individual needs. Smart home assistants, wearable health monitors, and personalized learning platforms are just a few examples of systems designed to adapt to users' preferences and behaviors.

Swarm Intelligence Inspired by nature, swarm intelligence involves the collective behavior of decentralized systems. Autonomous drones and robots operating as coordinated swarms could revolutionize fields like agriculture, disaster response, and military operations.

Space Exploration Autonomous systems are critical for exploring distant planets and moons. NASA's Mars rovers and future missions to the outer solar system rely on autonomous systems capable of operating in remote and harsh environments.

Integration with Emerging Technologies

The convergence of autonomous systems with technologies like quantum computing, 5G, and blockchain could unlock unprecedented capabilities. These integrations will enable faster decision-making, enhanced security, and greater scalability.

Autonomous Systems in Various Industries

Autonomous systems are transforming industries by improving efficiency, reducing costs, and enabling new possibilities. Here's an overview of their impact across key sectors:

Manufacturing

The manufacturing industry has long been a leader in adopting autonomous systems. Robots equipped with AI and vision systems can perform intricate tasks like assembling electronics and inspecting quality. Smart factories leverage IoT and autonomous systems to achieve real-time monitoring and adaptive production processes, minimizing downtime and waste.

Transportation and Logistics

Autonomous systems are revolutionizing transportation and logistics. Self-driving trucks and drones are streamlining delivery operations, while automated warehouses use robotic systems for inventory management and order fulfillment. These innovations enhance supply chain efficiency and reduce environmental impact by optimizing routes and resource usage.

Healthcare

In healthcare, autonomous systems are playing a vital role in diagnostics, treatment, and patient care. Robotic surgical systems, like the da Vinci Surgical System, allow for minimally invasive procedures with greater precision. AI-powered diagnostic tools analyze medical imaging to detect diseases at early stages, while autonomous robots assist in hospital logistics, such as delivering medications and cleaning rooms.

Agriculture

Autonomous systems are driving the transformation of agriculture through precision farming. Drones and autonomous tractors equipped with sensors and AI enable farmers to monitor crop health, optimize irrigation, and apply fertilizers more efficiently. These technologies help increase yield while minimizing environmental impact.

Energy

In the energy sector, autonomous systems are being used for monitoring and maintaining infrastructure. Drones inspect power lines and pipelines, while underwater robots assess offshore oil rigs. Autonomous systems also optimize renewable energy production, such as adjusting wind turbine angles to maximize efficiency.

Retail

Autonomous systems are enhancing the retail experience through automation and personalization. Self-checkout systems, inventory robots, and AI-powered recommendation engines streamline operations and improve customer satisfaction. Autonomous delivery robots are also emerging as a solution for last-mile logistics.

Defense and Security

The defense industry leverages autonomous systems for surveillance, reconnaissance, and combat operations.

Unmanned aerial vehicles (UAVs) and autonomous submarines provide strategic advantages by reducing risk to human operators. In security, AI-driven systems monitor video feeds, detect anomalies, and respond to threats in real-time.

Entertainment and Media

Autonomous systems are reshaping entertainment and media production. AI-generated content, such as virtual actors and procedurally generated environments, is becoming more prevalent. Autonomous drones are also used for filming dynamic scenes, offering perspectives previously unattainable.

The evolution of autonomous systems represents a remarkable journey of technological progress. From ancient automata to today's AI-powered machines, these systems have continually redefined what is possible. Current trends in AI, IoT, and human-machine collaboration, coupled with advancements across industries, showcase the transformative potential of autonomous systems. Looking to the future, their integration with emerging technologies promises to unlock new possibilities, paving the way for a world where autonomy enhances efficiency, safety, and quality of life.

Chapter 48 The Intersection of AI and Human Emotions

Emotional intelligence (EI) in AI refers to the system's ability to recognize, understand, and appropriately respond to human emotions. While traditional AI focused on solving logical and analytical problems, advancements in machine learning, natural language processing (NLP), and affective computing have enabled AI to process complex emotional data.

Affective computing is a key driver behind emotional intelligence in AI. It involves the development of systems that can detect emotions through facial expressions, voice modulation, text sentiment, and physiological signals such as heart rate or skin conductivity. For instance, AI-powered tools like facial recognition software can analyze micro-expressions to gauge an individual's emotional state. Similarly,

NLP algorithms can interpret sentiment in text or speech to understand mood or intent.

AI's ability to recognize emotions is largely dependent on data training. Machine learning models are exposed to vast datasets of labeled emotional cues, enabling them to identify patterns and make predictions. For example, sentiment analysis algorithms are trained on annotated text data to classify emotions like happiness, sadness, anger, or fear. However, the effectiveness of these models relies on the diversity and quality of the training data, as biases in datasets can lead to skewed interpretations of emotions.

The development of emotional intelligence in AI serves various purposes. In customer service, chatbots and virtual assistants equipped with EI can provide empathetic responses to frustrated users, improving user satisfaction. In healthcare, emotionally intelligent AI can assist therapists by analyzing patients' emotional states or offering companionship to individuals facing loneliness. However, achieving truly human-like emotional intelligence in AI remains a significant challenge, as emotions are deeply subjective and context-dependent.

The Role of AI in Human-AI Emotional Interaction

AI's role in human emotional interaction is expanding rapidly, affecting domains ranging from personal relationships to professional environments. Emotional interaction between humans and AI involves two primary components: perception and response.

Perception: AI's ability to perceive emotions enhances communication and builds trust. Virtual assistants like Siri, Alexa, and Google Assistant increasingly incorporate tone recognition to modify their responses based on user emotions. In mental health applications, AI-driven tools analyze user inputs for signs of stress, anxiety, or depression, providing support or escalating concerns to professionals if necessary.

Response: Beyond recognizing emotions, AI systems are designed to simulate empathy. For instance, Replika, a chatbot designed for companionship, uses machine learning to engage users in emotionally resonant conversations. Similarly, AI therapists like Woebot offer cognitive behavioral therapy (CBT) techniques tailored to the user's emotional state, blending emotional intelligence with practical guidance.

AI's presence in human emotional interaction extends into entertainment, where emotionally responsive characters in video games or movies adapt to player or viewer behavior. In education, emotionally intelligent AI tutors can identify when a student is frustrated or confused and adjust teaching methods accordingly.

However, AI's involvement in emotional interaction is not without limitations. The absence of genuine feelings in AI systems means that their responses, although contextually accurate, lack the authenticity of human empathy. This gap can lead to a paradox where users might feel comforted by an AI's emotional response but simultaneously recognize its artificiality.

Ethical and Social Considerations

The integration of emotional intelligence in AI raises profound ethical and social questions. As AI becomes more adept at understanding and simulating emotions, its impact on society must be carefully scrutinized.

Privacy Concerns: Emotionally intelligent AI often relies on sensitive data, including facial expressions, voice recordings, and biometric signals. This level of data collection poses significant privacy risks. Users may not fully understand how their emotional data is being collected, stored, or used, leading to potential misuse or breaches. For instance, organizations could exploit emotional data for manipulative advertising or surveillance.

Bias and Fairness: AI models trained on biased datasets may misinterpret emotions, particularly across different cultural or demographic groups. An AI system might associate certain facial expressions or tones of voice with specific emotions inaccurately, leading to unfair treatment or discrimination. Ensuring fairness requires diverse and representative datasets, along with continuous monitoring for biases in AI systems.

Emotional Manipulation: The ability of AI to recognize and simulate emotions could be exploited for manipulation. For instance, emotionally intelligent AI could be used in advertising to exploit users' vulnerabilities by tailoring emotionally charged messages. In social media, algorithms could amplify emotionally polarizing content to increase engagement, potentially leading to societal division.

Dependence on AI for Emotional Support: As AI becomes more integrated into emotional domains, there is a risk of individuals becoming overly reliant on AI for emotional support. This dependence could lead to reduced human-to-human interaction and weaken interpersonal relationships. For instance, users who find solace in AI companions might avoid addressing underlying issues with real people, potentially exacerbating feelings of isolation.

Authenticity and Ethical Design: The simulated empathy of AI systems raises questions about authenticity. While an AI's empathetic response might be effective in certain contexts, it is ultimately an algorithmic output devoid of genuine understanding. Designers of emotionally intelligent AI must strike a balance between providing comfort and maintaining transparency about the system's limitations. Ethical guidelines should ensure that users are not misled into believing that AI systems possess human-like consciousness or emotions.

Societal Impacts: AI's role in emotional interaction could reshape societal norms. For instance, the increasing use of AI companions might alter perceptions of relationships and redefine what constitutes emotional connection. Similarly, emotionally intelligent AI in workplaces could influence how employees interact with technology and each other, potentially blurring boundaries between professional and personal spheres.

Balancing Opportunities and Challenges

The intersection of AI and human emotions offers immense opportunities for innovation and societal benefit. Emotionally intelligent AI has the potential to revolutionize mental health care, education, customer service, and beyond. However, realizing these benefits requires addressing the associated challenges through ethical design, robust privacy protections, and ongoing societal dialogue.

Regulatory frameworks should prioritize transparency, fairness, and accountability in AI systems. Organizations developing emotionally intelligent AI must adopt responsible AI principles, including ethical data collection, unbiased training, and user empowerment. Public awareness campaigns can also play a crucial role in educating individuals about the capabilities and limitations of emotionally intelligent AI, fostering informed interactions.

The intersection of AI and human emotions is a frontier rich with possibilities and complexities. Emotional intelligence in AI enables systems to engage with humans in more nuanced and meaningful ways, enhancing user experiences across various domains. However, this technological advancement comes with ethical, social, and psychological implications that must be thoughtfully addressed.

As AI continues to evolve, fostering a collaborative approach involving technologists, ethicists, policymakers, and the public is essential. By prioritizing ethical considerations and embracing diverse perspectives, society can harness the potential of emotionally intelligent AI while mitigating its risks. The journey toward harmonizing AI and human emotions is not just about creating smarter systems but also about ensuring that these systems contribute positively to humanity's well-being.

Chapter 49 Agentic AI and Human Rights

Autonomous artificial intelligence (AI), or agentic AI, refers to systems capable of making decisions and executing actions without direct human input. These advanced systems, while offering tremendous potential for innovation, also pose significant challenges to human rights. As AI becomes increasingly embedded in areas such as healthcare, law enforcement, and employment, its capacity to influence, and potentially infringe upon, fundamental human rights grows exponentially.

One major area of concern is the right to privacy. Autonomous AI systems often rely on vast amounts of data to function effectively, including sensitive personal information. Surveillance systems powered by AI, for example, can analyze behavior patterns, identify individuals in crowds, and predict future actions. Such capabilities, while beneficial for crime prevention and national security, risk creating a society where individuals are under constant watch. This pervasive surveillance can stifle free expression and erode trust in institutions.

Another significant impact is on the right to equality. AI systems, if not carefully designed and tested, can perpetuate and even exacerbate existing biases. For instance, algorithmic decision-making in hiring, lending, or law enforcement can lead to discriminatory outcomes if the training data reflects historical inequalities. Such biases can disadvantage marginalized groups, entrenching social divisions and undermining efforts to achieve equality.

Moreover, autonomous AI raises concerns about accountability and justice. When an AI system makes a decision that harms an individual—whether through an incorrect medical diagnosis, an unfair denial of a loan, or a wrongful arrest—determining responsibility can be challenging. Traditional legal frameworks, which assume human agency, struggle to address situations where the decision-making process is opaque or driven by a machine.

The right to life is also at stake in contexts where AI systems are used in lethal autonomous weapons or critical healthcare applications. Autonomous weapons, capable of making life-

or-death decisions without human intervention, pose ethical dilemmas about the value of human oversight in warfare. In healthcare, while AI can enhance diagnostic accuracy and treatment efficiency, errors in autonomous decision-making could have dire consequences for patients.

Finally, the rise of agentic AI threatens economic and social rights. Automation driven by AI has already displaced numerous jobs, and as AI systems grow more sophisticated, this trend is likely to continue. While AI can create new opportunities, the transition period may exacerbate unemployment and inequality, particularly for those in roles most susceptible to automation. Access to education and retraining becomes crucial to ensure that individuals can adapt to an AI-driven economy.

The Need for Legal Frameworks to Protect Individuals

The rapid development of autonomous AI underscores the urgent need for comprehensive legal frameworks to protect human rights. Current regulatory approaches are often reactive and fragmented, struggling to keep pace with technological advancements. Proactive, globally coordinated efforts are essential to mitigate risks while fostering innovation.

A cornerstone of such frameworks should be the principle of transparency. AI systems must be designed to allow scrutiny of their decision-making processes. This includes making algorithms auditable and ensuring that outputs can be explained in terms understandable to non-experts. Transparent systems not only foster trust but also enable individuals to challenge decisions that affect their rights.

Accountability mechanisms are equally critical. Legal systems must clarify who is responsible when AI systems cause harm. This may involve attributing liability to developers, operators, or even organizations deploying the technology. Ensuring accountability also requires that AI systems undergo rigorous testing and certification before deployment, akin to safety standards in industries like aviation and pharmaceuticals.

Another essential component is privacy protection. Legal frameworks should establish clear limits on data collection, storage, and use, emphasizing informed consent and data minimization. For AI systems operating in sensitive areas, such as healthcare or criminal justice, stricter safeguards are necessary to prevent misuse and abuse of personal information.

Anti-discrimination measures are vital to address biases in AI systems. Regulators must require developers to use diverse and representative data sets, conduct regular audits for bias, and implement corrective measures when disparities are identified. Additionally, affected individuals should have access to legal remedies if they experience discrimination resulting from AI decisions.

The integration of ethical guidelines into AI development is another crucial step. Governments, academic institutions, and private companies should collaborate to create standards that prioritize human dignity, fairness, and equity. These guidelines should inform both the design and deployment of AI systems, ensuring that they align with societal values.

International cooperation is also imperative. The global nature of AI development and deployment necessitates harmonized regulations that prevent regulatory arbitrage—where companies exploit less stringent laws in certain jurisdictions. Collaborative initiatives, such as the establishment of an international AI ethics board or the adoption of treaties governing autonomous weapons, can provide a unified approach to managing AI's impact on human rights.

Balancing Innovation with Ethical Responsibility

The challenge of managing autonomous AI lies in balancing the need for innovation with ethical responsibility. AI has the potential to revolutionize industries, improve quality of life, and address pressing global challenges such as climate change and disease. However, unbridled innovation without ethical safeguards risks creating technologies that harm individuals and society.

One approach to achieving this balance is through the concept of "ethical innovation." This entails embedding ethical considerations into every stage of the AI lifecycle, from research and development to deployment and monitoring. Developers should adopt a "do no harm" philosophy, proactively identifying and mitigating risks before systems are released.

Governments play a pivotal role in fostering an environment where ethical innovation thrives. This includes investing in public research initiatives, providing grants for projects that prioritize social good, and creating regulatory sandboxes where companies can test AI systems under controlled conditions. Such measures can encourage responsible innovation while minimizing potential harms.

The private sector must also embrace its responsibility. Companies developing autonomous AI should adopt corporate social responsibility (CSR) practices that emphasize ethical AI development. This includes establishing internal ethics committees, training employees on human rights considerations, and conducting impact assessments to evaluate how AI systems affect individuals and communities.

Public awareness and education are equally important. As AI becomes more integrated into daily life, individuals must understand how these systems operate and their rights in relation to them. Governments, educational institutions, and civil society organizations should collaborate to provide accessible resources and training, empowering individuals to navigate an AI-driven world confidently.

Additionally, fostering interdisciplinary collaboration is crucial. Ethical AI development requires input from diverse fields, including computer science, law, philosophy, sociology, and psychology. Such collaboration ensures that AI systems are not only technically robust but also socially and ethically aligned with human values.

Innovation and ethical responsibility are not mutually exclusive; rather, they can complement each other. By prioritizing ethical considerations, developers can build AI systems that gain public trust and acceptance, ultimately enhancing their adoption and success. For instance, an autonomous medical AI system that demonstrates transparency, fairness, and accuracy is more likely to be embraced by healthcare professionals and patients alike.

The rise of autonomous AI presents both unprecedented opportunities and profound challenges for human rights. While these technologies have the potential to transform society for the better, they also risk infringing on fundamental rights if left unchecked. Addressing these risks requires the establishment of robust legal frameworks that prioritize transparency, accountability, and fairness.

Balancing innovation with ethical responsibility is critical to ensuring that AI serves as a force for good. This involves embedding ethical considerations into AI development, fostering international cooperation, and empowering individuals to understand and assert their rights in an AI-driven world. By taking proactive measures today, society can harness the benefits of autonomous AI while safeguarding the rights and dignity of all individuals.

Chapter 50 AI and Its Role in Global Sustainability

AI can address complex ecological challenges effectively.

Biodiversity Monitoring and Wildlife Conservation

AI-powered tools such as image recognition and acoustic sensors have become invaluable in monitoring biodiversity. For instance, camera traps equipped with AI algorithms can identify and track animal species in real-time, providing critical data for wildlife conservation. Similarly, AI-driven drones monitor remote habitats, detect poaching activities, and assist in reforestation efforts.

Combating Climate Change

AI plays a significant role in combating climate change by analyzing vast amounts of climate data to identify trends and predict future scenarios. Machine learning algorithms can optimize renewable energy production by forecasting solar and wind energy outputs based on weather patterns. Additionally, AI-powered systems are used to monitor deforestation and carbon emissions, enabling timely intervention to mitigate environmental damage.

Enhancing Resource Efficiency

AI can optimize resource usage in industries and urban settings, reducing waste and minimizing environmental impact. For example, smart irrigation systems driven by AI ensure that water is used efficiently in agriculture, while AI-powered energy management systems reduce electricity consumption in buildings.

Ocean Health Monitoring

The health of marine ecosystems is critical for global sustainability. AI technologies are employed to analyze satellite imagery and underwater data to monitor coral reefs, track illegal fishing activities, and measure ocean pollution levels. These insights help in the formulation of policies to protect marine biodiversity.

Addressing Global Challenges with AI

Beyond environmental protection, AI offers innovative solutions to a range of global challenges, including poverty, hunger, healthcare, and education.

Poverty Alleviation

AI-driven data analytics can identify poverty hotspots by analyzing socioeconomic and geospatial data. Governments and NGOs can use this information to target interventions, allocate resources effectively, and design programs that address the specific needs of underserved populations.

Combating Hunger and Ensuring Food Security

AI is instrumental in creating sustainable agricultural practices that can combat hunger and ensure food security. Precision agriculture, powered by AI, uses sensors and drones to monitor soil health, crop growth, and pest infestations. These insights enable farmers to optimize crop yields while reducing resource wastage. Furthermore, AI algorithms are used to predict food supply chain disruptions, ensuring timely distribution of food to areas in need.

Healthcare Innovation

AI-driven technologies are transforming healthcare by improving diagnosis, treatment, and patient care. AI algorithms analyze medical data to detect diseases at early stages, develop personalized treatment plans, and optimize hospital operations. In low-resource settings, AI-powered diagnostic tools help healthcare workers deliver quality care, bridging the gap in medical infrastructure.

Improving Education Access

AI has the potential to make education more accessible and inclusive. Personalized learning platforms powered by AI adapt to individual learning styles, ensuring effective education for students worldwide. Additionally, AI tools enable remote learning, breaking down barriers for students in remote or underserved areas.

Disaster Management

AI technologies are pivotal in disaster management and risk reduction. Predictive analytics models assess natural disaster risks, enabling early warnings and evacuation planning. AI-driven drones and robots assist in search and rescue operations, while satellite data helps monitor post-disaster recovery efforts.

Building a Sustainable Future with AI

To build a sustainable future, AI must be integrated into long-term strategies that address environmental, social, and economic dimensions of sustainability.

Promoting Circular Economy

A circular economy aims to minimize waste and make the most of resources. AI plays a crucial role in achieving this by optimizing recycling processes, predicting material lifecycles, and designing products with sustainability in mind. For example, AI algorithms can identify and sort recyclable materials in waste streams, increasing recycling efficiency.

Smart Cities and Urban Sustainability

AI is a cornerstone of smart city development, which focuses on enhancing urban living while minimizing environmental impact. Smart city technologies powered by AI include traffic management systems that reduce congestion and emissions, energy-efficient infrastructure, and waste management systems that promote recycling and resource conservation.

Fostering Renewable Energy Adoption

AI facilitates the transition to renewable energy by optimizing power generation, storage, and distribution. Smart grids use AI to balance energy supply and demand in real-time, integrating renewable energy sources seamlessly into the energy mix. This reduces reliance on fossil fuels and supports a low-carbon future.

Encouraging Sustainable Consumer Behavior

AI-powered platforms can influence consumer behavior by promoting sustainable choices. For instance, recommendation systems on e-commerce platforms can highlight eco-friendly products, while AI-driven apps educate users about their carbon footprint and suggest ways to reduce it.

Supporting Policy and Decision-Making

AI provides policymakers with actionable insights by analyzing large datasets and simulating the impact of various policy scenarios. These insights help in crafting evidence-based policies that address sustainability challenges effectively. AI tools also facilitate transparency and accountability in governance.

Accelerating Scientific Research

AI accelerates research and innovation in fields critical to sustainability, such as renewable energy, climate science, and biotechnology. By analyzing complex datasets and simulating experiments, AI helps scientists develop breakthrough solutions to pressing global issues.

While AI offers immense potential for sustainability, it also poses ethical and practical challenges. Addressing these challenges is crucial to ensure that AI's benefits are equitably distributed and its risks minimized.

Bias and Fairness

AI systems can perpetuate existing biases in data, leading to unfair outcomes. Efforts must be made to ensure that AI models are trained on diverse datasets and are transparent in their decision-making processes.

Energy Consumption

Training and deploying AI models require significant computational power, which can contribute to carbon emissions. Developing energy-efficient AI technologies and leveraging renewable energy for data centers can mitigate this issue.

Data Privacy

The collection and analysis of vast amounts of data raise concerns about privacy and security. Establishing robust data protection frameworks is essential to safeguard individual and organizational information.

Accessibility and Equity

Ensuring that AI technologies are accessible to all, particularly in developing regions, is critical for equitable progress. Collaboration between governments, private sectors, and international organizations can bridge the digital divide.

AI has the potential to transform global sustainability efforts, addressing environmental challenges, socio-economic disparities, and resource inefficiencies. By integrating AI into conservation, agriculture, healthcare, and urban planning, societies can create innovative solutions for a sustainable future. However, ethical considerations and practical challenges must be addressed to harness AI's full potential responsibly. Through collaborative efforts and thoughtful implementation, AI can serve as a powerful tool in building a resilient and equitable world.

Chapter 51 The Future of Agentic AI: Visions and Possibilities

The emergence of artificial intelligence (AI) as a transformative force has not only reshaped the contours of technology but also stirred profound questions about its implications for humanity. Among its myriad forms, agentic AI, characterized by autonomous decision-making and goal-oriented behavior, stands at the frontier of innovation. This exploration delves into predictions for the future of AI and agency, the evolution of AI in human society, and the ethical and philosophical considerations that accompany this unfolding reality.

Predictions for the Future of AI and Agency

Agentic AI—systems capable of independently formulating objectives and strategies—will play a pivotal role in defining the future of human civilization. Several trends and predictions underscore its trajectory:

1. Enhanced Autonomy and Adaptability

Future AI systems will exhibit unprecedented levels of autonomy, capable of interpreting complex environments, making informed decisions, and adapting dynamically to new scenarios. These systems may function in domains as varied as autonomous vehicles, precision medicine, and space exploration. Imagine healthcare robots autonomously diagnosing and administering treatments tailored to individual patients, or AI-powered drones executing intricate rescue operations in disaster zones.

2. Integration Across Domains

Agentic AI will likely transcend singular applications to operate seamlessly across interconnected ecosystems. Smart cities could harness such AI to optimize energy use, manage traffic, and respond to emergencies in real time. In agriculture, agentic systems might oversee entire supply chains, from predicting crop yields to automating distribution networks.

3. Rise of Artificial General Intelligence (AGI)

The leap toward AGI—systems possessing the ability to understand and perform any intellectual task that humans can—will redefine agency in AI. With general reasoning capabilities, AGI could participate in solving global challenges, such as climate change or economic inequality. However, such advancements necessitate rigorous safeguards to align AI's goals with humanity's welfare.

4. Collaborative Intelligence

The future will likely see humans collaborating with agentic AI in increasingly complex ways. Rather than replacing human effort, these systems will augment human capabilities, enabling collaborative intelligence where both parties bring their unique strengths to the table. For instance, architects could co-design urban landscapes with AI, balancing aesthetic vision with structural optimization.

5. Economic and Workforce Transformations

The proliferation of agentic AI will disrupt traditional industries, creating opportunities for new economic models while displacing certain job categories. Governments and organizations must proactively prepare for these shifts by fostering education systems that emphasize creativity, emotional intelligence, and adaptability—traits less easily replicated by machines.

The Evolution of AI in Human Society

The integration of agentic AI into society is a gradual yet transformative process that will influence every aspect of human life. This evolution can be examined through three critical phases: adoption, normalization, and symbiosis.

Phase 1: Adoption

In this initial stage, agentic AI systems are introduced to specific sectors. Early adopters include industries requiring precise, high-stakes decision-making, such as healthcare, finance, and logistics. While adoption is driven by efficiency gains, it is often accompanied by skepticism and resistance due to concerns about job displacement and trust in autonomous systems.

Phase 2: Normalization

As agentic AI demonstrates reliability and value, its presence becomes normalized. Systems become more user-friendly, and their integration into daily life fosters widespread acceptance. Autonomous assistants could become as ubiquitous as smartphones, assisting with scheduling, shopping, and even maintaining social connections.

Phase 3: Symbiosis

In the symbiosis phase, human-AI interaction reaches a harmonious state. Rather than being distinct entities, agentic AI and humans operate as partners, each enhancing the other's strengths. Personalized education systems driven by AI could empower lifelong learning, while AI-enhanced governance might ensure transparency and efficiency in public administration.

Ethical and Philosophical Considerations for a Future with Agentic AI

The rise of agentic AI is not without its challenges. The delegation of agency to machines necessitates a careful examination of ethics, responsibility, and the fundamental nature of intelligence.

1. Alignment of Objectives

A primary ethical challenge is ensuring that agentic AI systems align with human values. Misaligned objectives can lead to unintended consequences, ranging from benign inefficiencies to catastrophic outcomes. Establishing robust alignment protocols, such as value learning algorithms and rigorous testing environments, is critical to mitigating these risks.

2. Accountability and Responsibility

Who bears responsibility for the actions of agentic AI? This question becomes particularly pressing when autonomous systems cause harm or act contrary to human expectations. A framework of accountability must be developed, potentially blending corporate, governmental, and individual oversight.

3. Bias and Fairness

Agentic AI systems often inherit biases present in their training data, which can perpetuate or amplify societal inequalities. Ensuring fairness in decision-making processes—from hiring algorithms to criminal justice applications—requires transparent data practices and ongoing audits.

4. Privacy and Surveillance

The capabilities of agentic AI in data collection and analysis pose significant threats to individual privacy. Safeguarding personal freedoms requires stringent regulations on data usage, emphasizing consent and anonymity. Striking a balance between societal benefits and individual rights will be a key challenge.

5. Existential Risks

Philosophical debates about agentic AI often touch on existential risks. Scenarios such as AI surpassing human control or prioritizing its own survival over human welfare are explored in speculative contexts. While such outcomes may seem distant, their nonzero probability demands proactive measures, including kill switches, ethical guidelines, and global cooperation.

6. Redefining Humanity

As agentic AI blurs the boundaries between human and machine intelligence, it prompts reflection on what it means to be human. Could the rise of AI dilute the uniqueness of human creativity, empathy, or consciousness? Philosophers and scientists alike must grapple with these questions, ensuring that technological progress enriches rather than diminishes the human experience.

7. Equitable Access

Ensuring that the benefits of agentic AI are equitably distributed is crucial to preventing a digital divide. Socioeconomic disparities could widen if access to advanced AI systems becomes a privilege reserved for a select few.

Governments and organizations must work toward inclusive policies that democratize AI access.

The future of agentic AI is rife with possibilities, each carrying profound implications for human society. By predicting its trajectory, understanding its evolution, and addressing its ethical challenges, humanity can navigate this transformative era with foresight and responsibility. Agentic AI has the potential to be a powerful ally in solving humanity's greatest challenges, provided its development is guided by ethical principles and a commitment to collective welfare. In embracing this future, we not only shape the trajectory of technology but also redefine our aspirations for what it means to live in a world shared with intelligent machines.

About the Author

Maria Johnsen is a dynamic storyteller, visionary, and multilingual digital marketing expert with a passion for blending art, technology, and communication. She published 86 books. Originally from the charming city of Trondheim, Norway, Maria grew up immersed in a rich cultural landscape, which honed her ability to create meaningful connections across diverse markets. Her expertise makes her an invaluable partner to investors and businesses seeking to expand their global reach.

A Lifelong Commitment to Learning and Growth

Maria's journey is a testament to her relentless pursuit of knowledge. From studying at a prestigious boarding school in Paris, where she quickly mastered French, to earning degrees in Information Technology, AI and Computer Engineering,

Informatics, Film Production, and Beauty Arts, she has continuously sought to broaden her horizons. Her education reflects her deep belief in the transformative power of learning both personally and professionally.

Her dedication to teaching has also played a key role in her career. Maria worked on a cross-cultural project between Russia and Norway, teaching Russian to Norwegian managers and bankers involved in an agricultural initiative in Arkhangelsk, Russia. This experience showcased her ability to bridge cultural divides and foster international collaboration.

A Passion for Teaching and Mentorship

Maria's impact extends beyond her own achievements. While teaching in Changchun, China, she inspired 170 students, with 70% securing scholarships to continue their studies in the U.S. and Canada. Her innovative teaching methods and dedication to student success highlight her commitment to nurturing future leaders, aligning with the goals of those investing in global talent.

In 2017, Maria began transforming her poetry into song lyrics, using her films as a platform for her evolving artistic expression. This marked the beginning of her journey as a songwriter. One of her standout tracks, *Unbreakable Spirit*, serves as a motivational anthem for those facing adversity, encouraging them to rise above challenges.

Maria's album, *Nordlysets Kamp*, delves into themes of resilience and hope, blending Folk, Rock, and Metal. Inspired by the breathtaking beauty of Norway's landscapes, the album captures the spirit of endurance in the face of life's struggles.

Crafting Stories Across Film, Books, and Beyond

Maria's storytelling extends beyond music. As a filmmaker and author, she has written 85 books and films, distributed in over 250 countries. Her work sparks conversations that bridge cultural divides and explores a wide range of topics, including:

- The Business of Filmmaking: Networking and Strategies in the Movie Industry

- The Future of Artificial Intelligence in Digital Marketing

- Blockchain in Digital Marketing: A New Paradigm of Trust

- Multilingual Digital Marketing: Managing for Excellence

- Sales in the Age of Intelligent Web

- Computer Engineering, Neural Networks, and Generative AI

- Nanotechnology, AI Alignment and Misalignment, and Large Language Models (LLMs)

- Each book is more than just a guide; it's an invitation to explore new ideas and inspire innovation.

- An Entrepreneurial Spirit Empowering Brands Worldwide

Maria's entrepreneurial spirit led her to establish *Golden Way Media*, a multilingual digital marketing agency. With a deep understanding of cultural dynamics, she helps brands connect authentically with their audiences, cutting through the digital noise with strategies that empower businesses to thrive in an ever-evolving market.

A Connector of Cultures, Ideas, and People

At her core, Maria is a connector a bridge between diverse cultures, ideas, and people. Whether mentoring aspiring filmmakers, guiding students, or collaborating with businesses, Maria values each relationship and approaches every interaction with empathy, a shared vision for growth, and the belief that collaboration can lead to meaningful change.

Maria Johnsen is more than an accomplished professional—she embodies the transformative power of creativity, passion, and innovation. Her journey invites others to explore new ideas, embrace diversity, and drive positive change in the world. As you discover her work, you're invited to join her on a path of growth and impact, unlocking endless possibilities to build a brighter future for businesses and communities alike.

Bibliography

Boden, Margaret A. (Ed.). *The Philosophy of Artificial Intelligence.* Oxford University Press, 1990.

Bostrom, Nick. *Superintelligence: Paths, Dangers, Strategies.* Oxford University Press, 2014.

Brynjolfsson, Erik & McAfee, Andrew. *The Second Machine Age: Work, Progress, and Prosperity in a Time of Brilliant Technologies.* W. W. Norton & Company, January 2014.

Calo, Ryan, Froomkin, A. Michael, & Kerr, Ian. *The Law of Artificial Intelligence and Smart Machines.* Aspen Publishers, August 2016.

Coeckelbergh, Mark. *AI Ethics.* MIT Press, October 2020.

Johnsen, Maria. *AI and Ethics.* Maria Johnsen Publishing, 2015.

Johnsen, Maria. *AI and Moral Dilemmas* first edition. Maria Johnsen Publishing, 2014. 2end edition 2024.

Johnsen, Maria. *AI and the Future of Humanity*. Maria Johnsen Publishing, May 2021.

Johnsen, Maria. *Generative AI*. Maria Johnsen Publishing, March 2024.

Johnsen, Maria. *AI Alignment*. Maria Johnsen Publishing, October 2024.

Johnsen, Maria. *AI Mislignment*. Maria Johnsen Publishing, October 2024.

Johnsen, Maria. *Large Language Models LLms*. Maria Johnsen Publishing, September 2024.

Johnsen, Maria. *Nanotechnology*. Maria Johnsen Publishing, June 2024.

Johnsen, Maria. *Neural Networks*. Maria Johnsen Publishing, first edition, September 2015, second edition July 2024.

Johnsen, Maria. *AI in Digital Marketing*. De Gruyter Inc. Mercury Learning and Information Publishing. July 2024.

Johnsen, Maria. *The Future of Artificial Intelligence in Digital Marketing*. Maria Johnsen Publishing, 2017

Johnsen, Maria. *AI in Healthcare: Transforming the Future of Medicine*. Maria Johnsen Publishing, March 2023.

Johnsen, Maria, *Self aware AI Robots.* Maria Johnsen Publishing, August 2024

Johnsen, Maria, *Machine Learning.* Maria Johnsen Publishing, July 2024

Johnsen, Maria, *The Future of Search Engines.* Maria Johnsen Publishing, February 2024

Johnsen, Maria, *Hunting for Aliens and the Cosmos,* Maria Johnsen Publishing, January 2024

Johnsen, Maria. *AI in Healthcare: Transforming the Future of Medicine.* Maria Johnsen Publishing, March 2015.

Johnsen, Maria. *Artificial Intelligence: Transforming Business and Society.* Maria Johnsen Publishing, February 2022.

Johnsen, Maria. *Autonomous Systems and AI: Navigating the Future.* Maria Johnsen Publishing, June 2021.

Lee, Kai-Fu. *AI 2041: Ten Visions for Our Future.* Currency, September 2021.

Lee, Kai-Fu. *AI Superpowers: China, Silicon Valley, and the New World Order.* Houghton Mifflin Harcourt, September 2018.

Latham, William S. *Robotics and Artificial Intelligence in Space.* Springer, November 2020.

Lapan, Maxim. *Deep Reinforcement Learning Hands-On.* Packt Publishing, May 2018.

Moravec, Hans. *Mind Children: The Future of Robot and Human Intelligence.* Harvard University Press, 1988.

O'Neil, Cathy. *Weapons of Math Destruction: How Big Data Increases Inequality and Threatens Democracy.* Crown Publishing Group, September 2016.

Russell, Stuart & Norvig, Peter. *Artificial Intelligence: A Modern Approach.* 4th Edition. Pearson, December 2019.

Schwab, Klaus. *The Fourth Industrial Revolution.* Crown Business, January 2017.

Sutton, Richard S. & Barto, Andrew G. *Reinforcement Learning: An Introduction.* 2nd Edition. MIT Press, December 2017.

Tegmark, Max. *Life 3.0: Being Human in the Age of Artificial Intelligence.* Alfred A. Knopf, August 2017.

The Microsoft AI for Earth Team. *AI for Earth: Harnessing the Power of AI for Sustainability.* Microsoft Press, 2019.

Woods, R. L. *Autonomous Vehicles and the Future of Mobility.* CRC Press, August 2019.

Glossary

AI Ethics: The branch of ethics focused on the moral implications and considerations of artificial intelligence development, deployment, and usage, including issues of autonomy, privacy, and accountability.

AI-Driven Threat Assessment: The use of AI systems to analyze and evaluate potential threats, often in defense or security contexts, using machine learning and data analysis to predict risks and recommend actions.

Autonomous Drones: Unmanned aerial vehicles (UAVs) equipped with AI systems that allow them to perform tasks such as surveillance, reconnaissance, or combat without direct human control.

Autonomous Rovers and Probes: AI-driven machines designed for space exploration, capable of independently navigating and performing tasks on other planets or moons without human intervention.

Autonomy in AI: The ability of AI systems to operate independently, make decisions, and take actions based on their programming and data inputs without direct human oversight.

Challenges in Autonomous Car Development: The obstacles faced in the development of self-driving vehicles, including legal, ethical, technological, and safety issues.

Climate Change Mitigation: Strategies and actions aimed at reducing the impact of climate change, often involving AI-driven analysis, prediction, and adaptation solutions.

Collaborative AI: AI systems that work alongside humans, enhancing human capabilities while respecting ethical boundaries and ensuring human oversight and decision-making.

Data Security: The protection of digital data from unauthorized access, corruption, or theft, which is a key concern when deploying autonomous and agentic AI systems.

Ethical Considerations in Autonomous Systems: The moral questions that arise when autonomous AI systems are designed, including questions of accountability, transparency, and fairness.

Ethics in Autonomous Systems: The study of the moral implications of autonomous AI, particularly its role in decision-making and actions that affect human lives.

Global AI Ethics Guidelines: International frameworks or guidelines designed to address the ethical challenges posed by AI, particularly in areas such as privacy, autonomy, and accountability.

Human Creativity and AI: The relationship between human creativity and AI's ability to produce novel or artistic work, raising philosophical questions about the nature of creativity and authorship.

Moral Responsibility in AI: The assignment of ethical responsibility for the actions and outcomes of AI systems, particularly when these systems act autonomously.

Reinforcement Learning: A type of machine learning where an AI system learns to make decisions by receiving rewards or penalties based on its actions, contributing to its decision-making capabilities.

Robustness Against Adversarial Attacks: The ability of AI systems to withstand and function effectively in the face of attacks or manipulations intended to deceive or disrupt their operations.

Scaling Agentic AI Systems: The challenges involved in increasing the capabilities of agentic AI systems, including computational power, efficiency, and managing their growing complexity.

Smart Cities: Urban environments that use AI and other digital technologies to optimize resource use, improve quality of life, and manage infrastructure, often featuring autonomous systems for transportation, energy, and public services.

Space Colonization and AI: The role of AI in enabling humanity's expansion into space, including autonomous rovers, probes, and life-support systems designed for long-term space missions and colonies.

Trust in Autonomous Agents: Public and professional confidence in autonomous systems' ability to function safely and ethically, a key consideration in the adoption of technologies like self-driving cars and drones.

Workforce Transformation with AI: The impact of AI on employment, including job displacement, the creation of new roles, and the transformation of existing jobs, as well as the societal and ethical implications of these changes.

Printed in Great Britain
by Amazon